HOW TO DRAW

CUTE STUFF

FOR KIDS

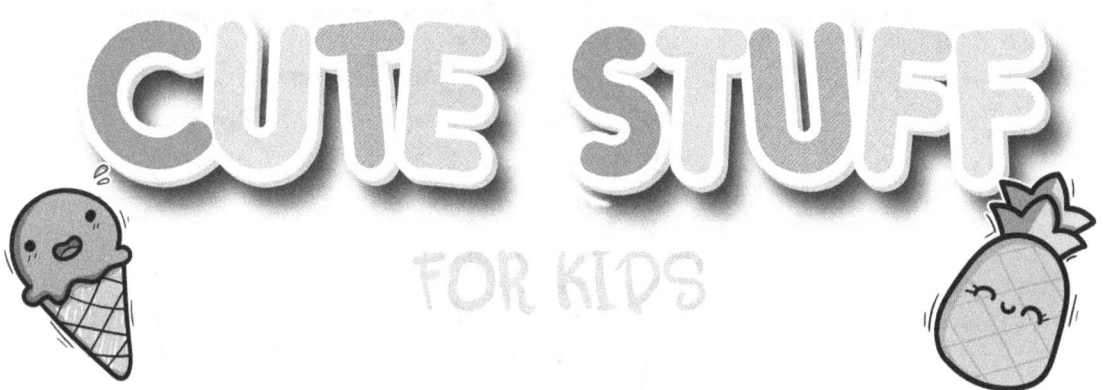

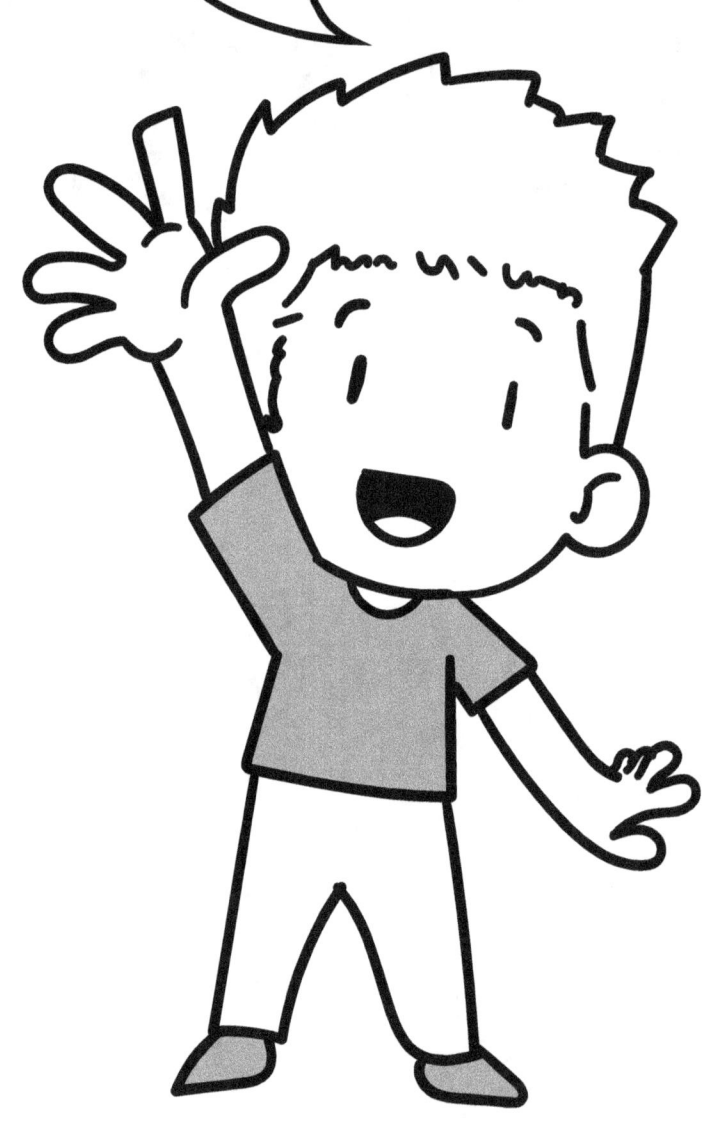

We will explore in this book

Animals

Emotions

Food

Objects

Insects

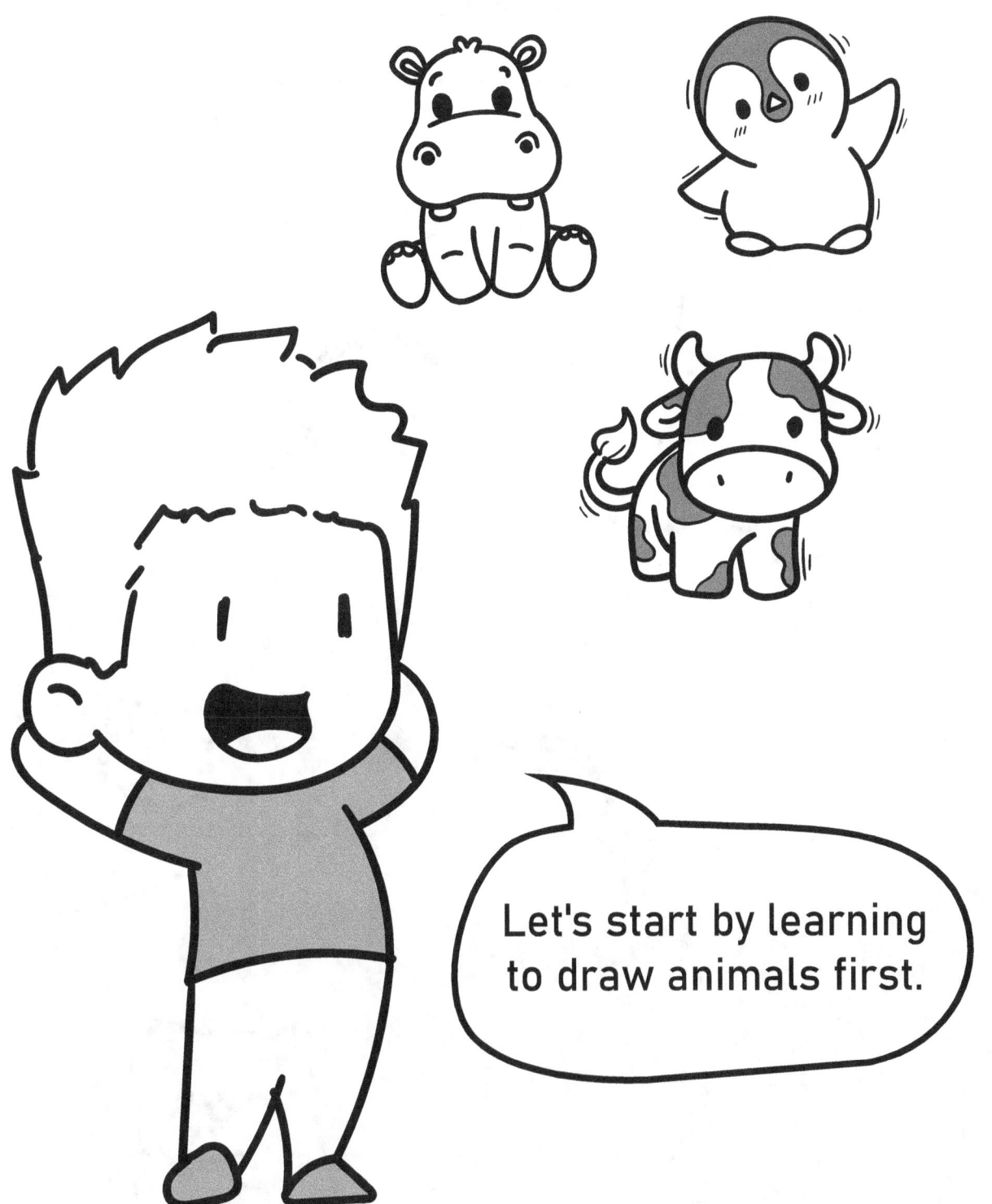

Let's start by learning to draw animals first.

Cat

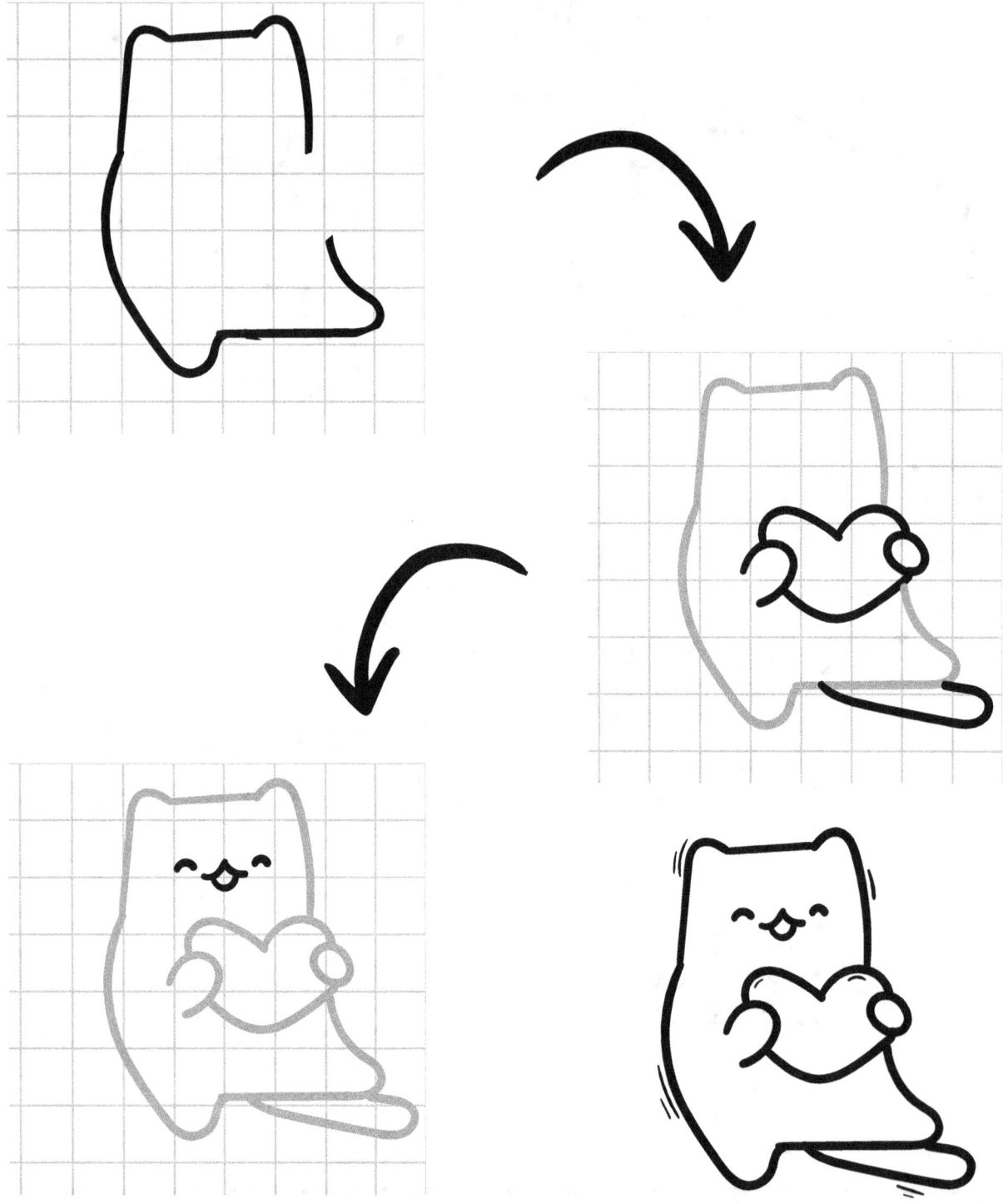

Try it

More than once

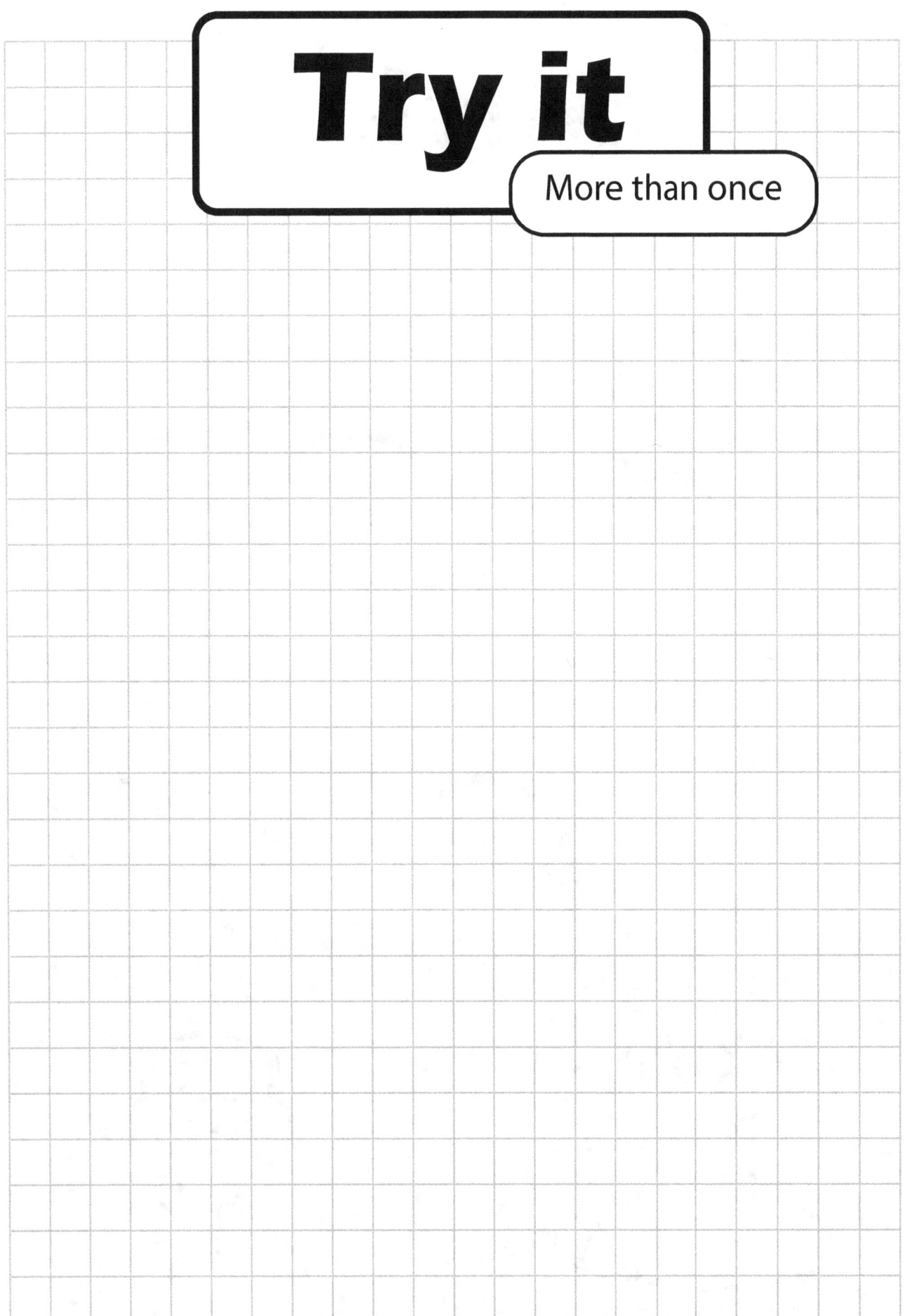

Duck

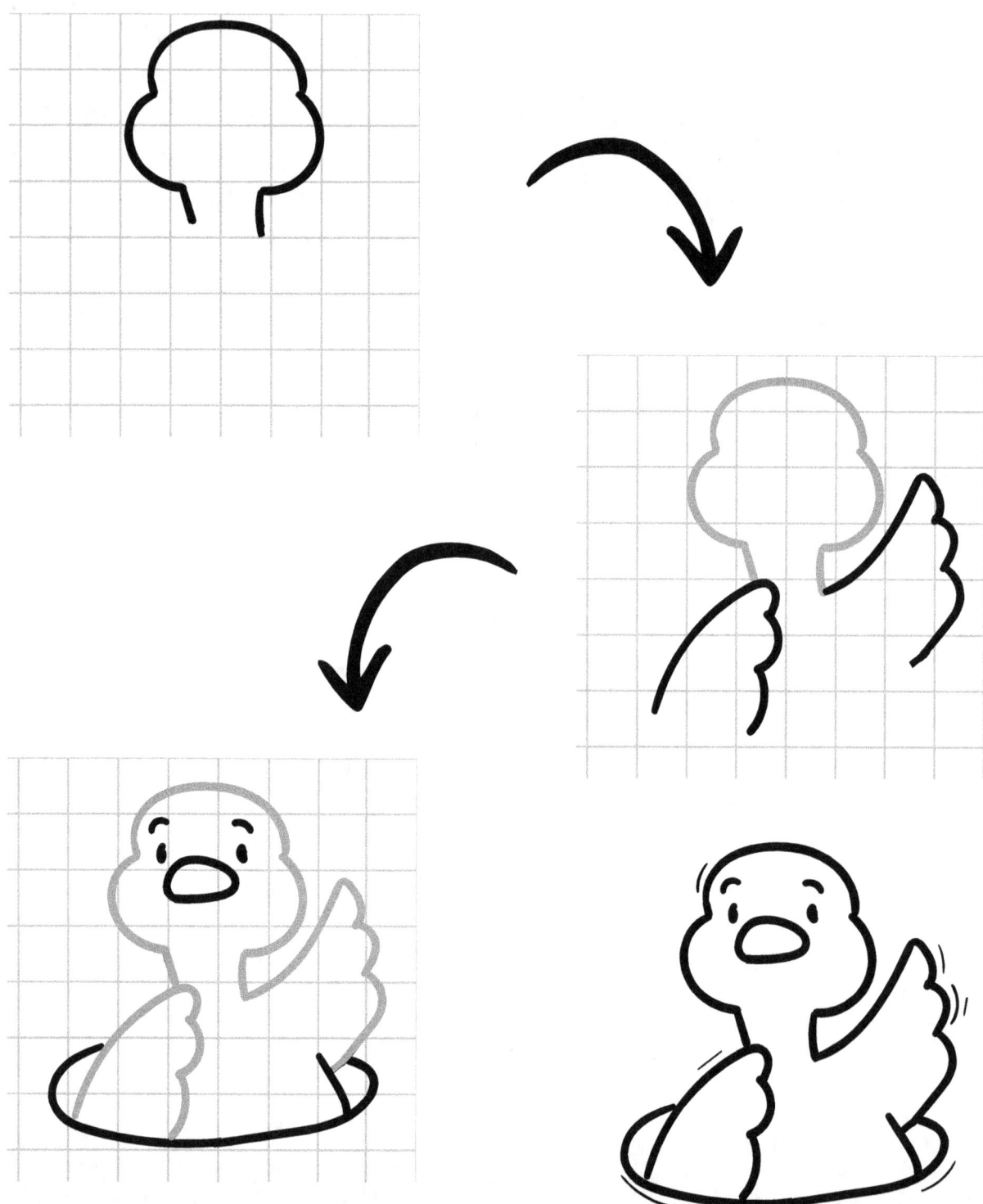

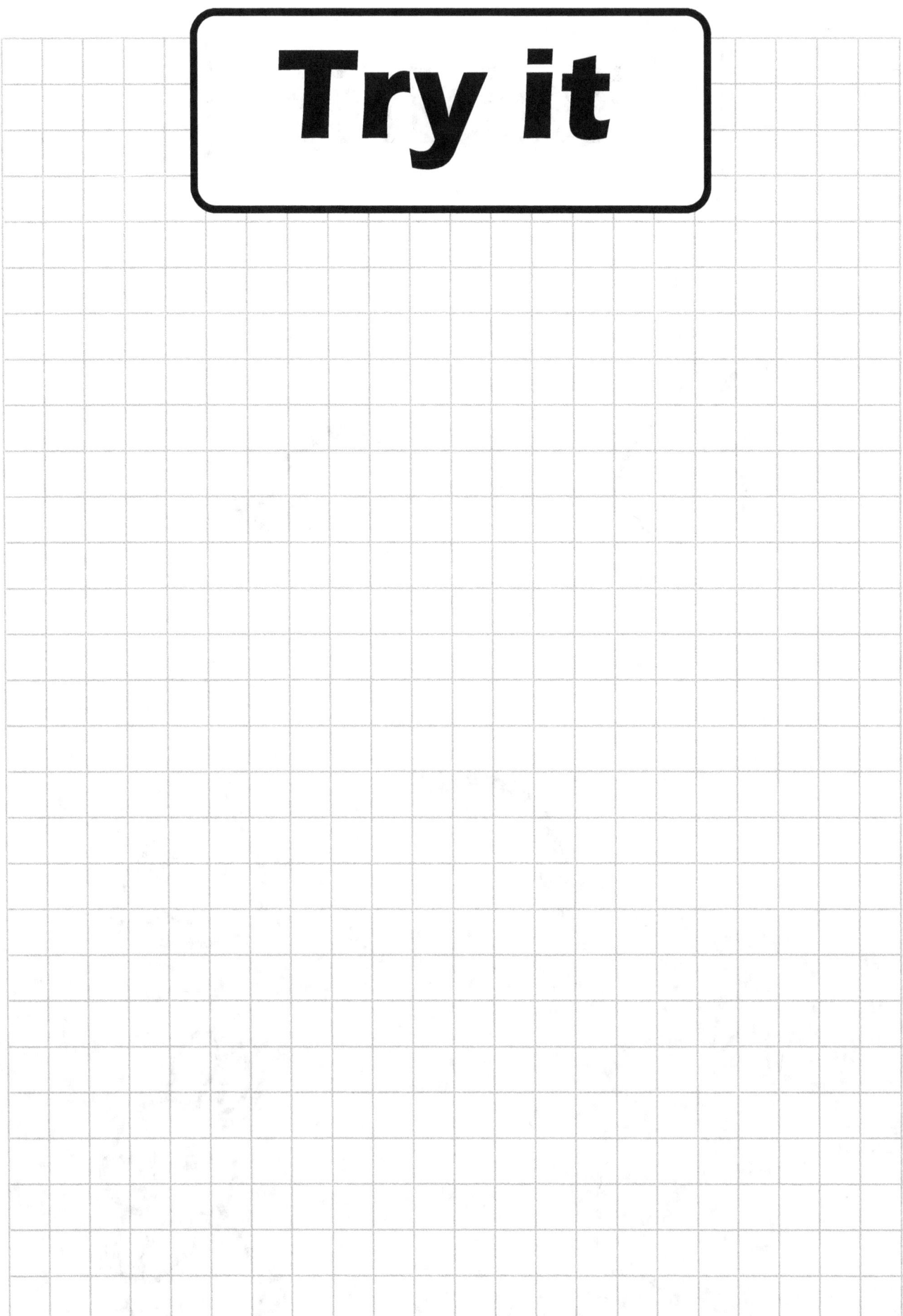

Try it

Rabbit

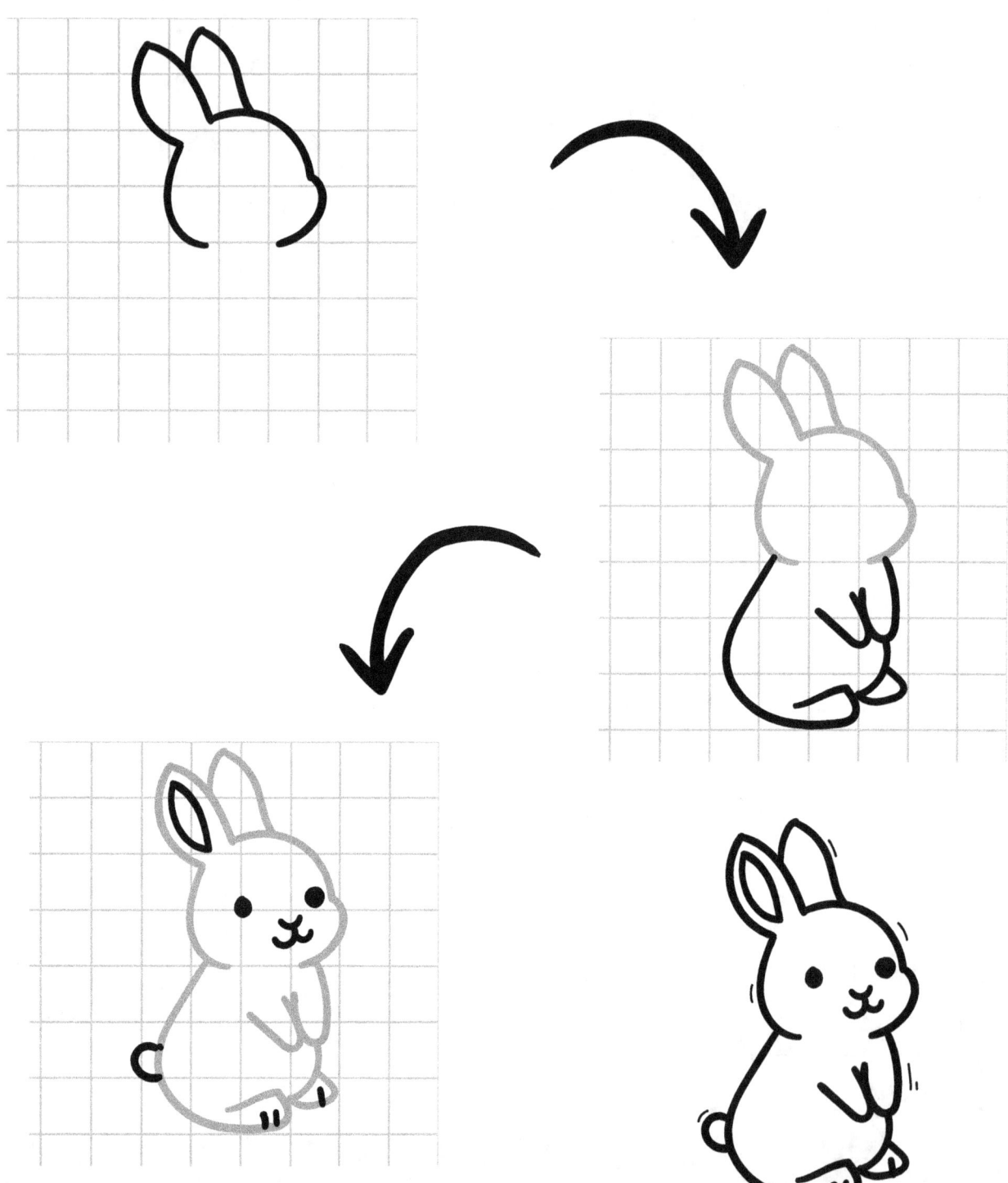

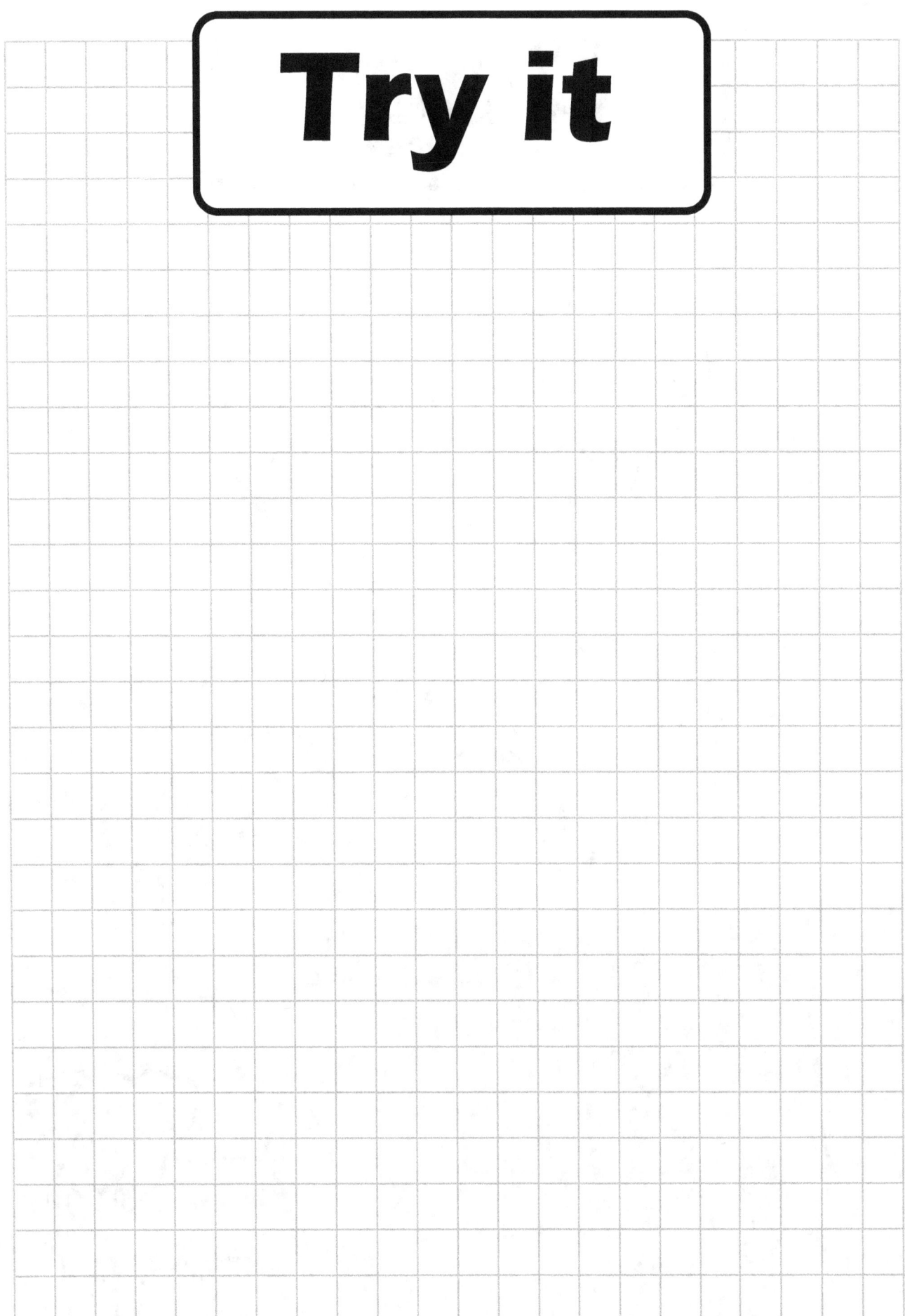

Try it

Dog

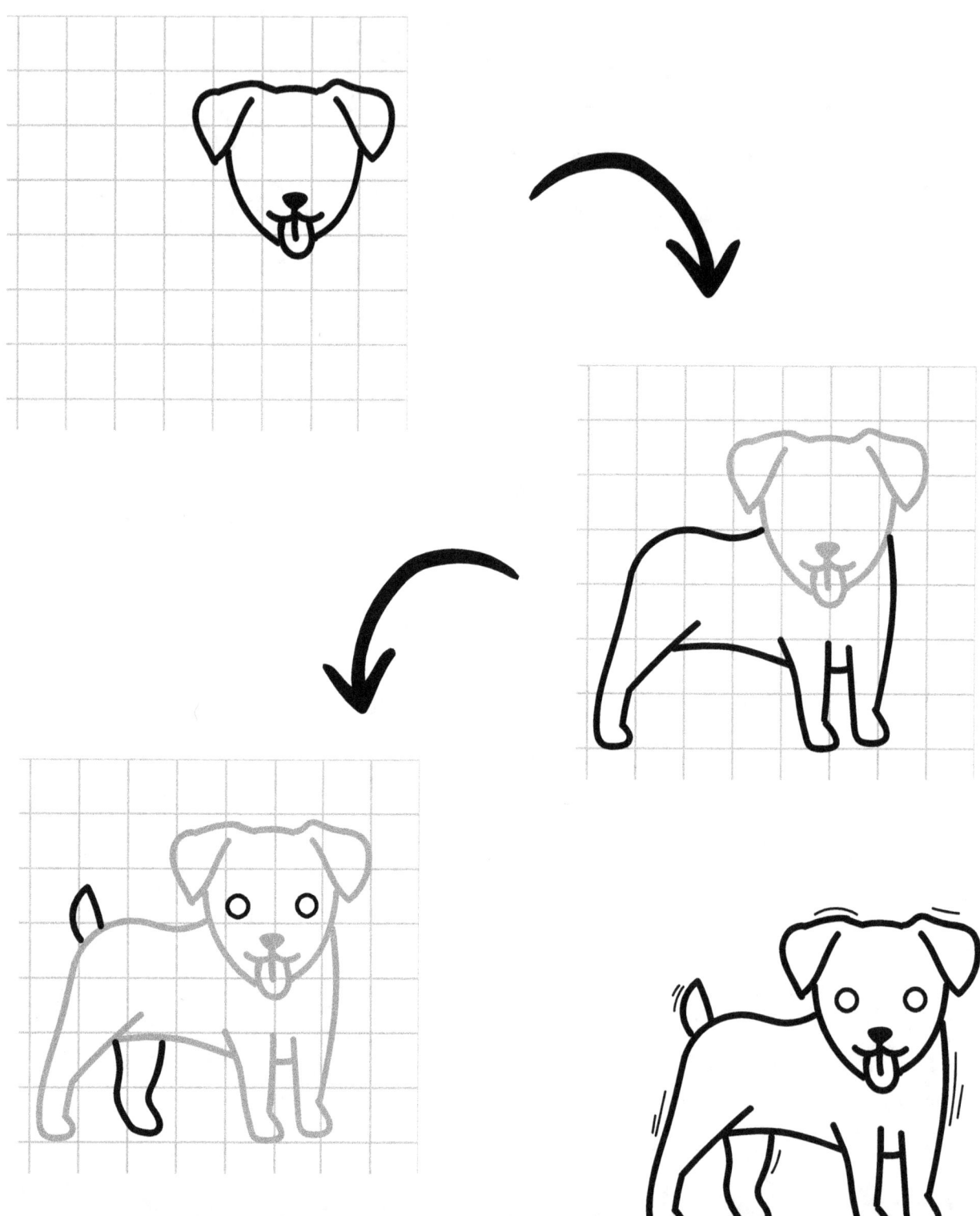

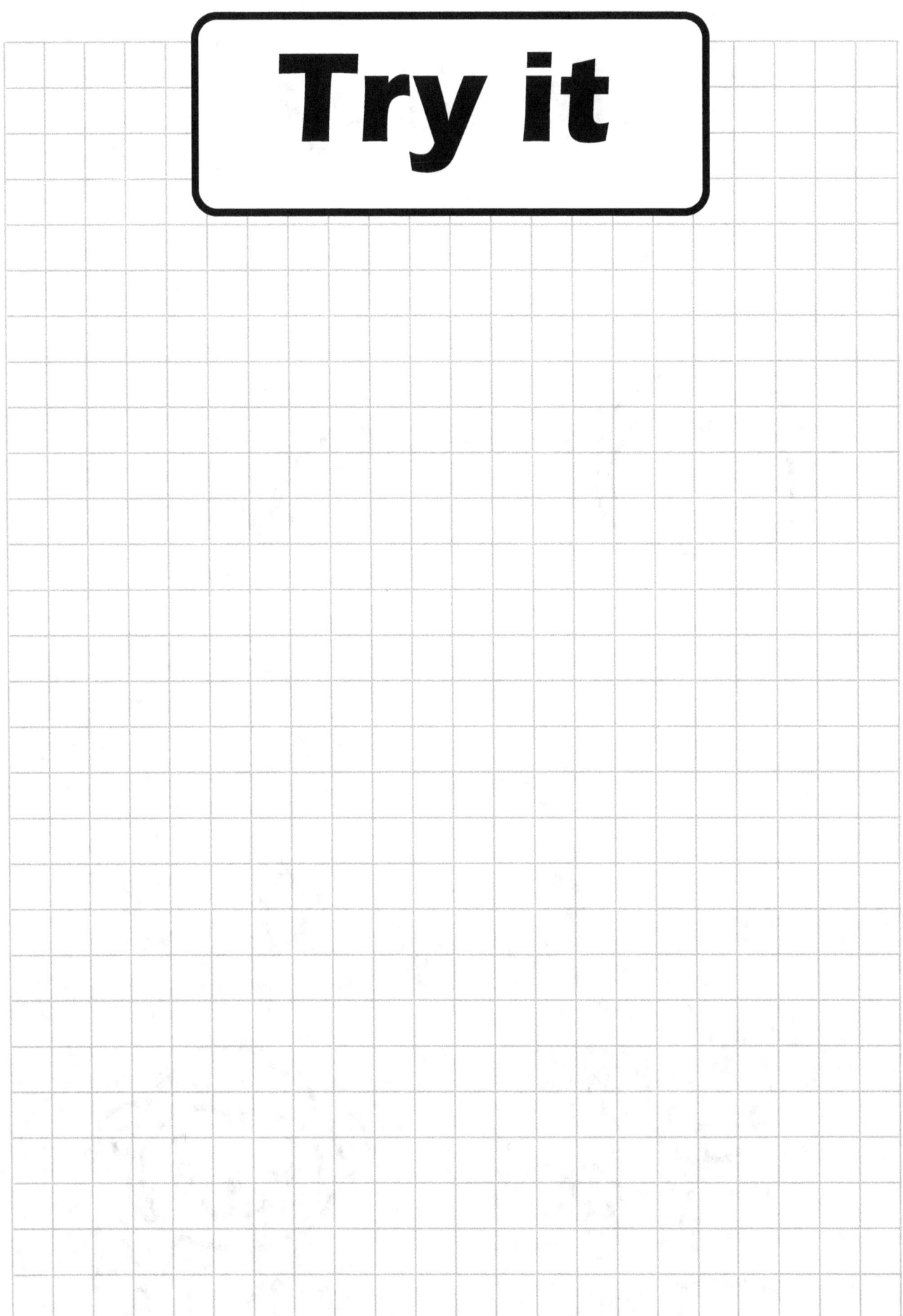

Try it

Monkey

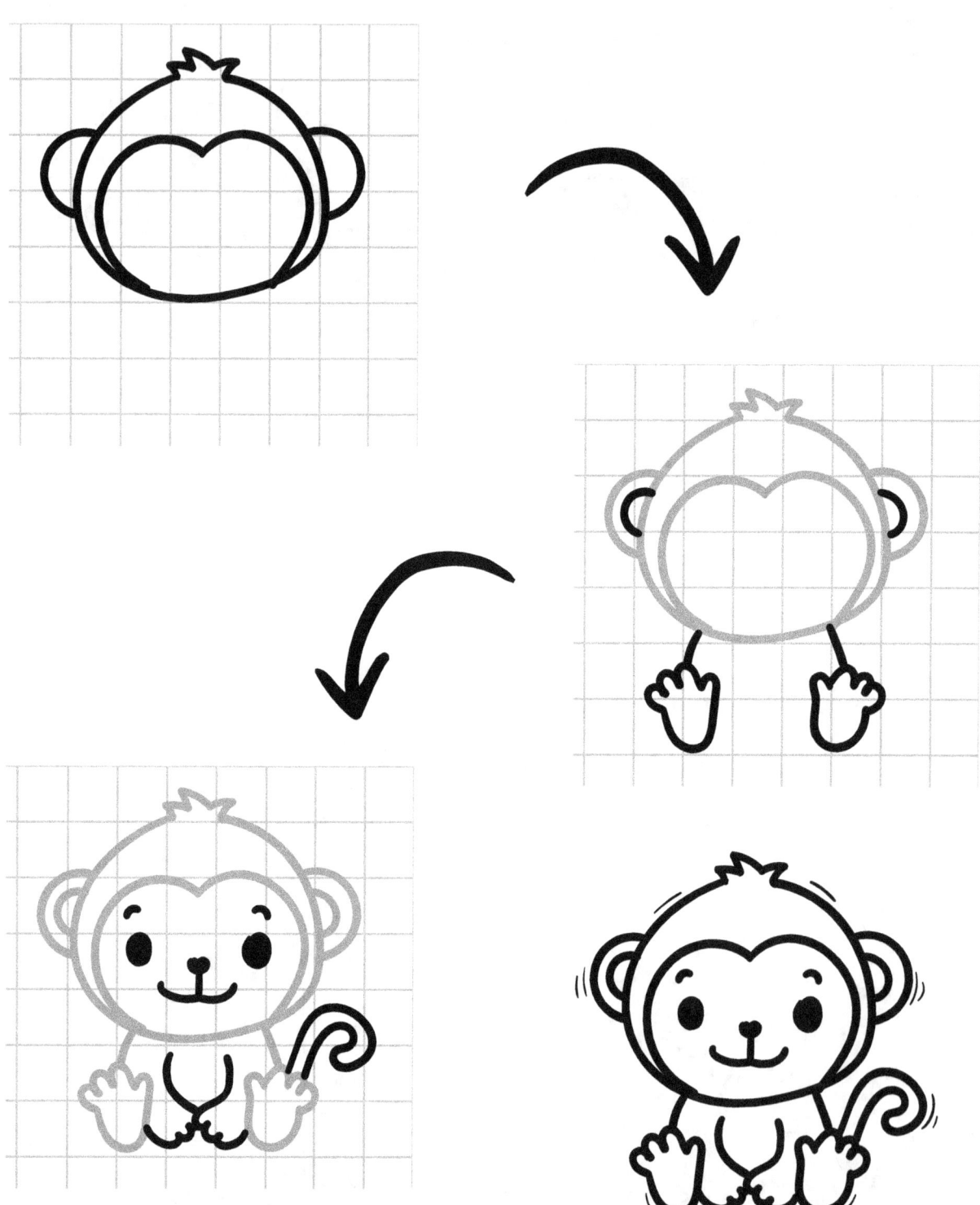

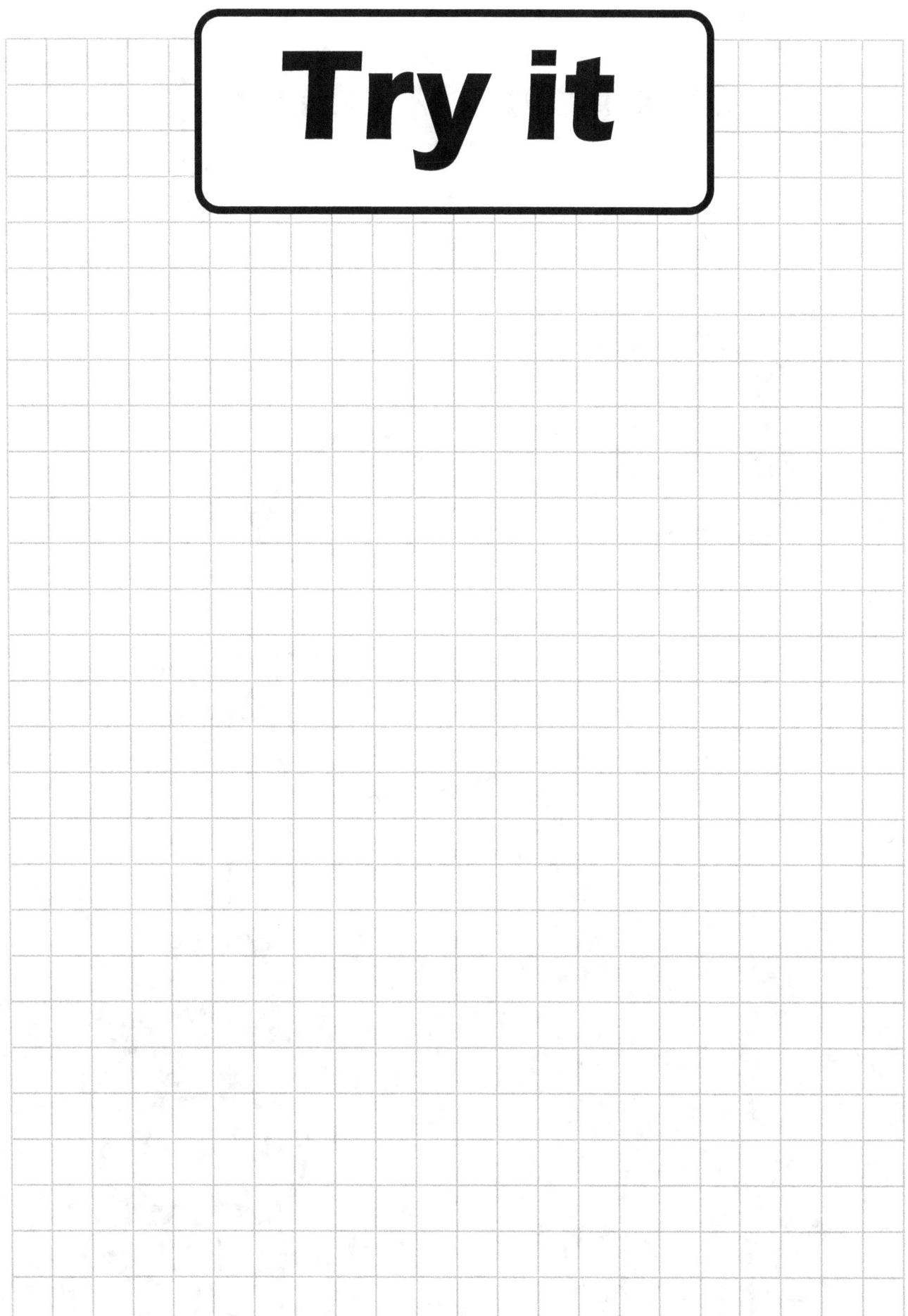

Try it

Hippopotamus

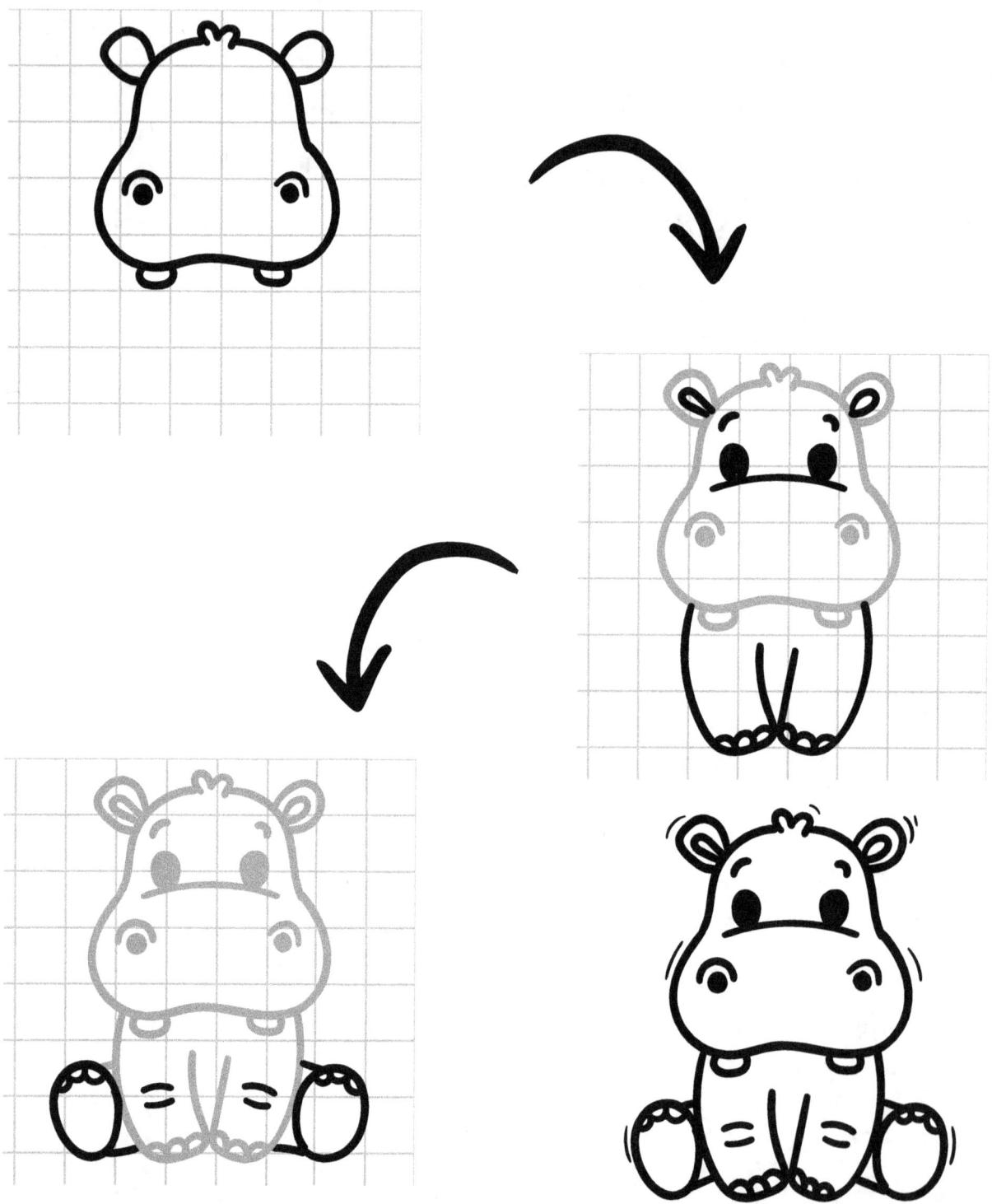

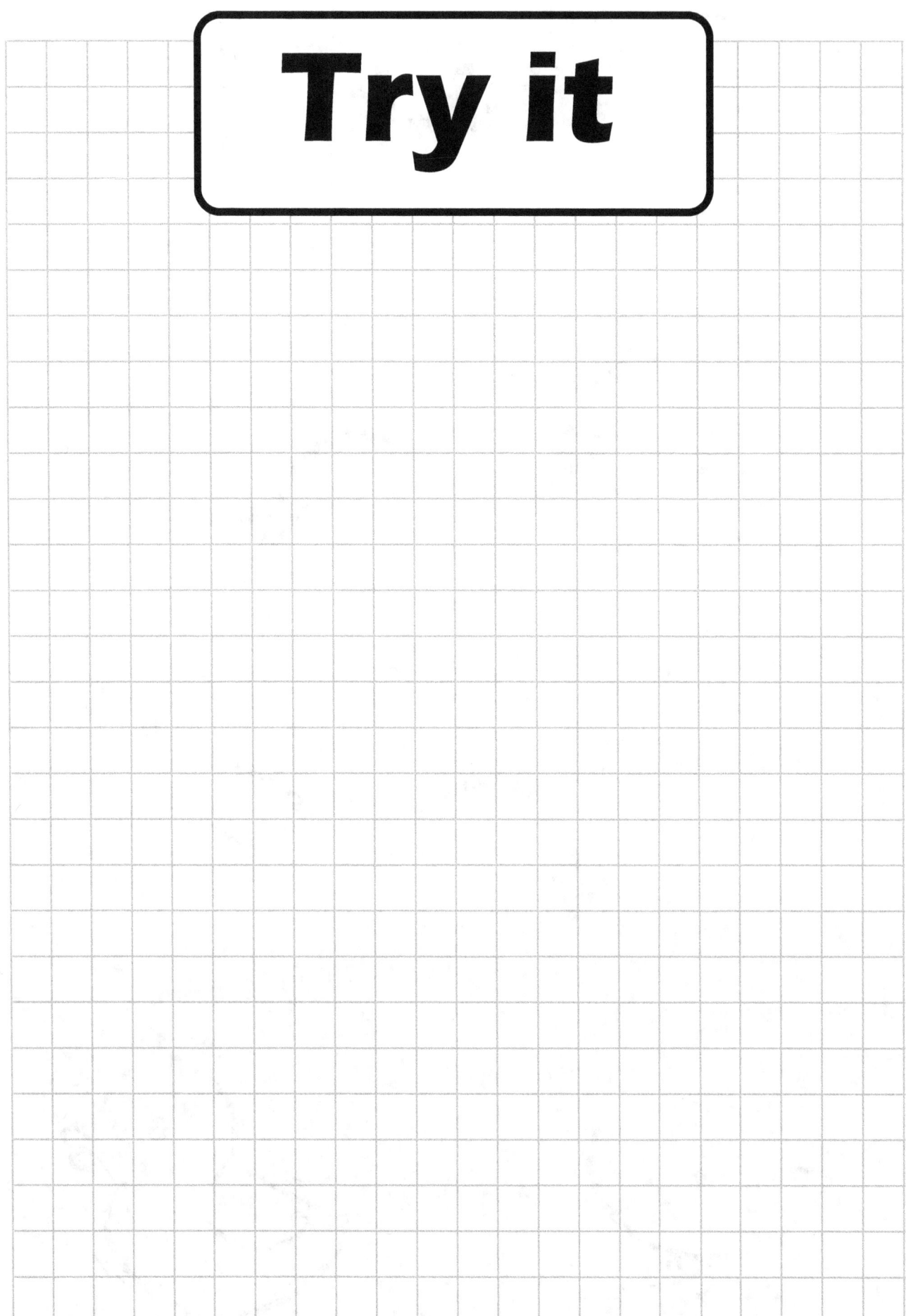

Try it

Chick

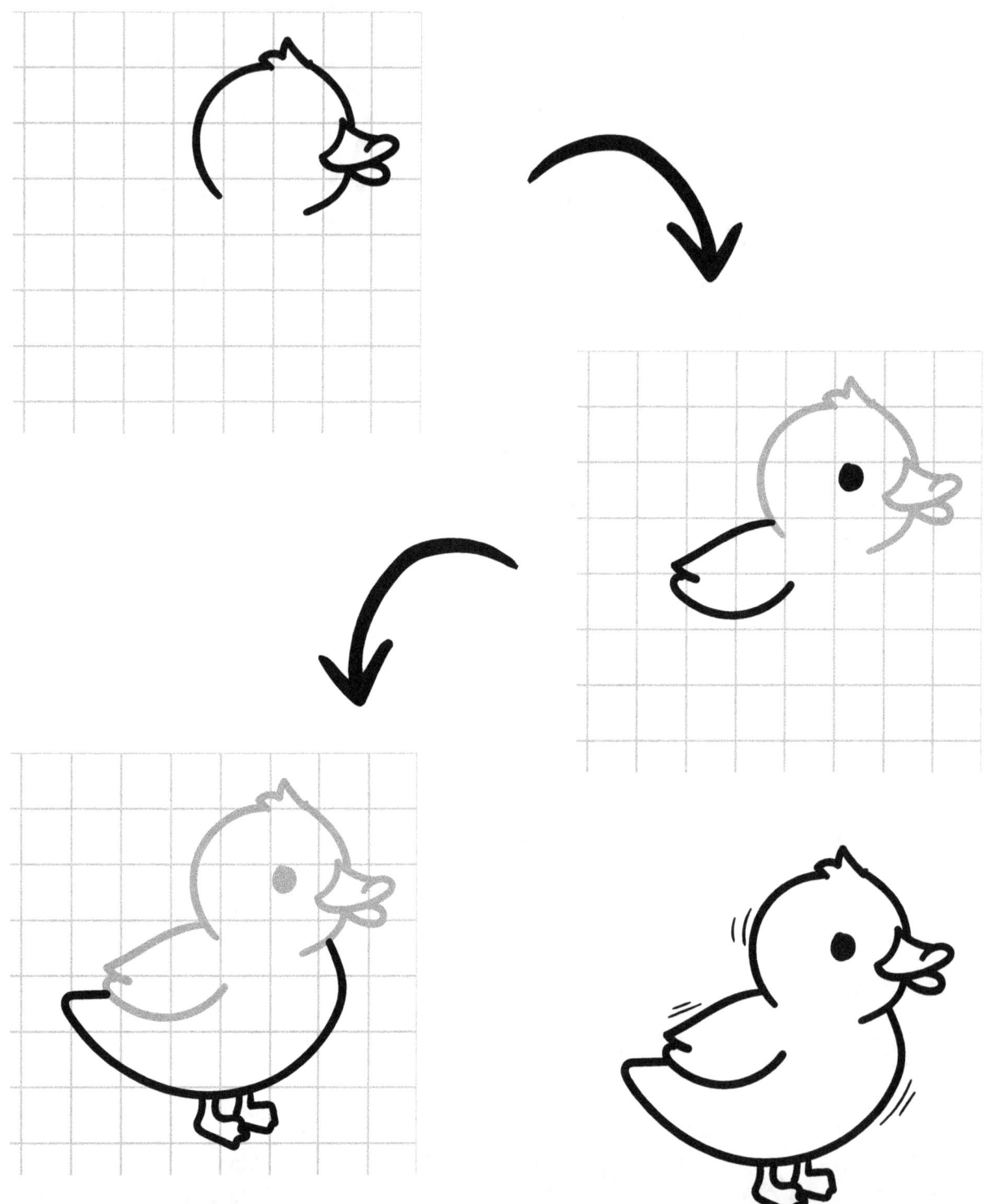

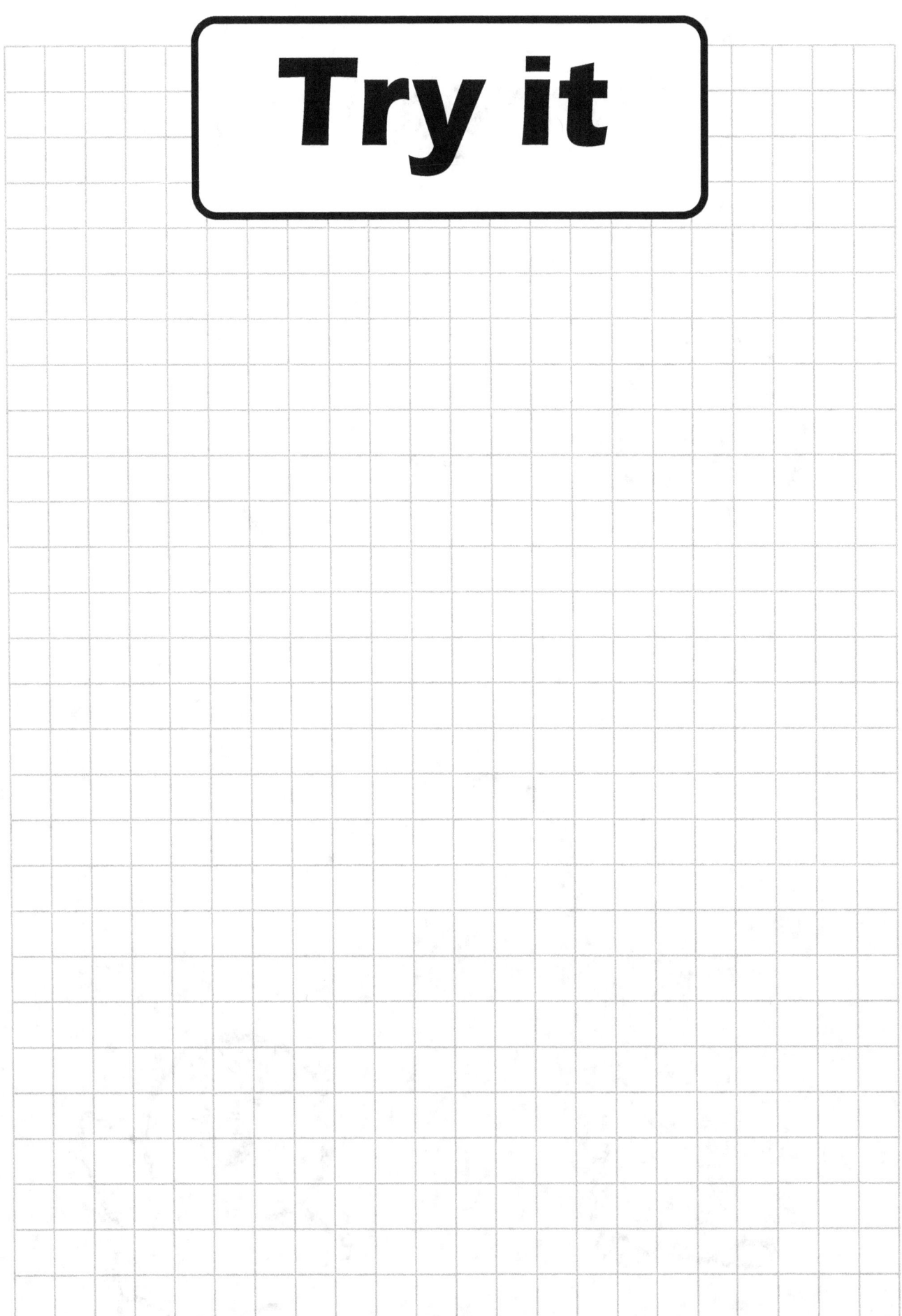

Try it

Penguin

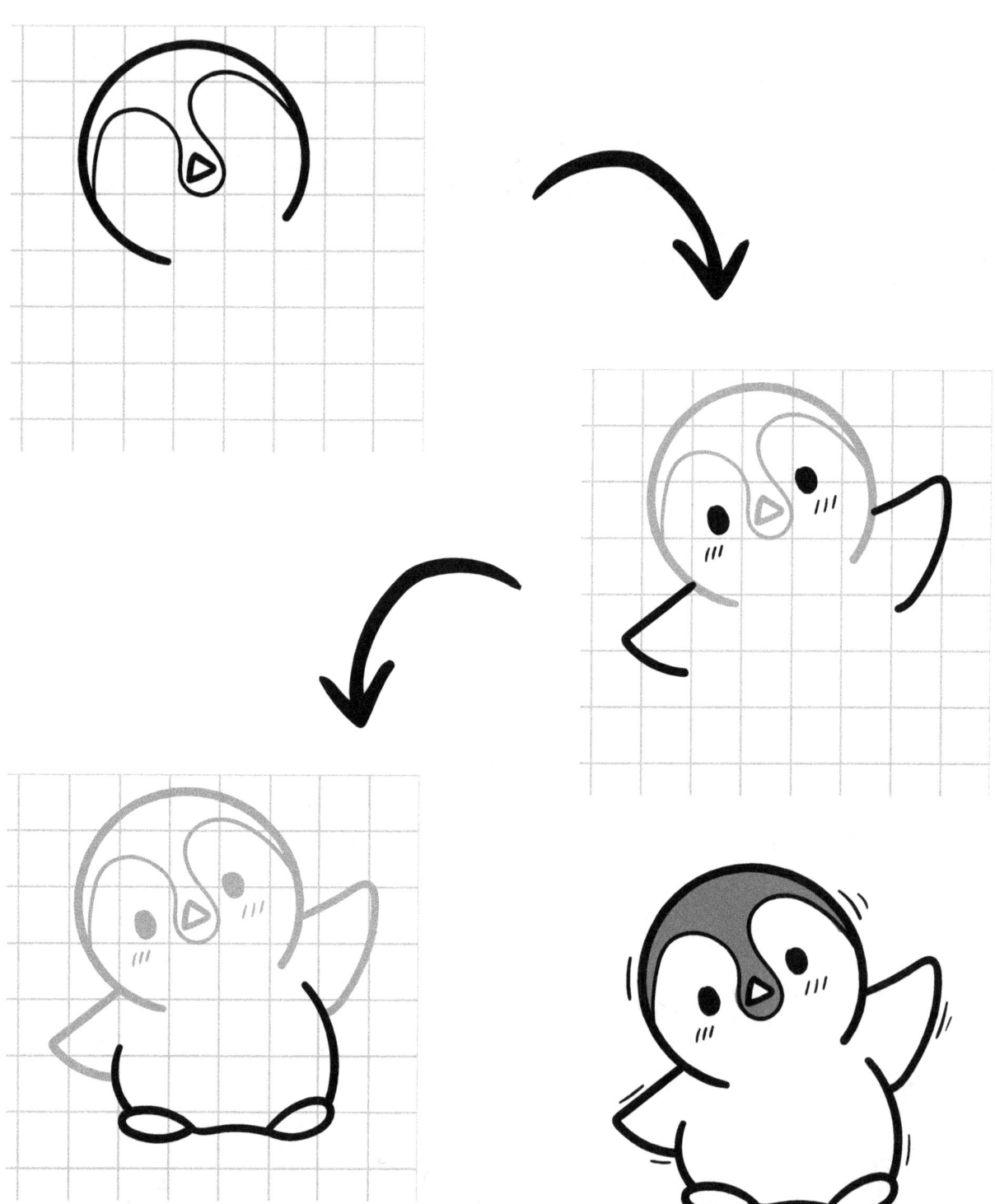

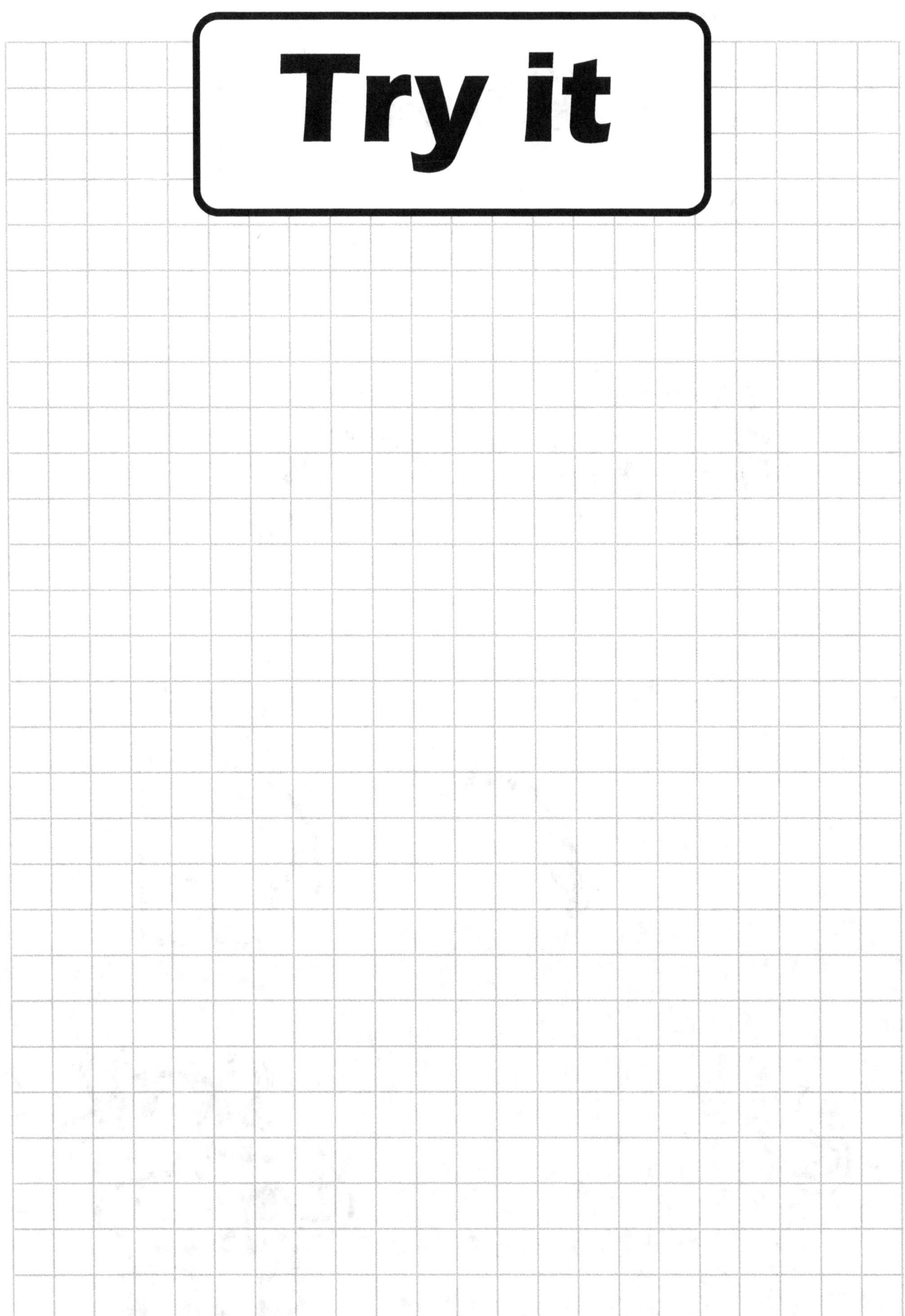

Try it

Cow

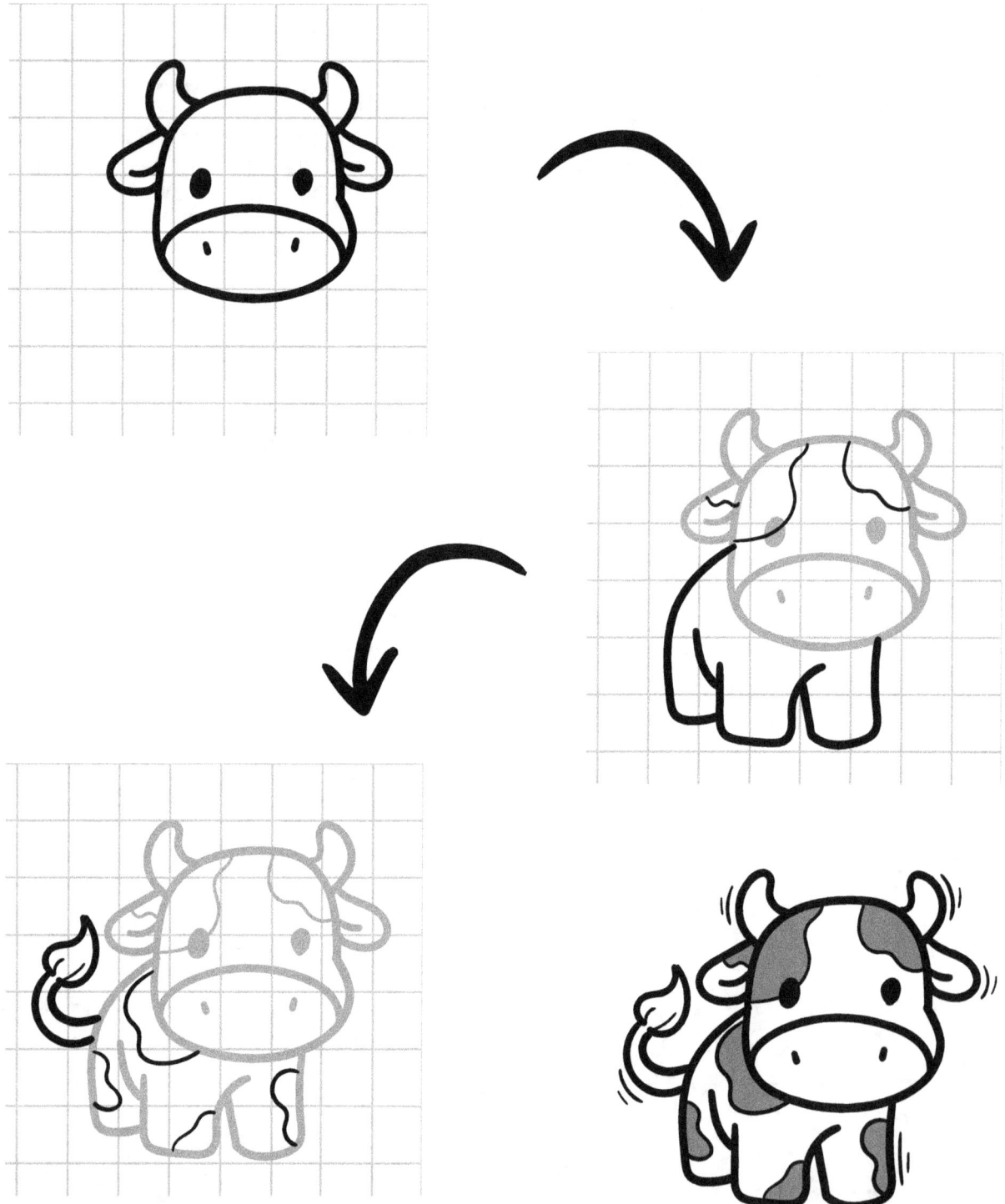

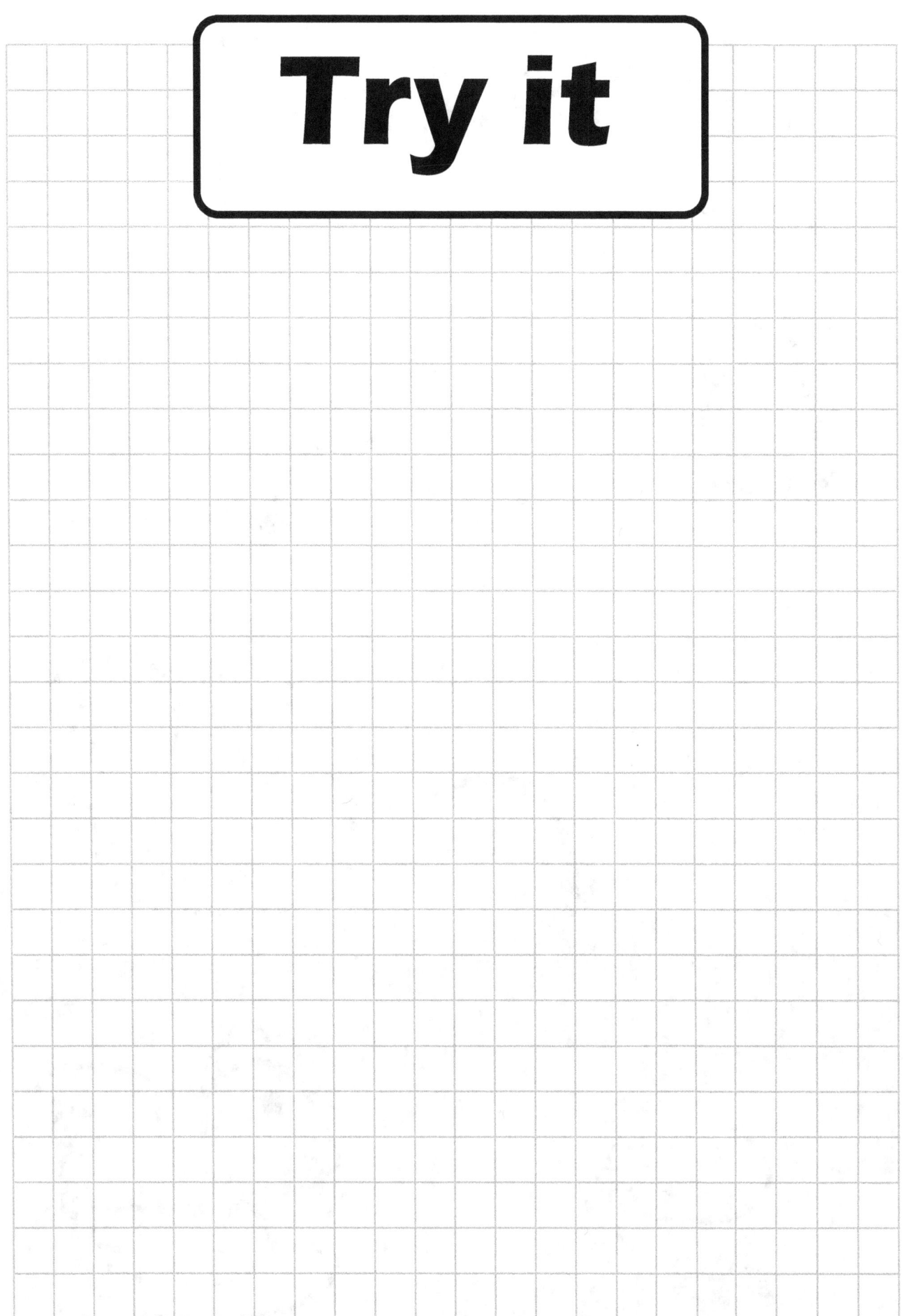

Try it

Chicken

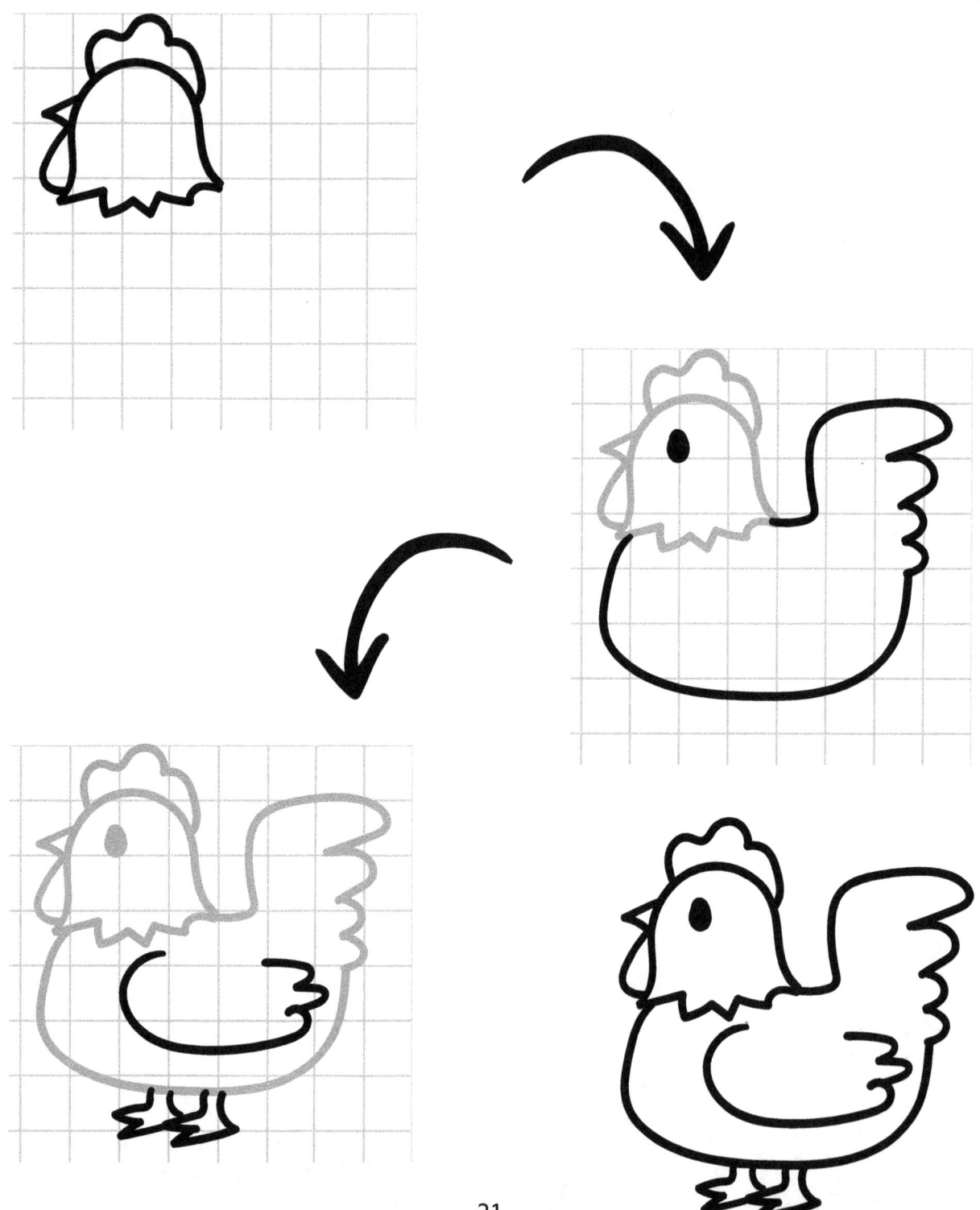

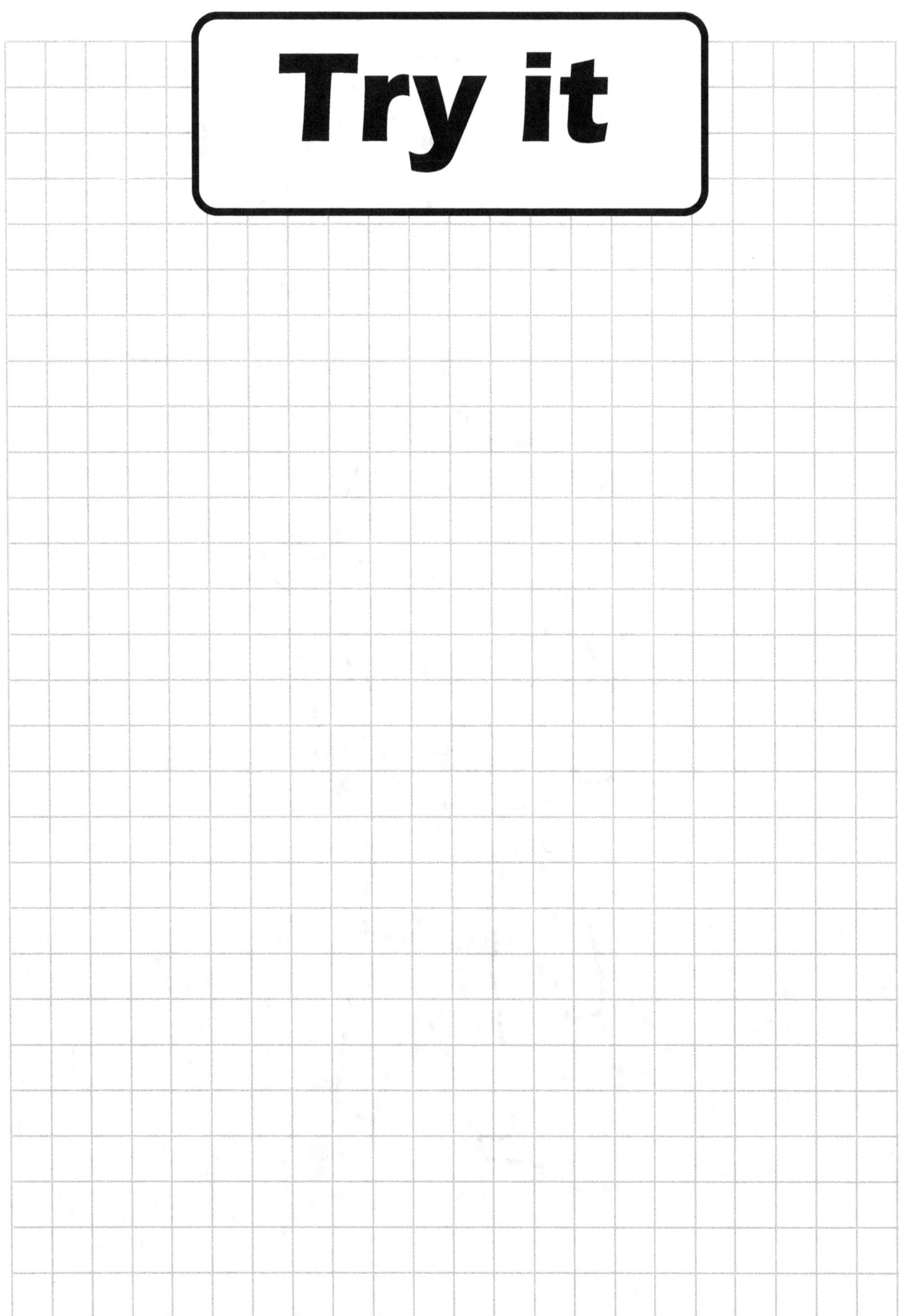

Try it

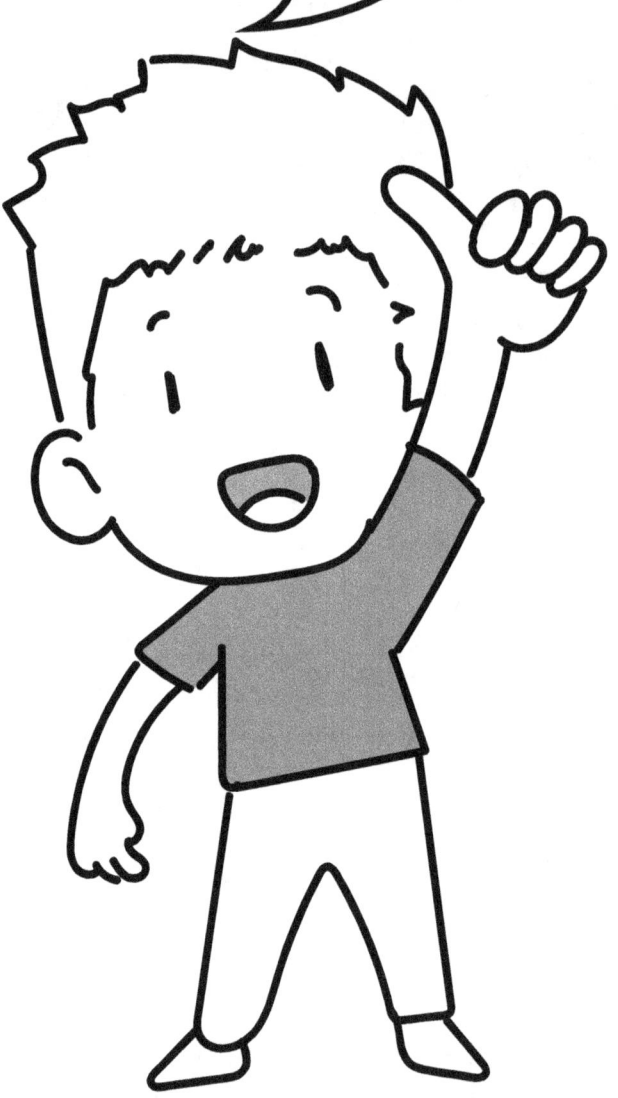

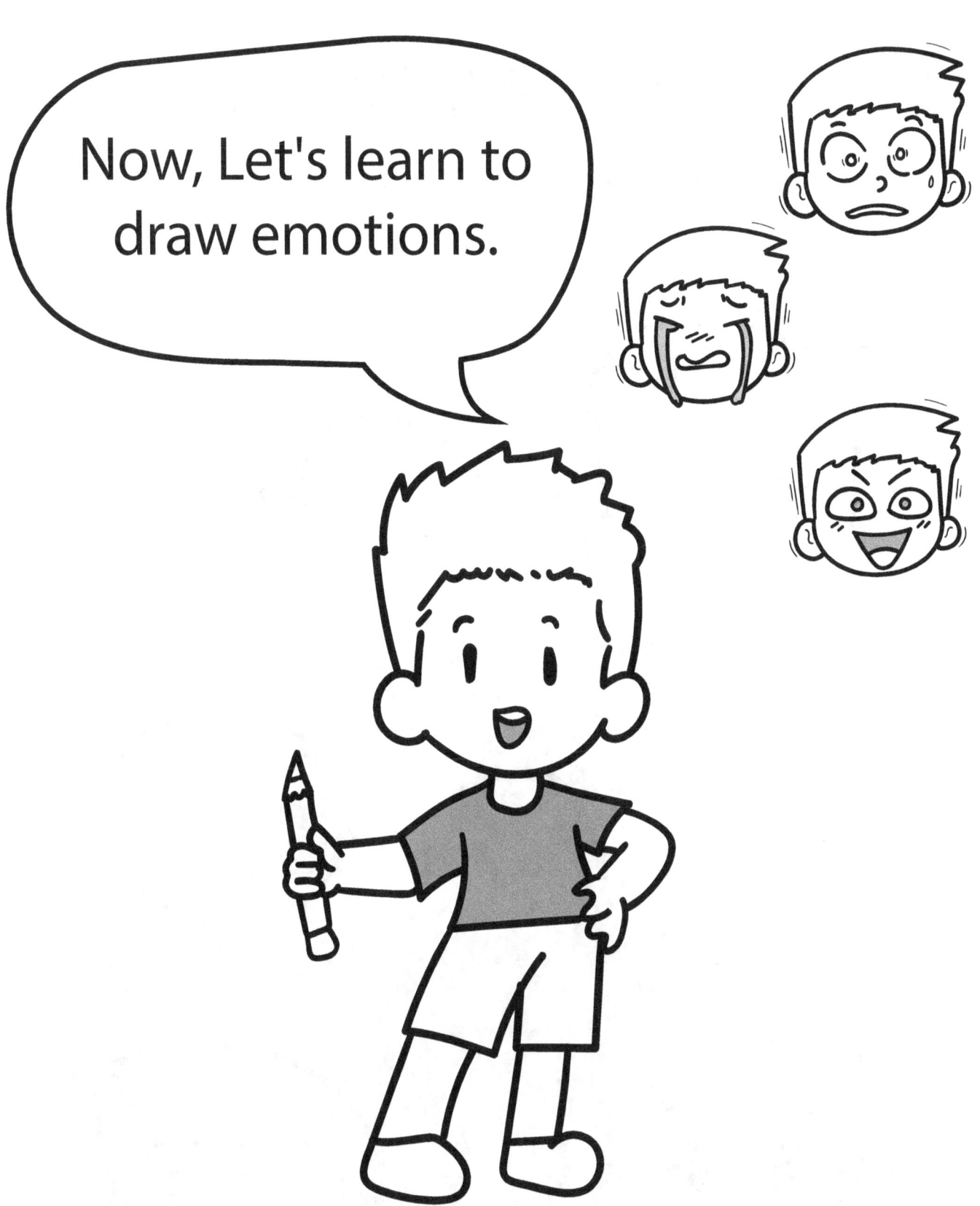

Happy

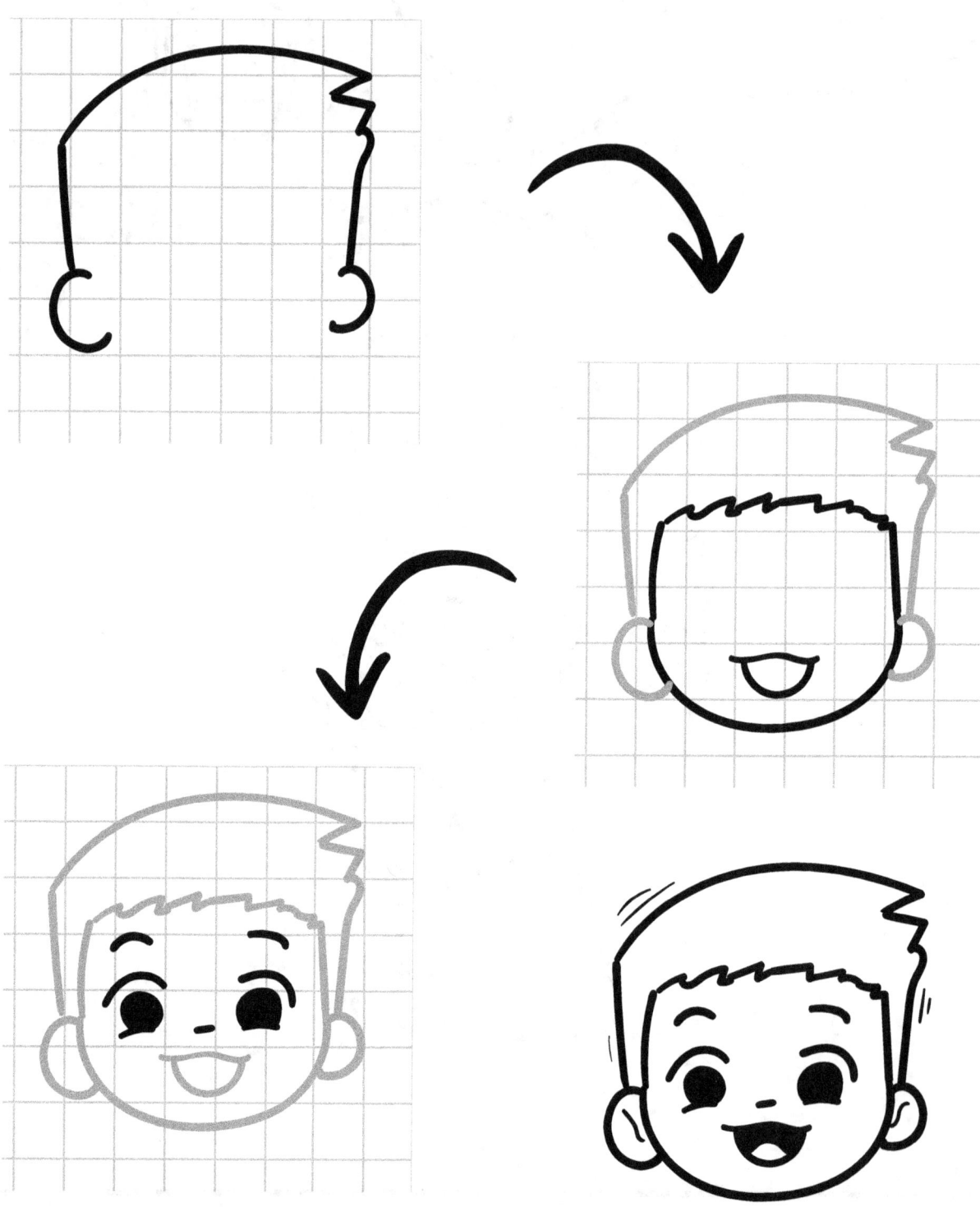

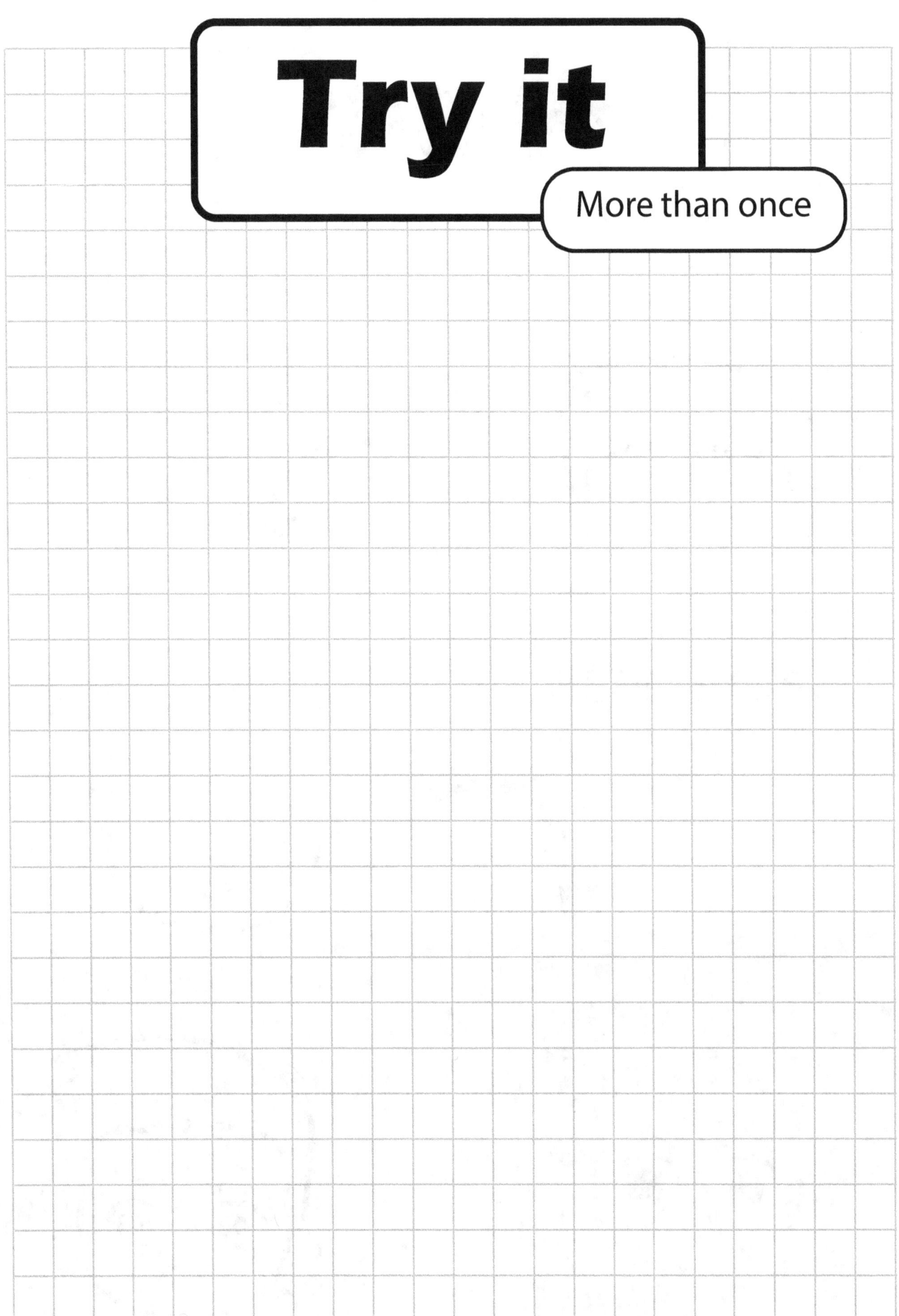

Try it

More than once

Angry

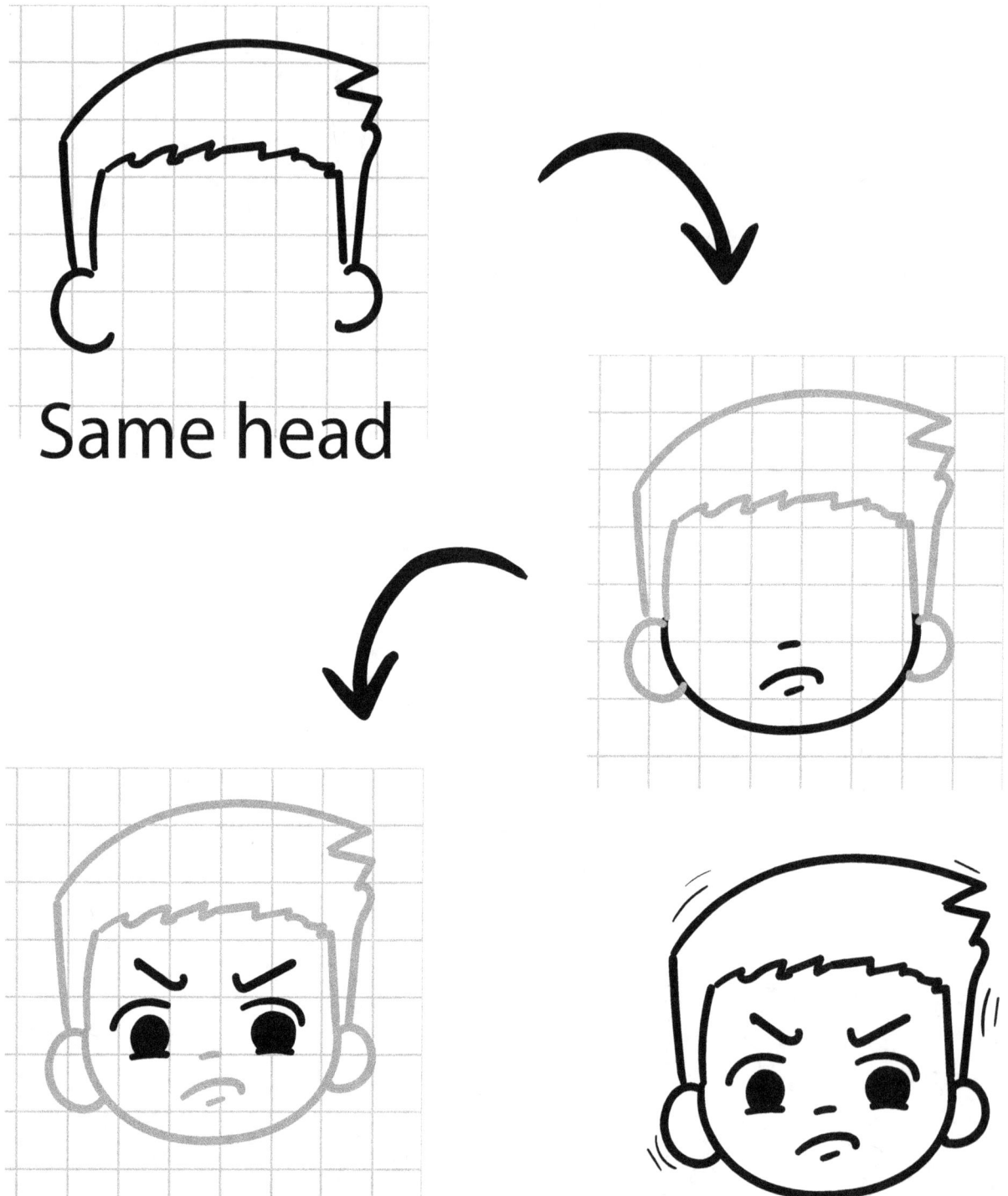

Same head

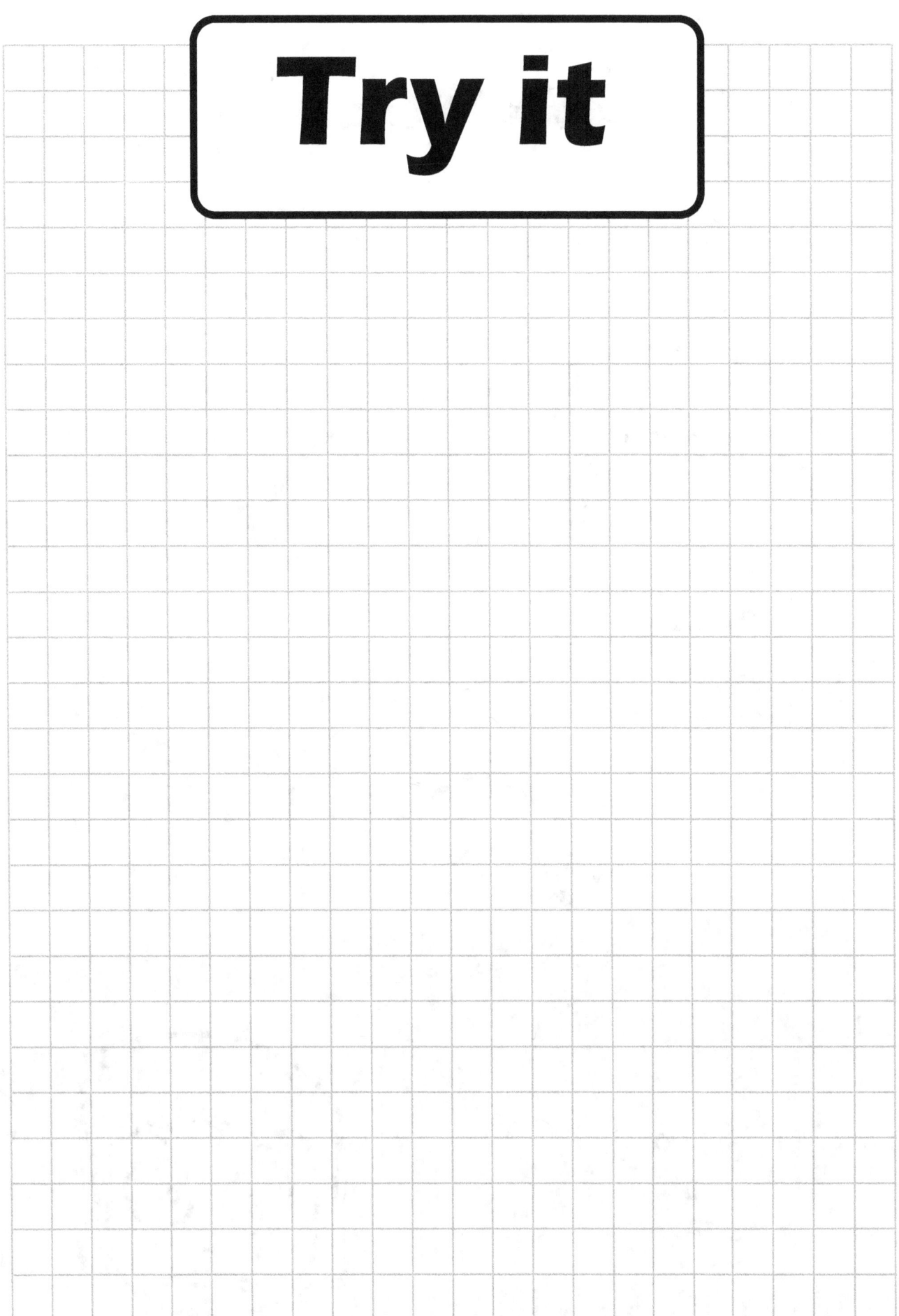

Try it

Scared

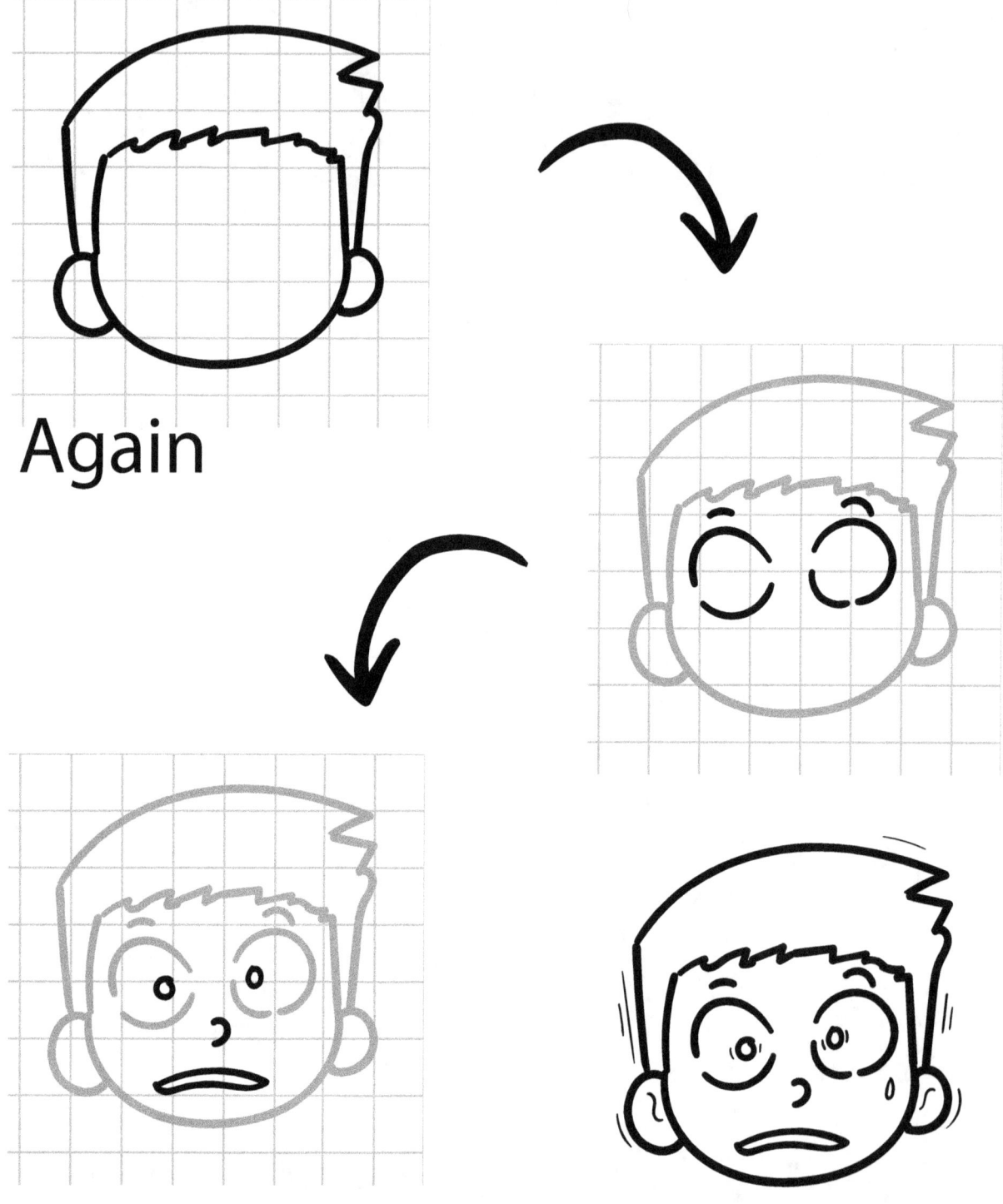

Again

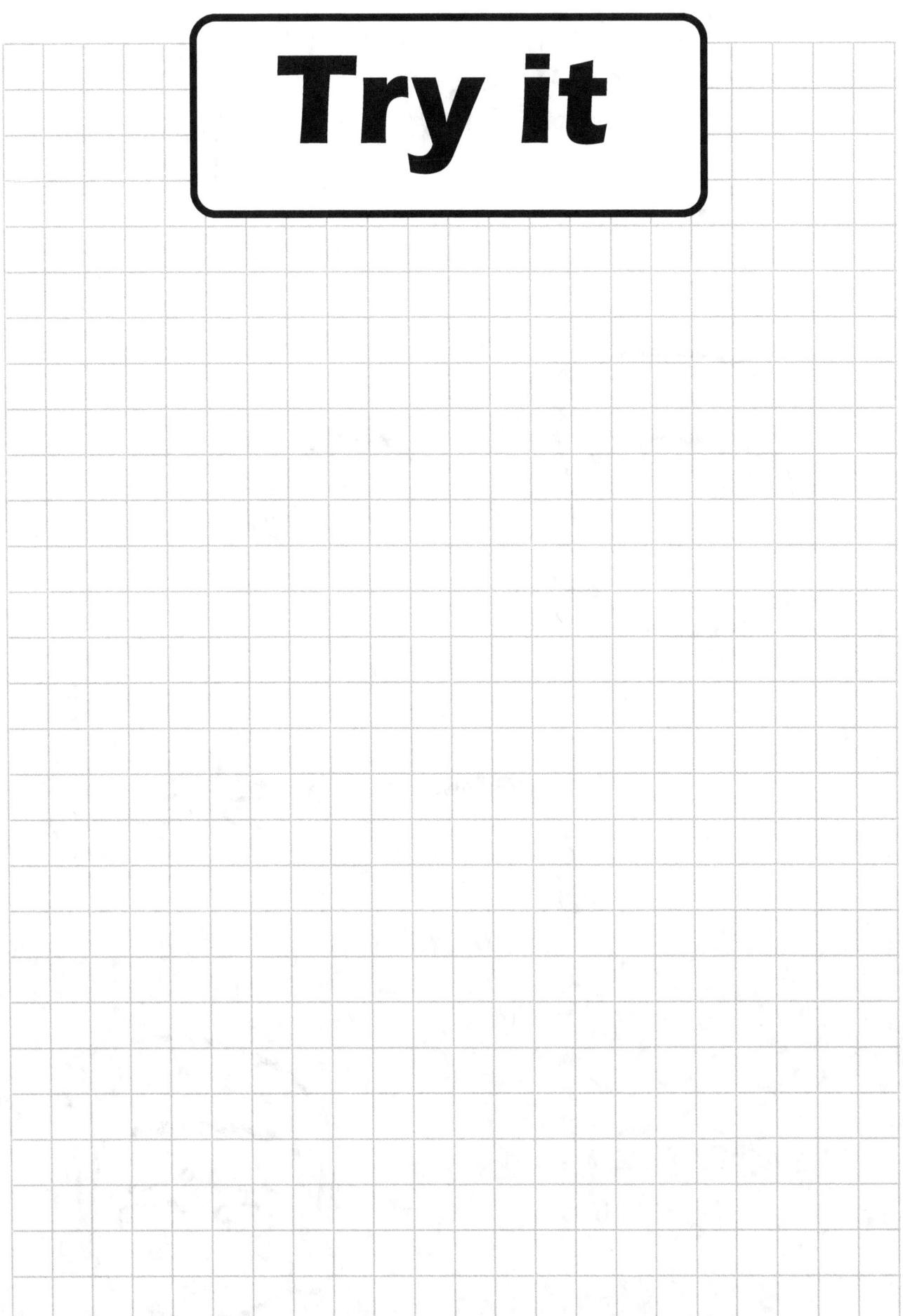

Try it

Shy

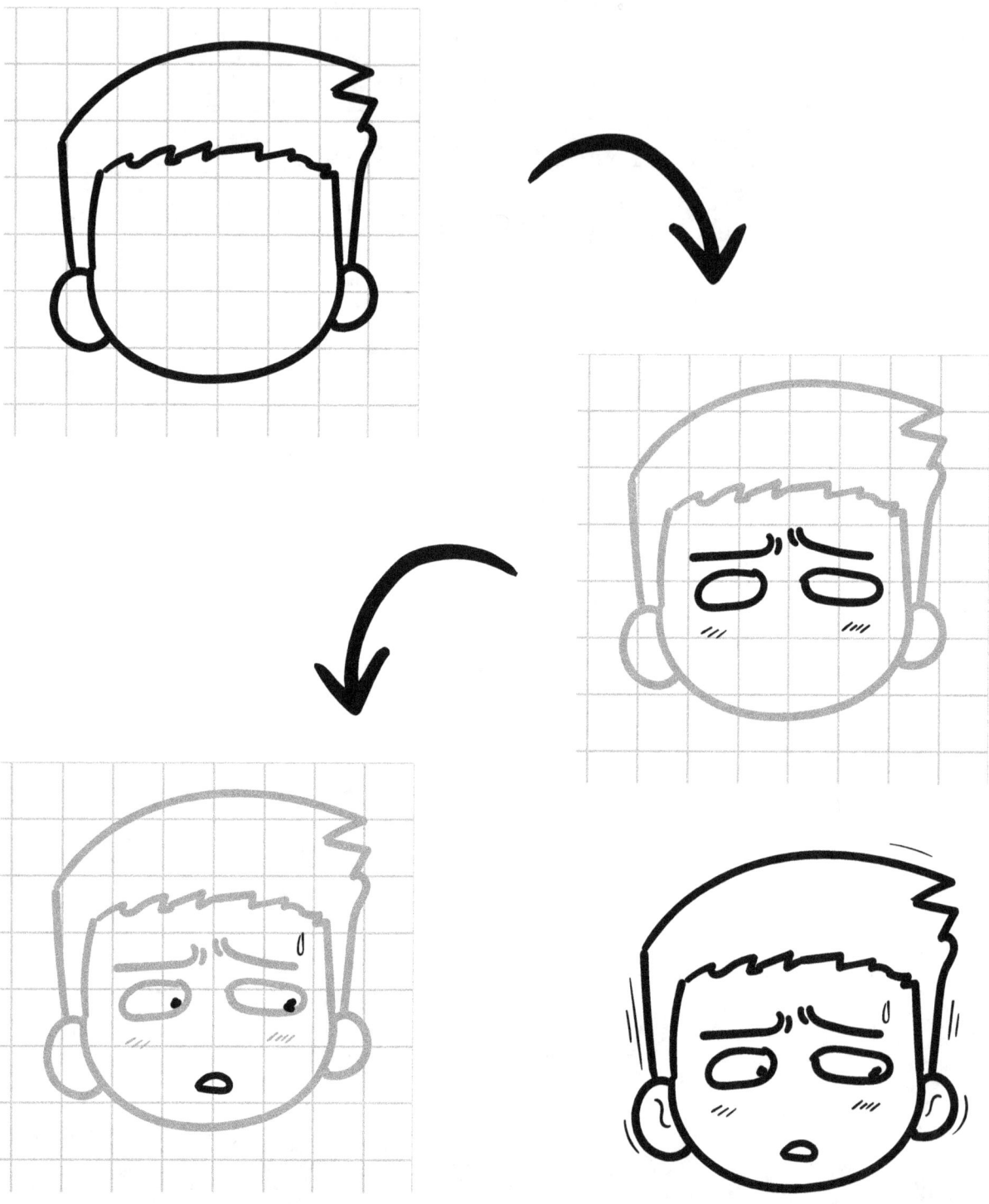

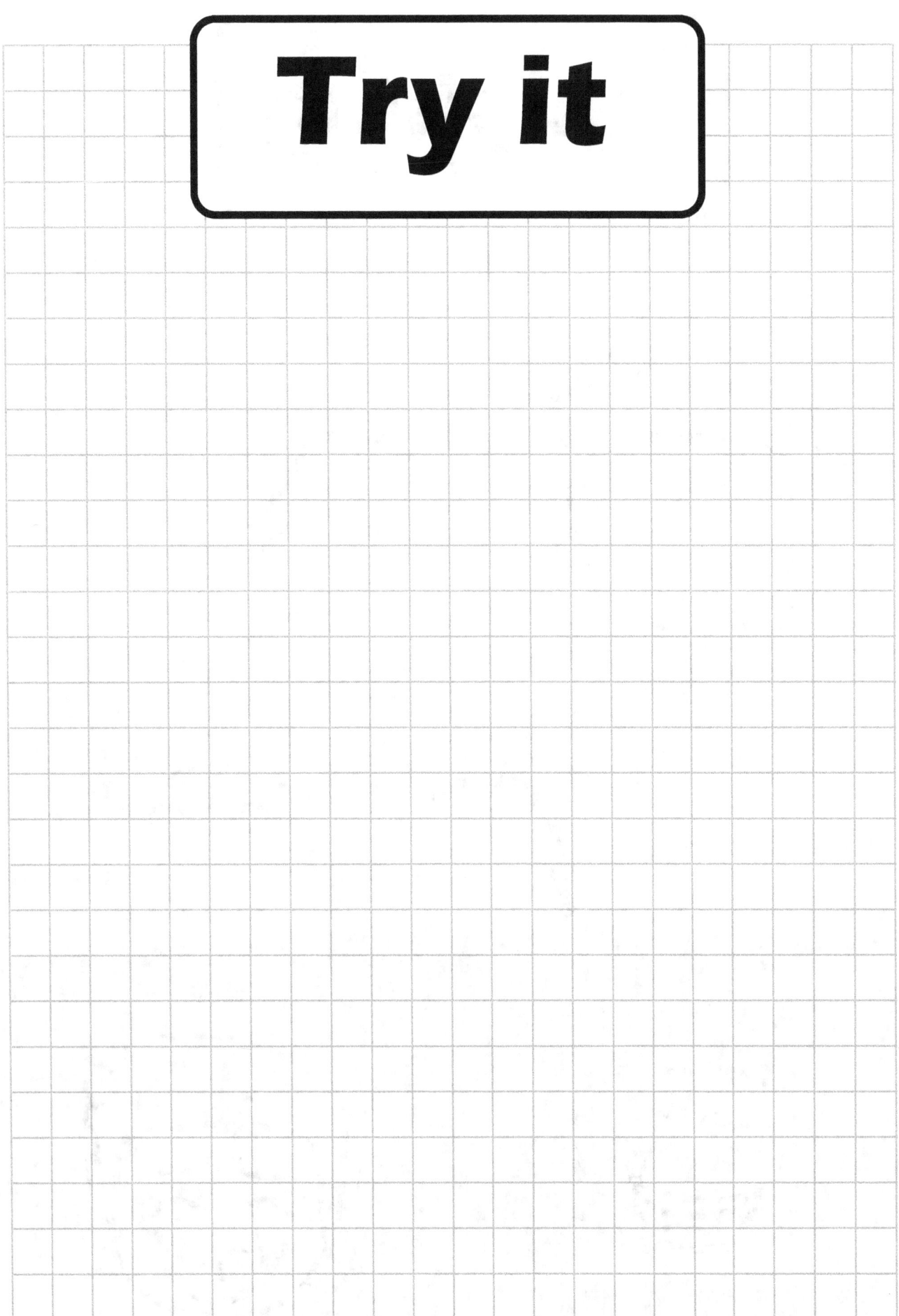

Try it

Laughing

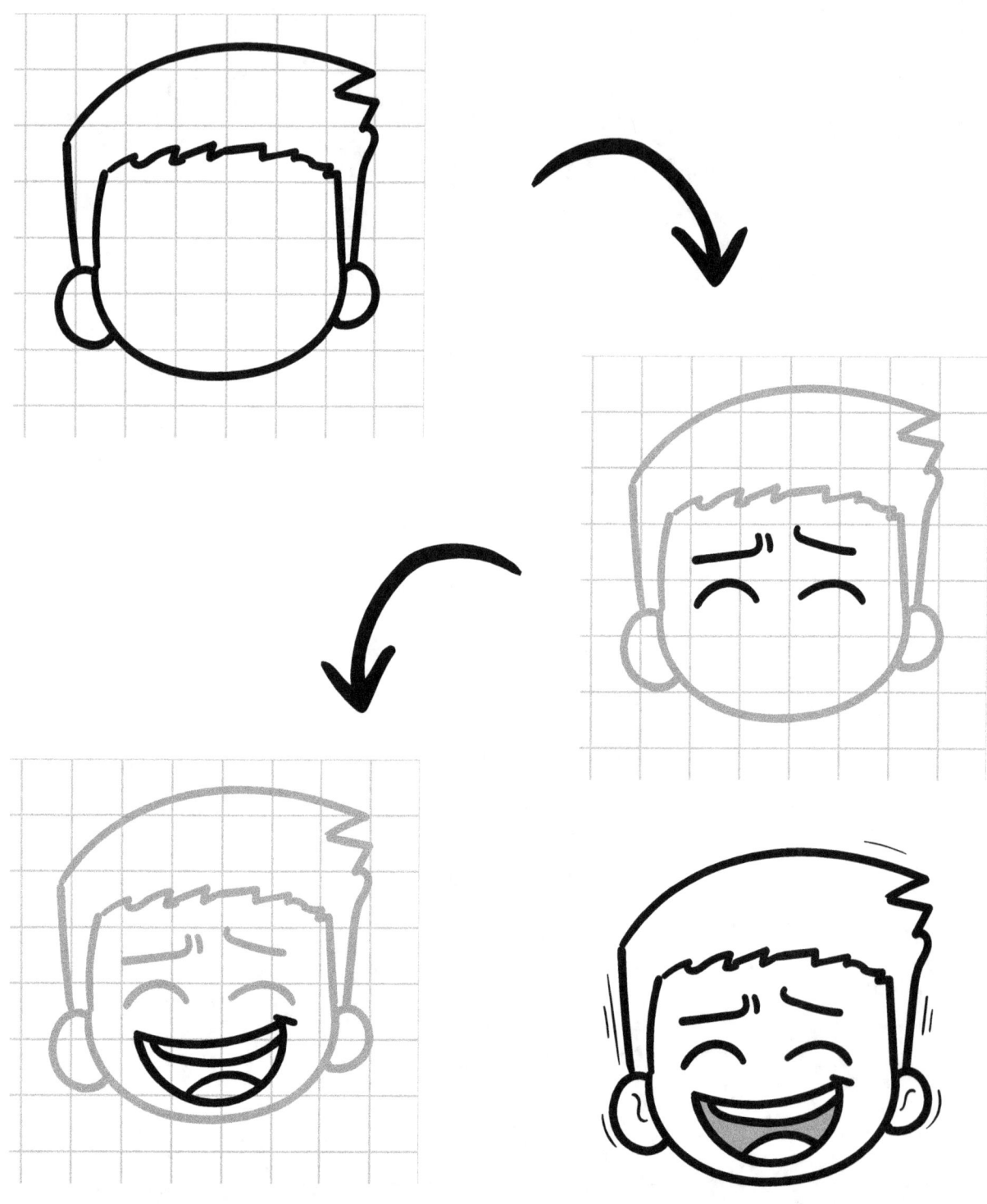

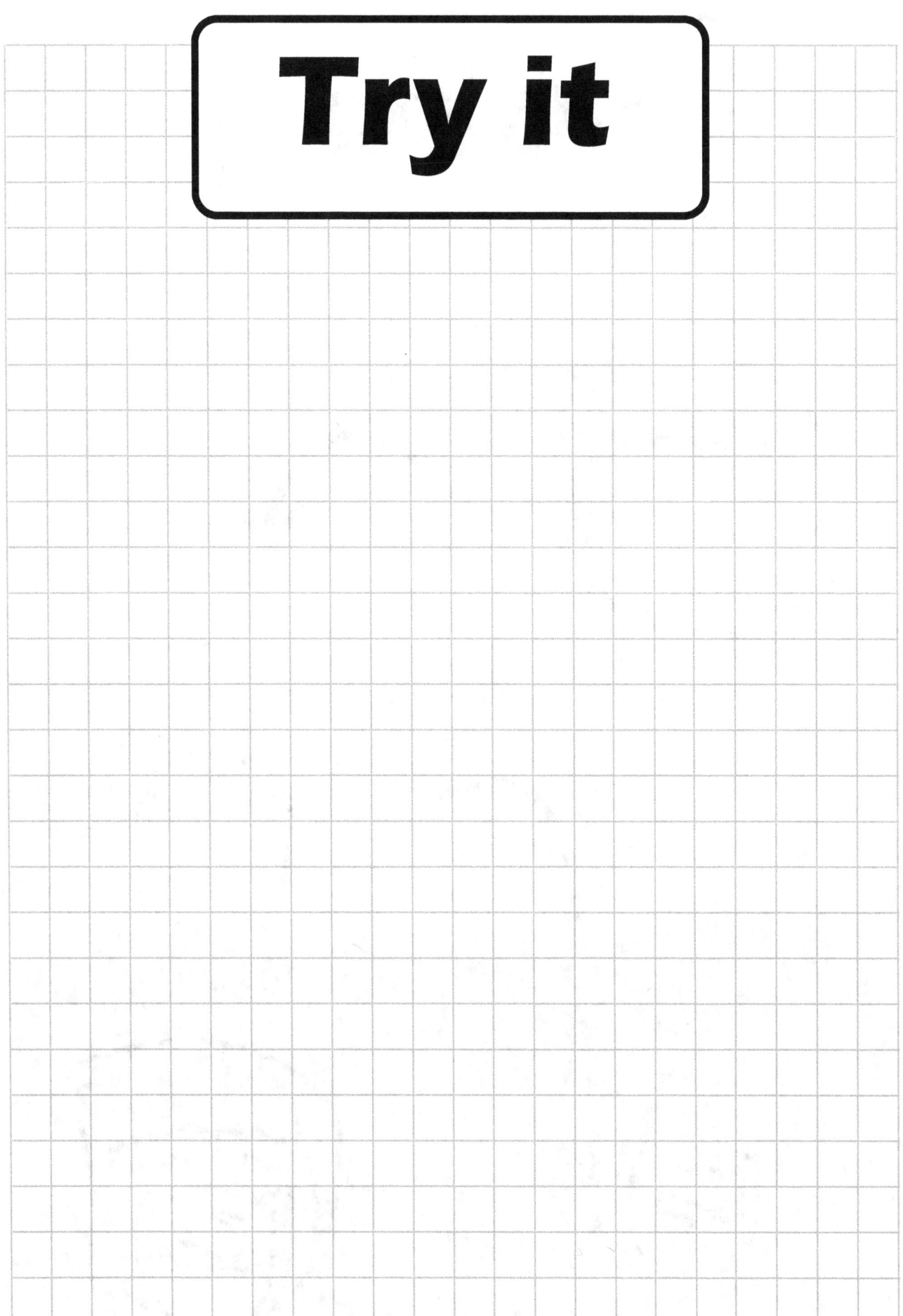

Try it

Crying

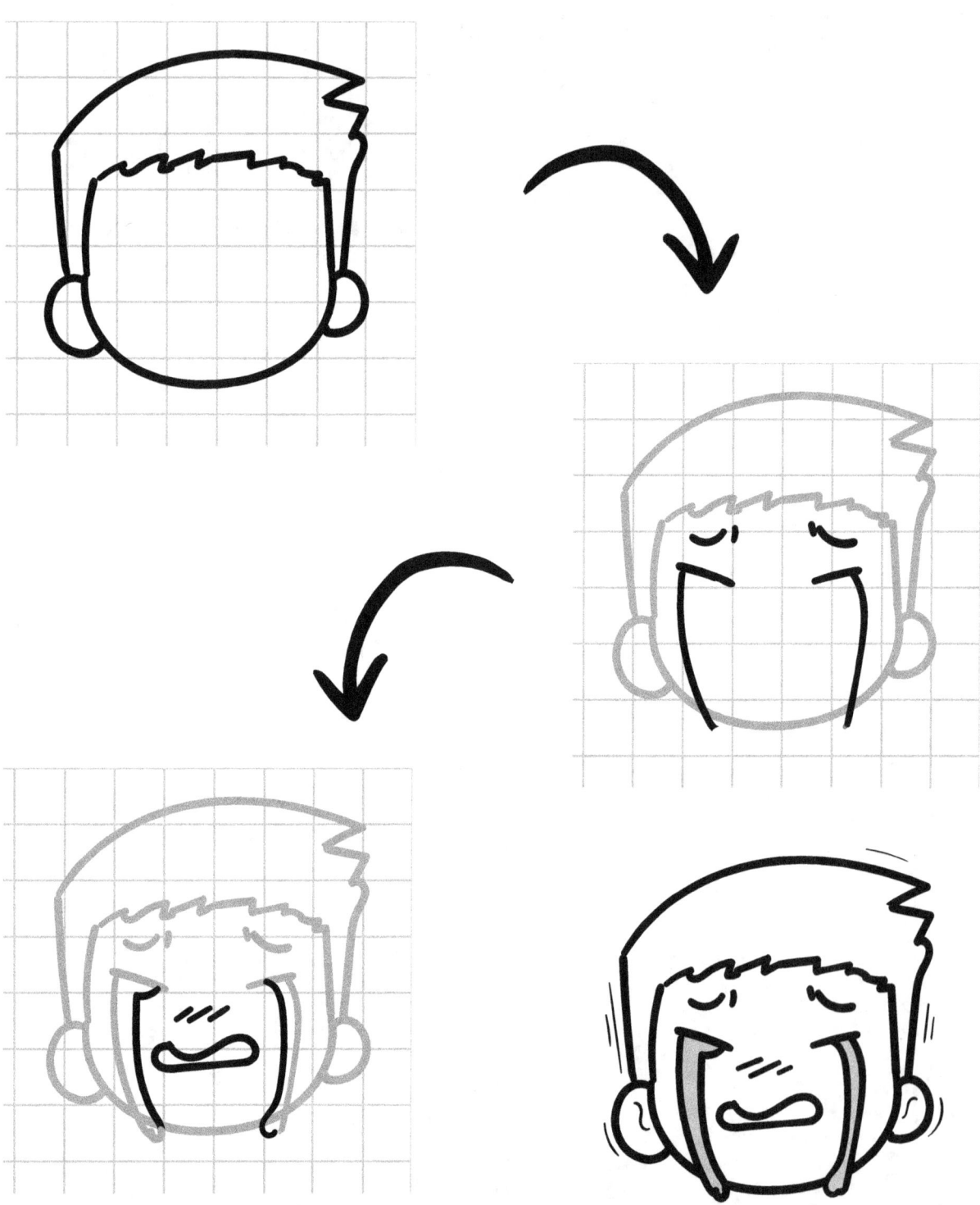

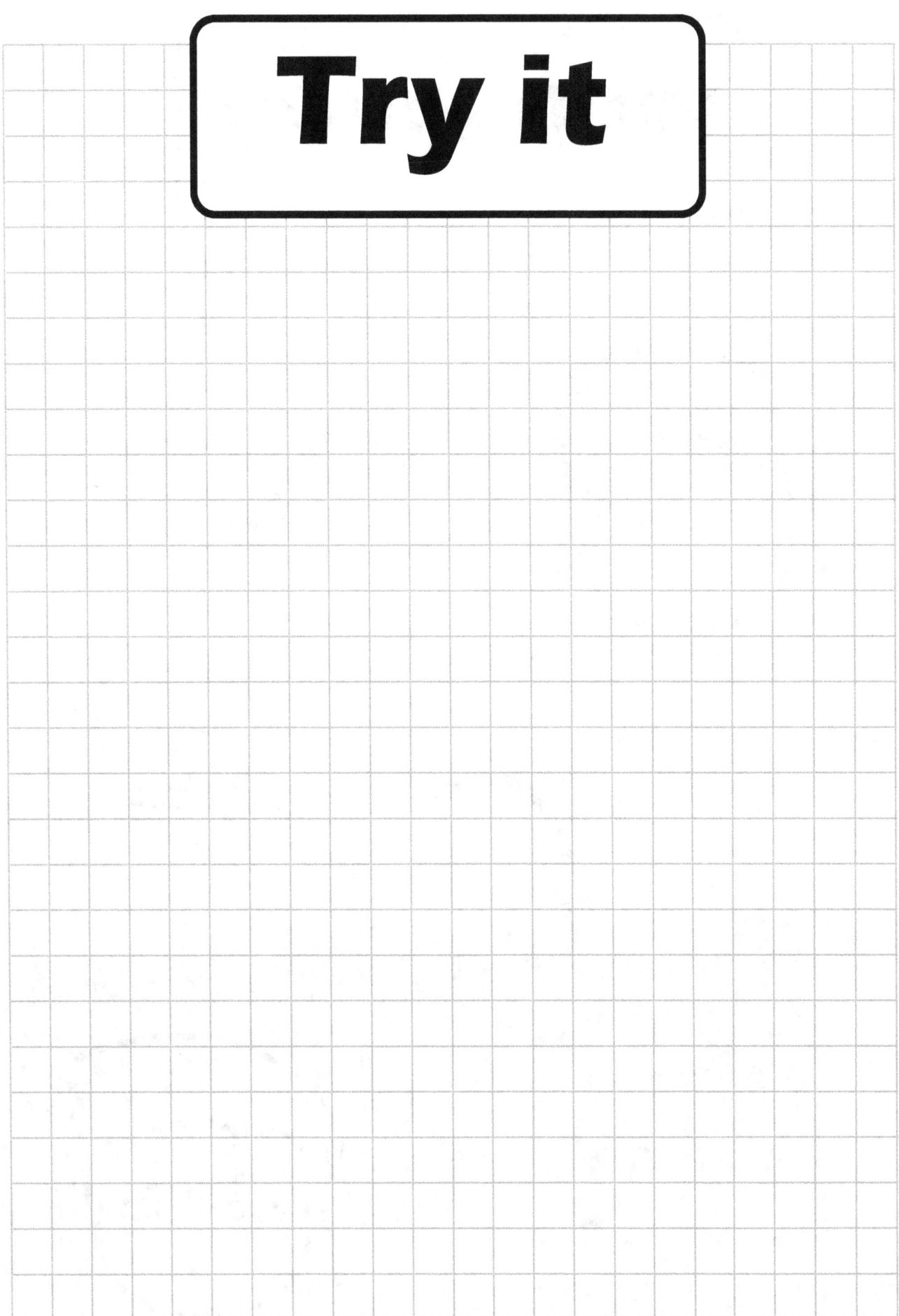

Try it

Wondering

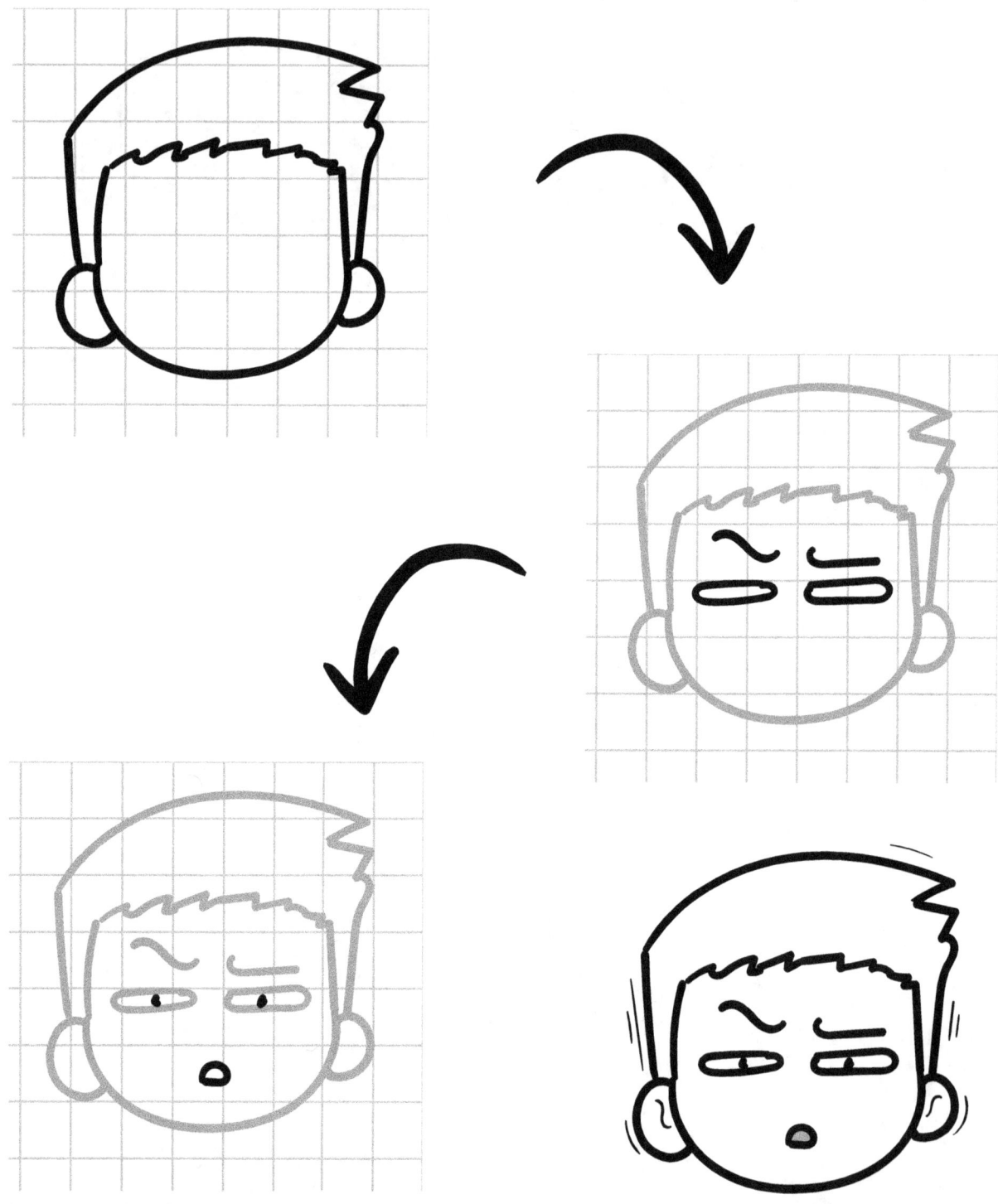

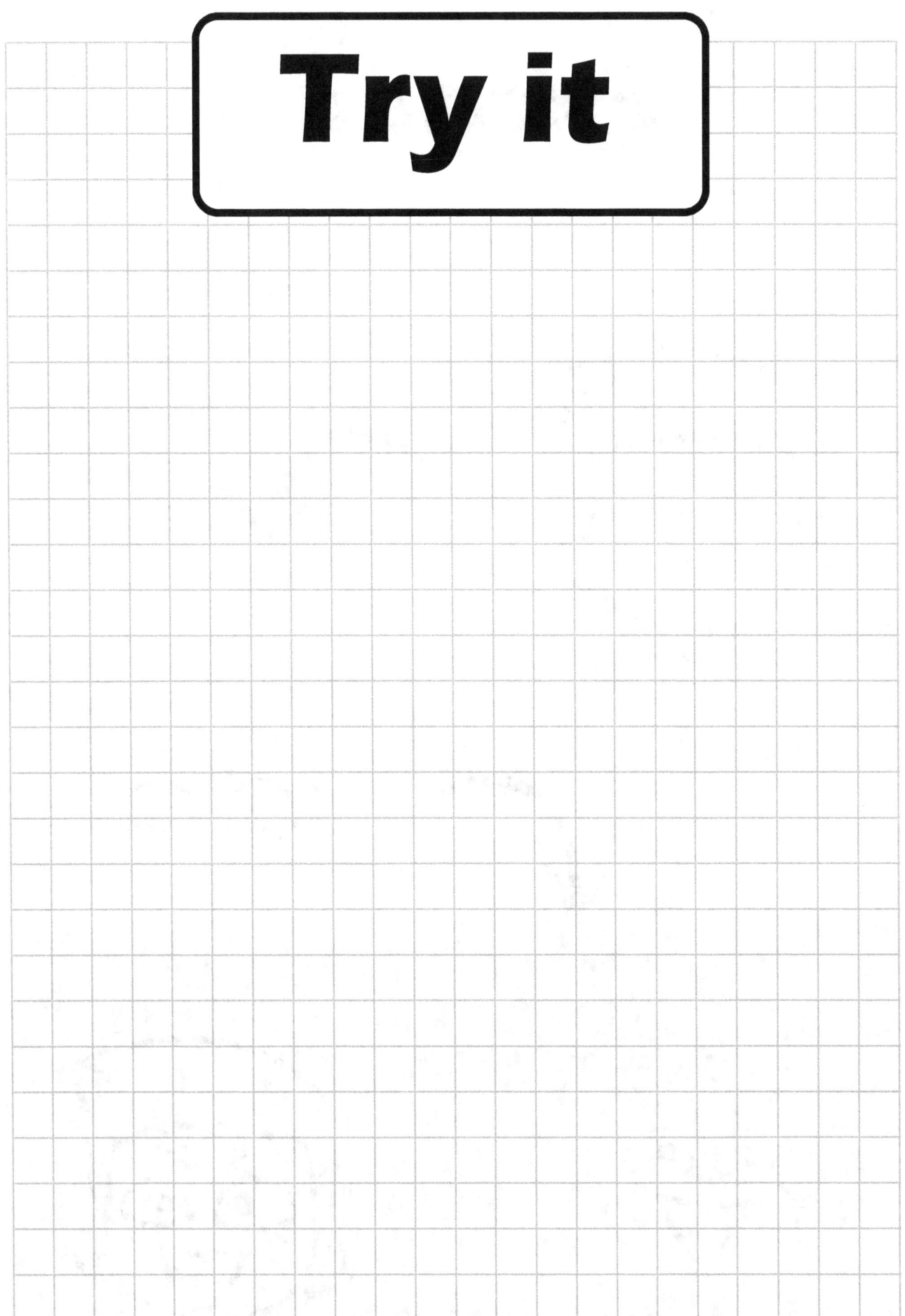

Try it

Excited

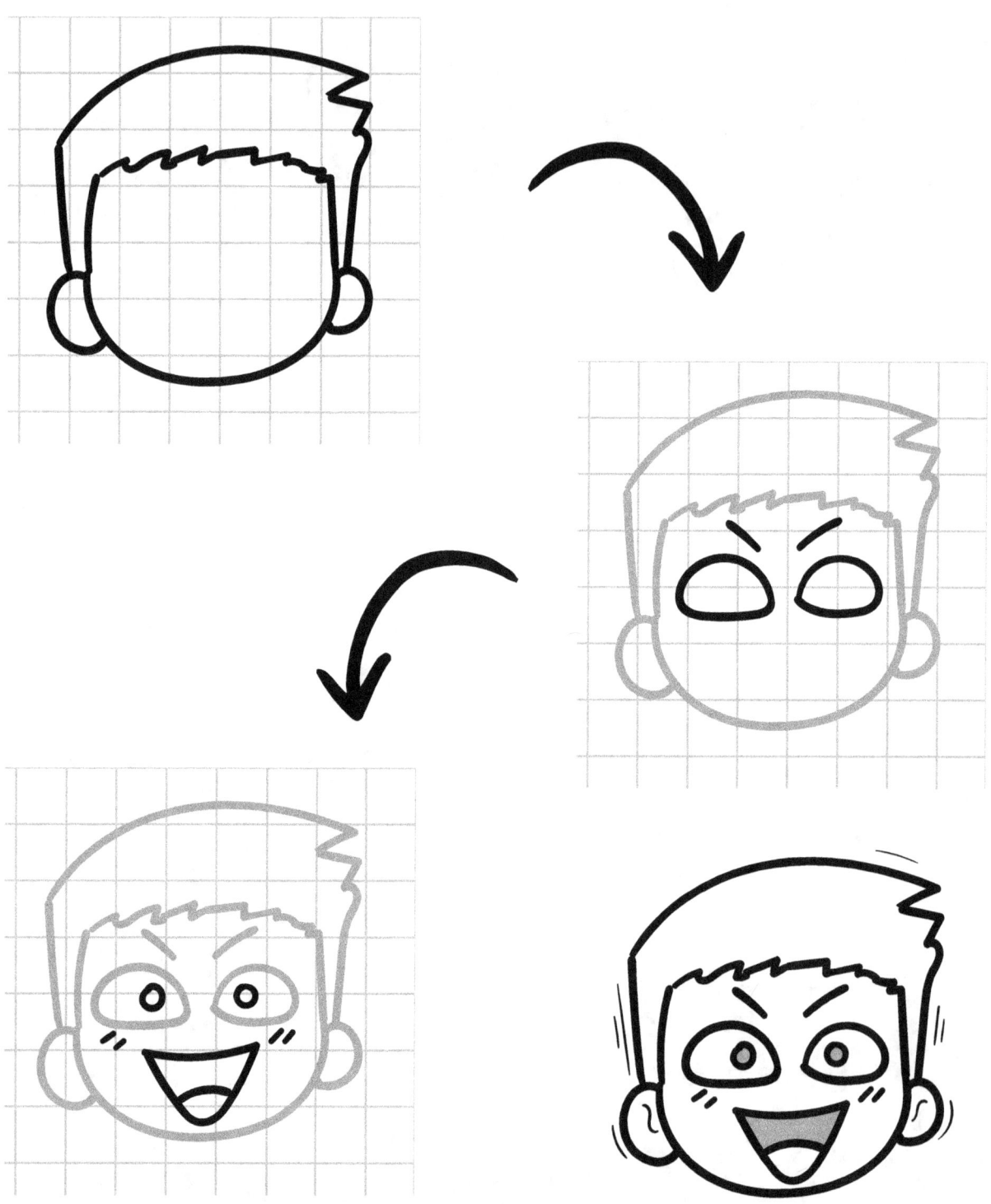

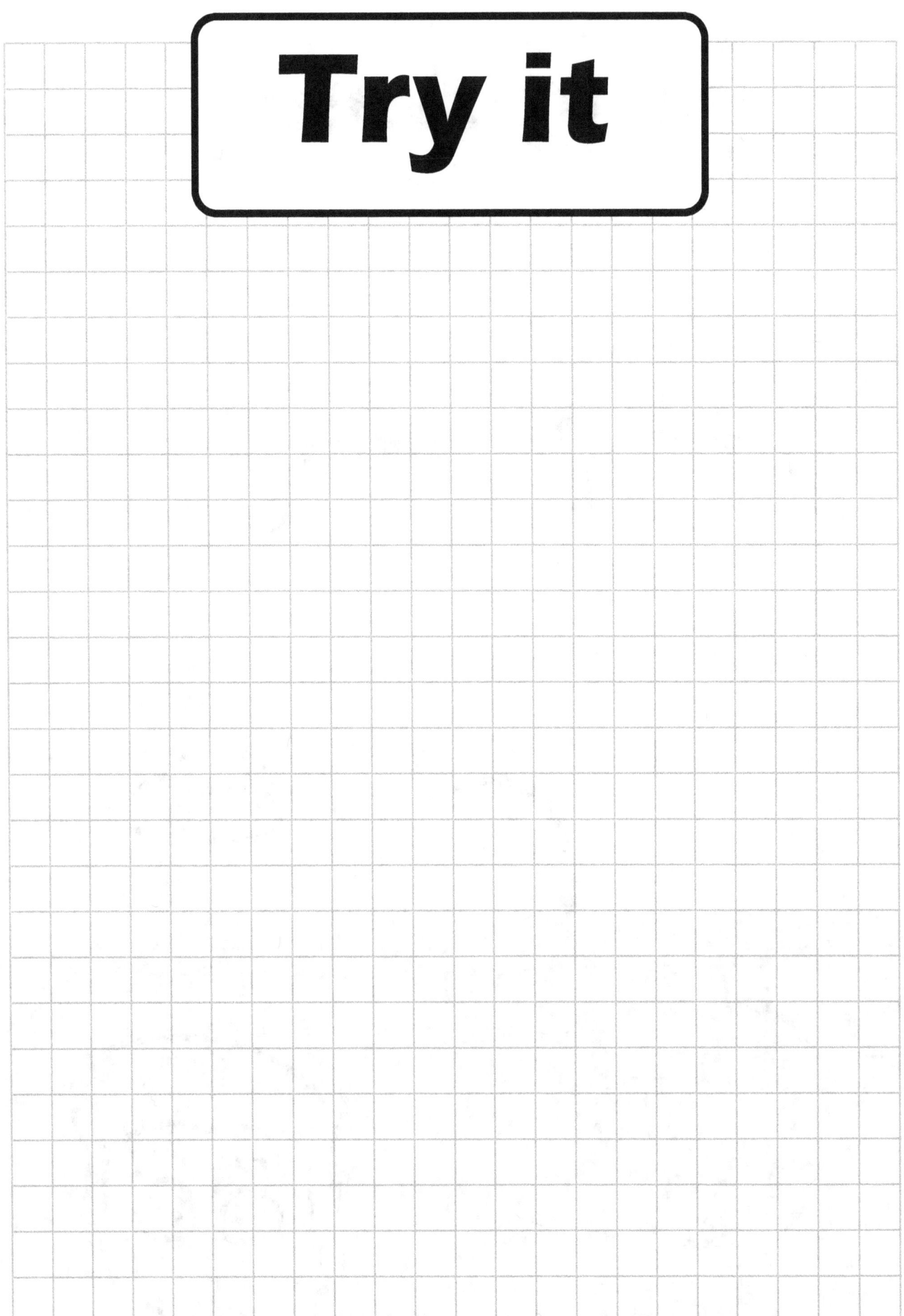

Try it

Surprised

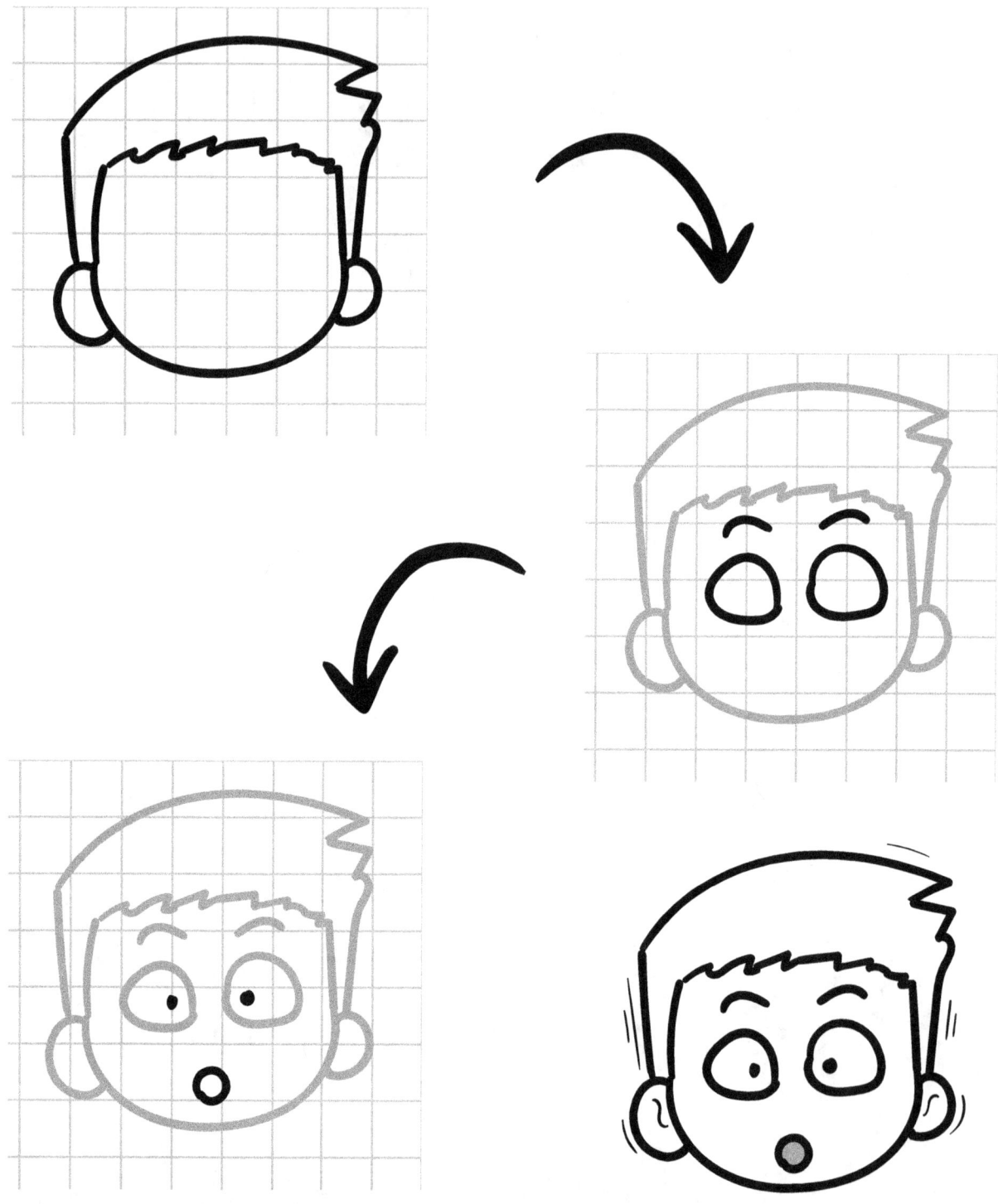

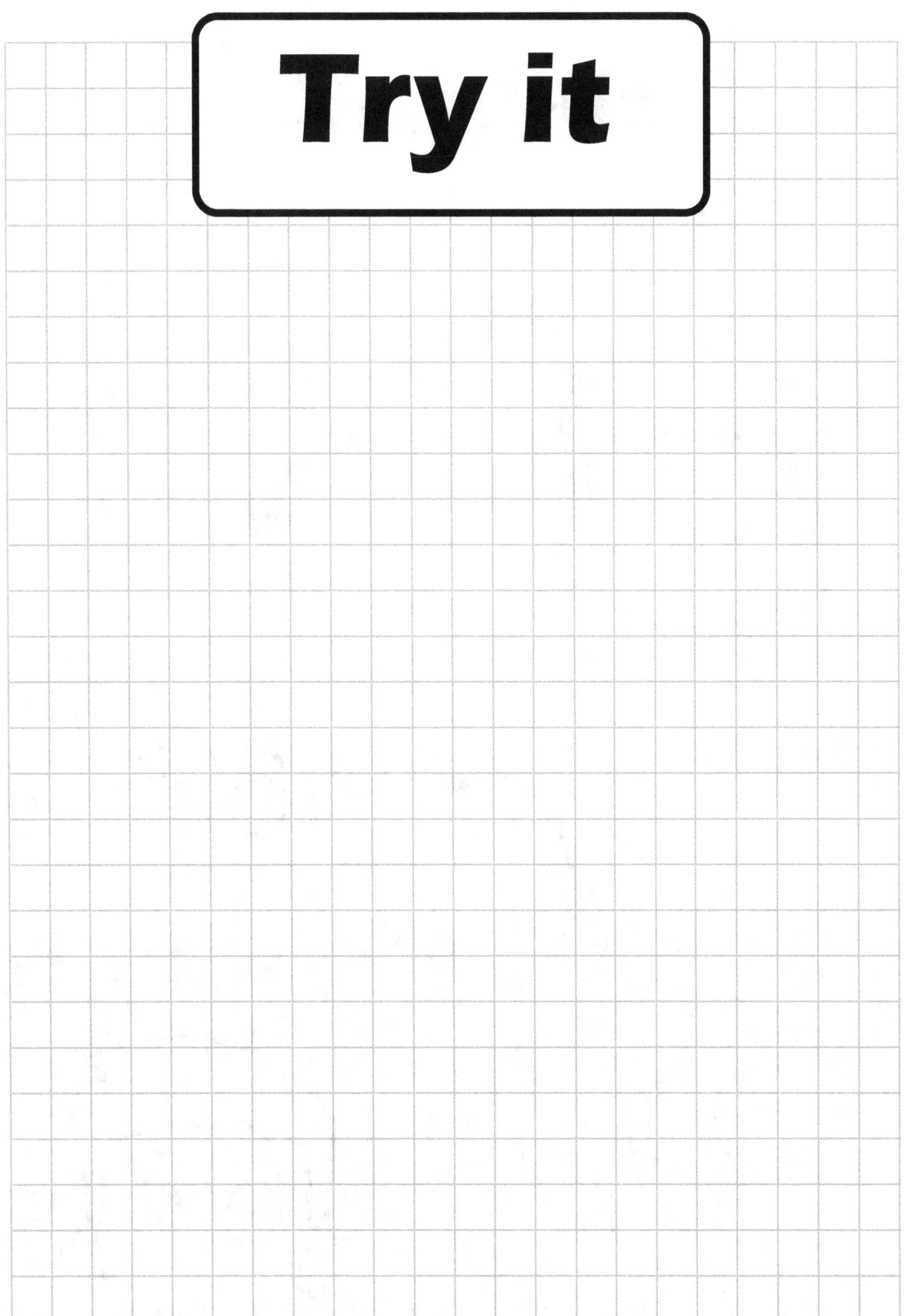

Try it

Neutral

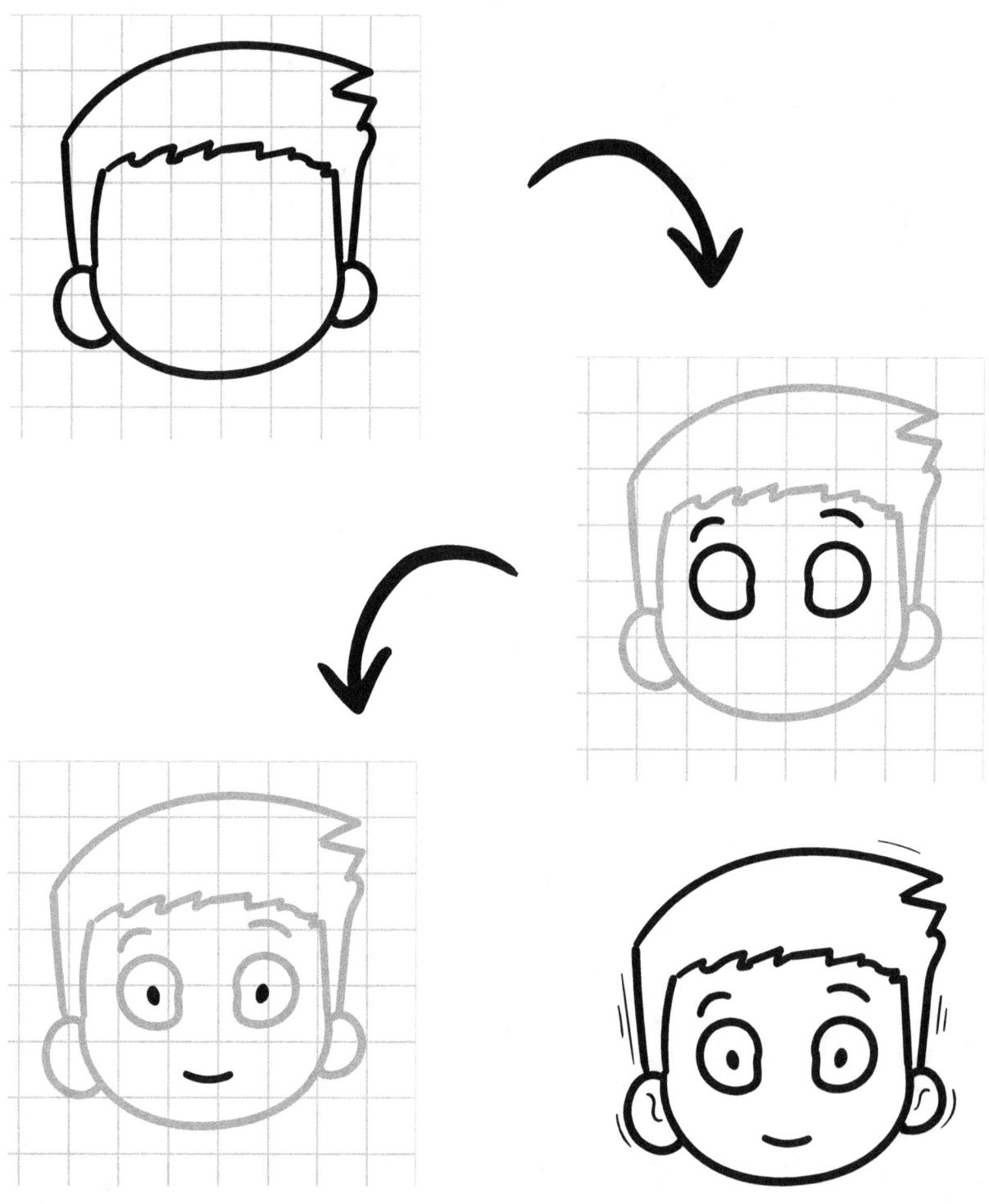

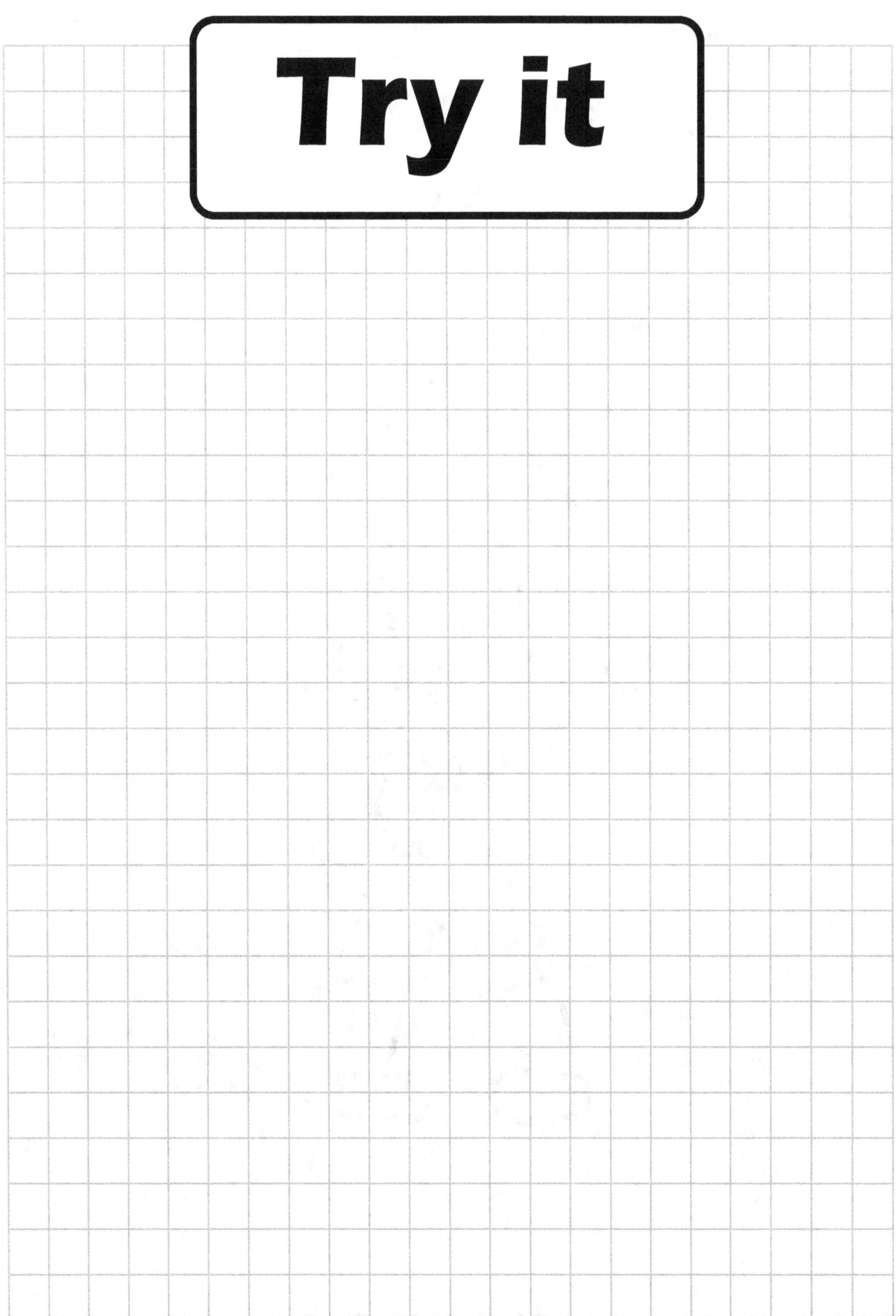

Try it

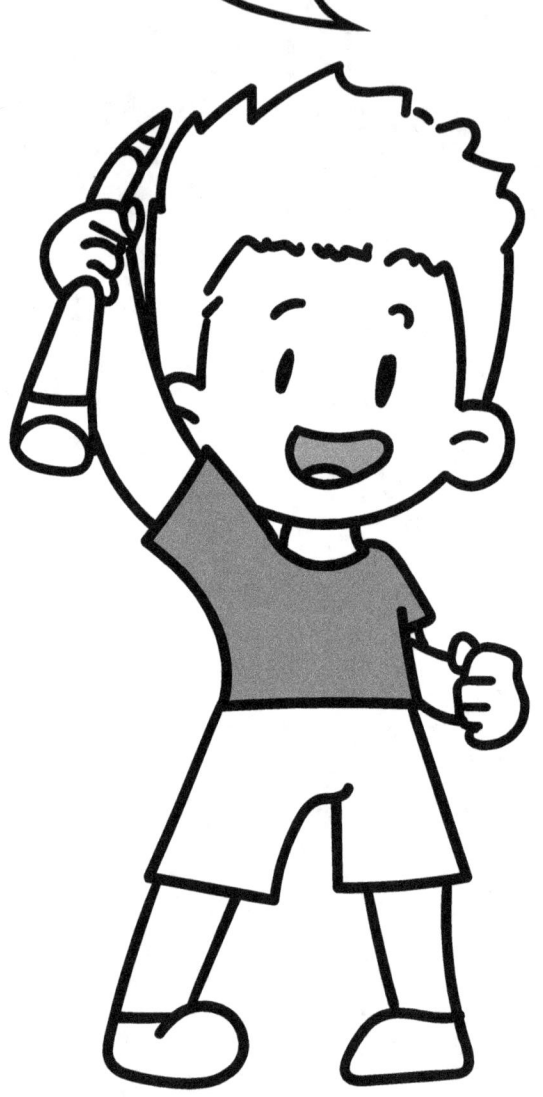

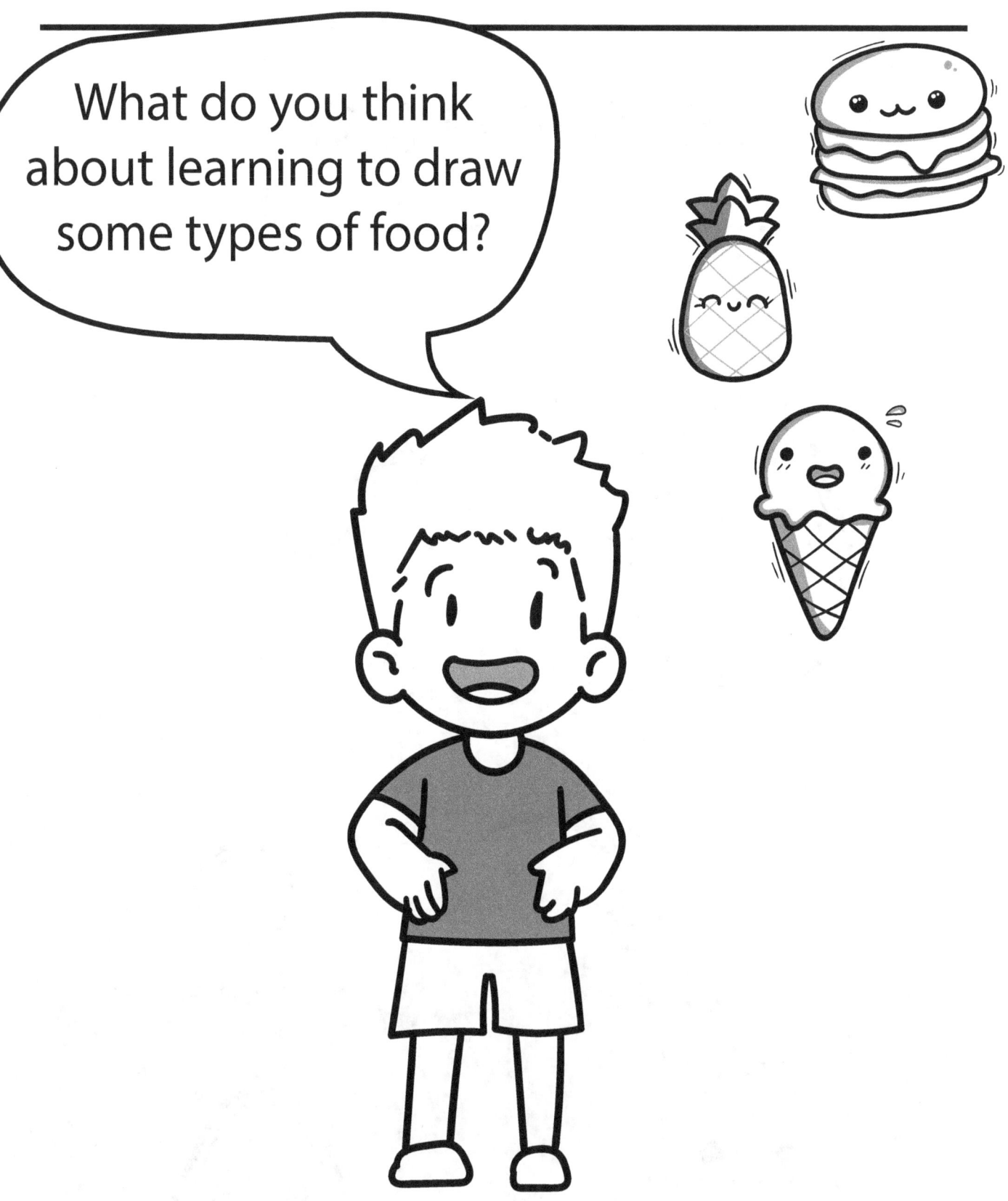

Avocado

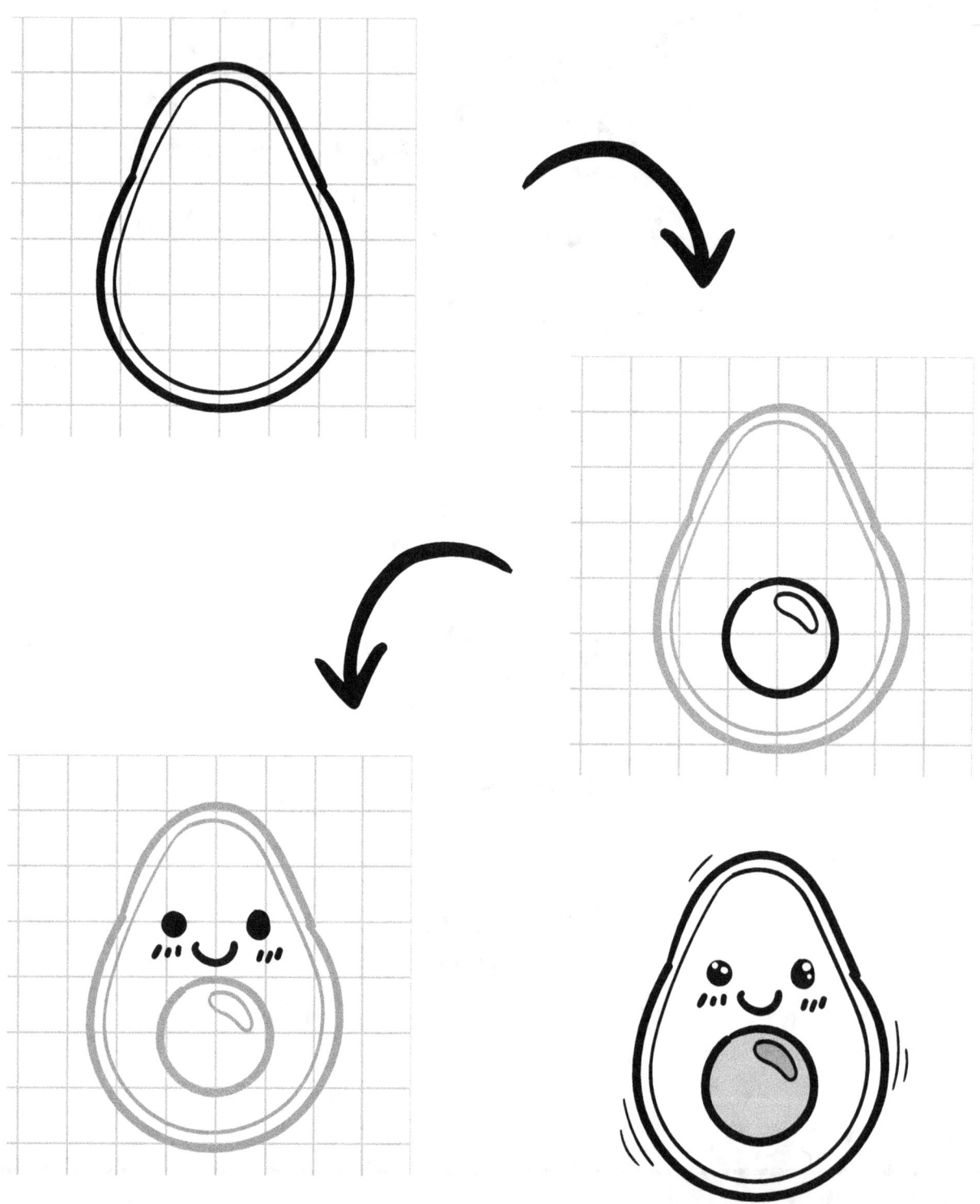

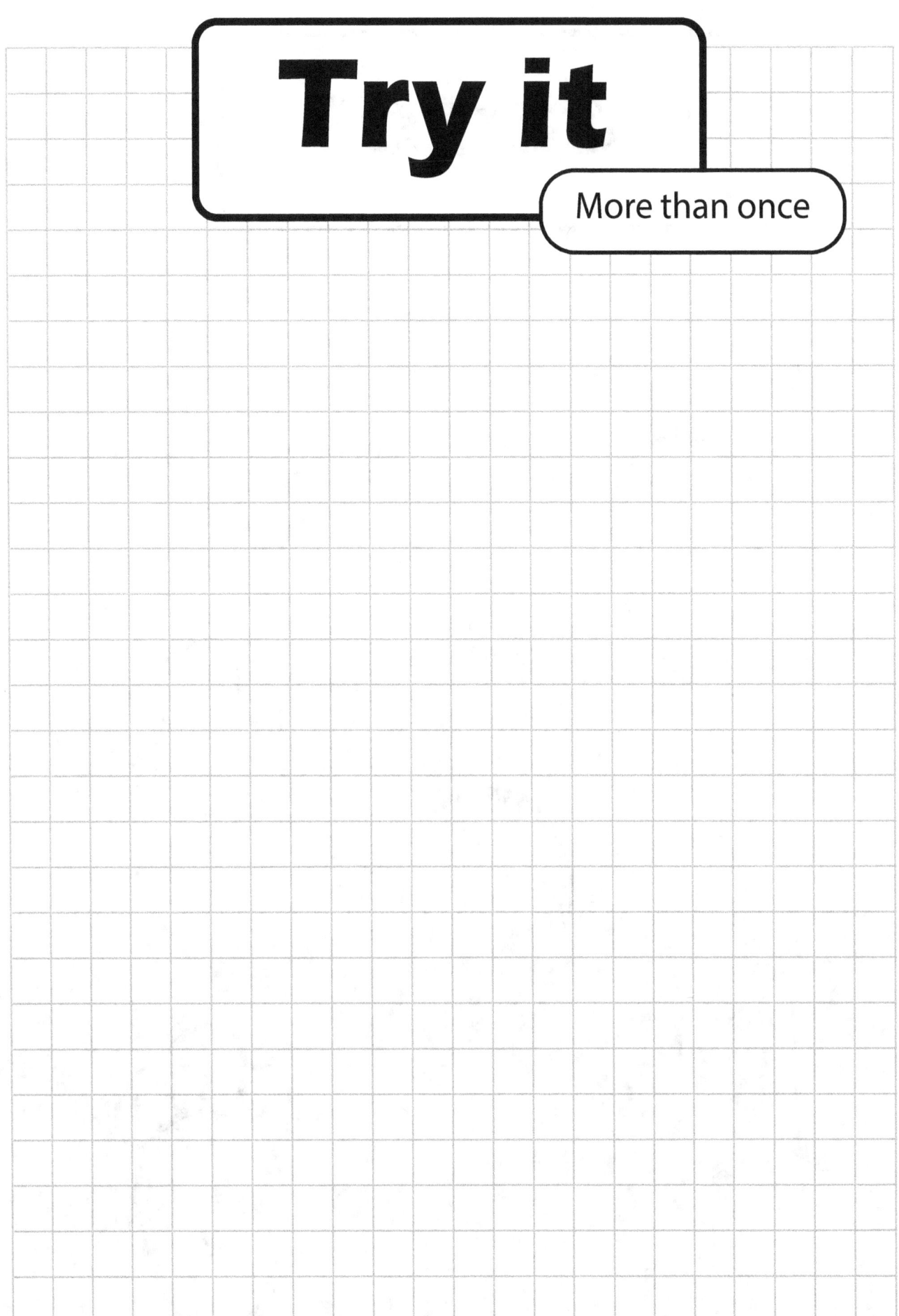

Try it

More than once

Carrot

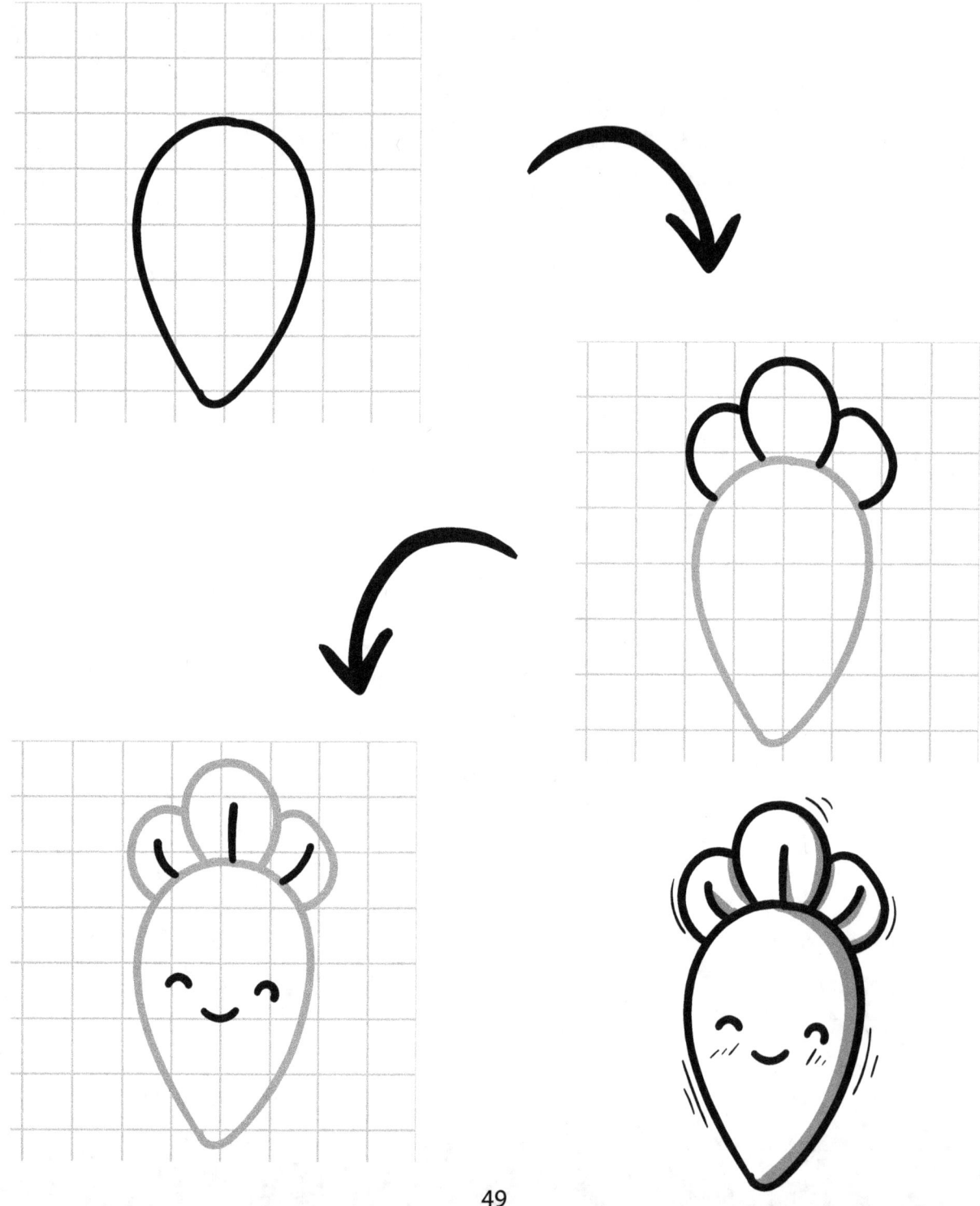

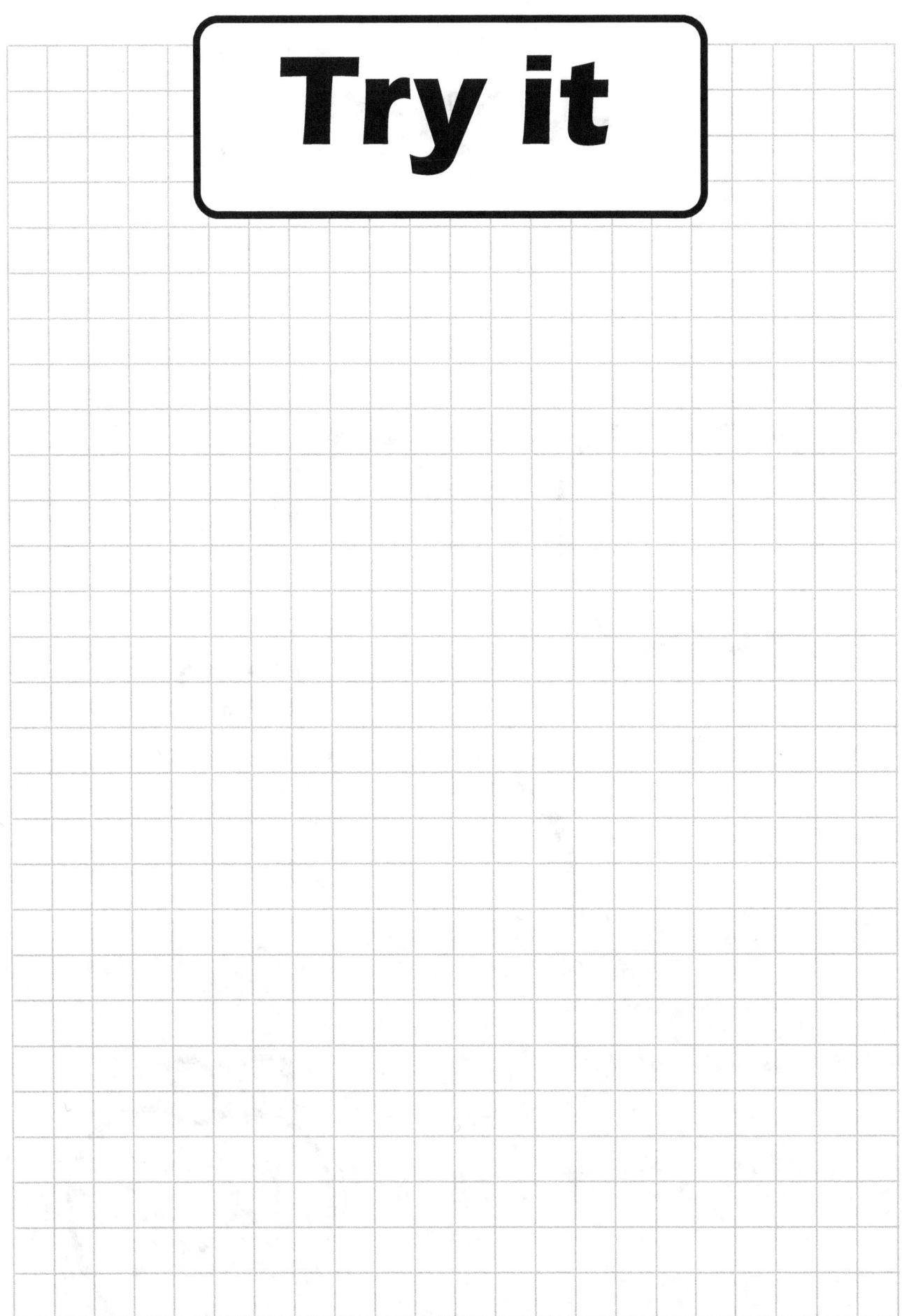

Try it

Apple

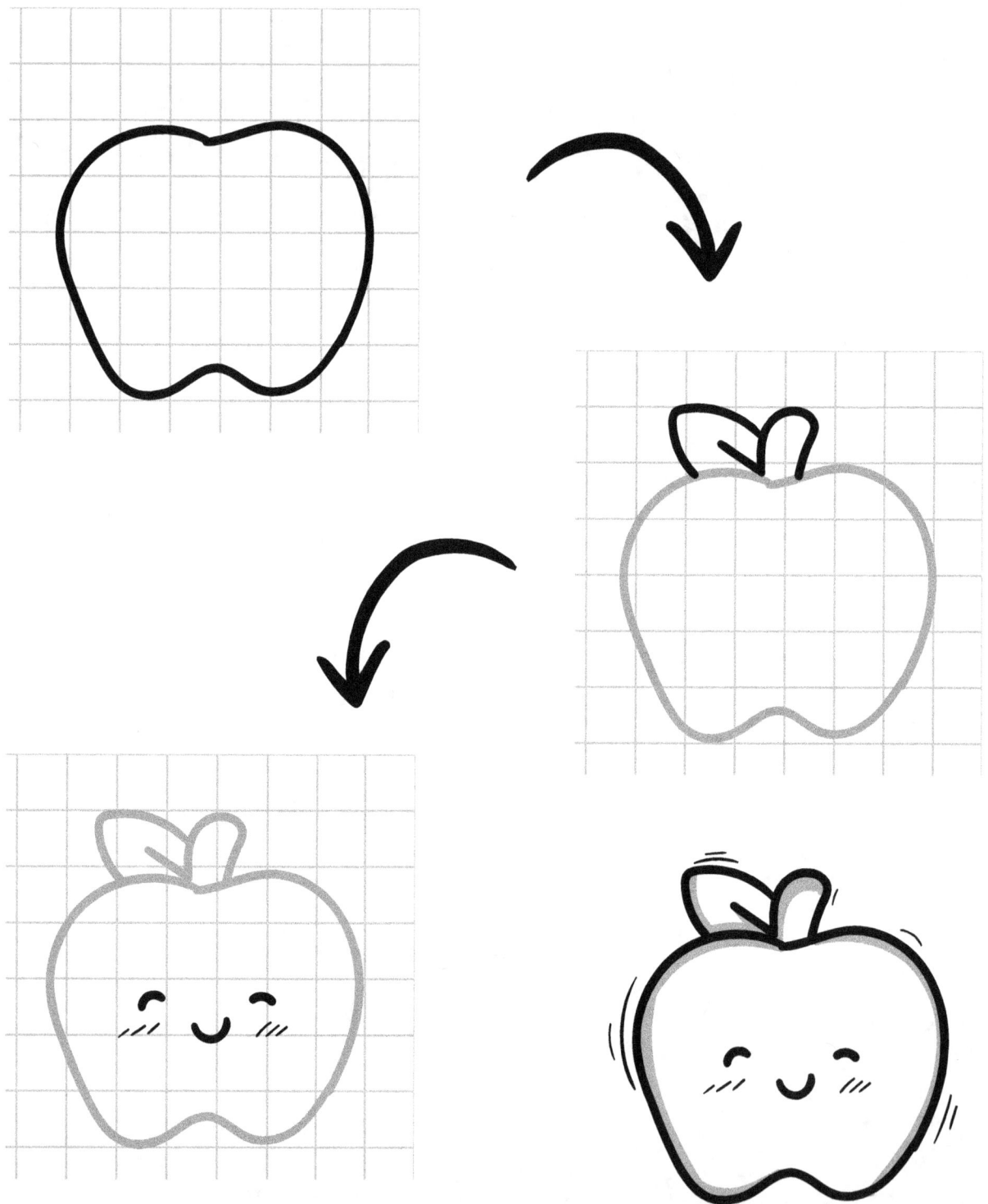

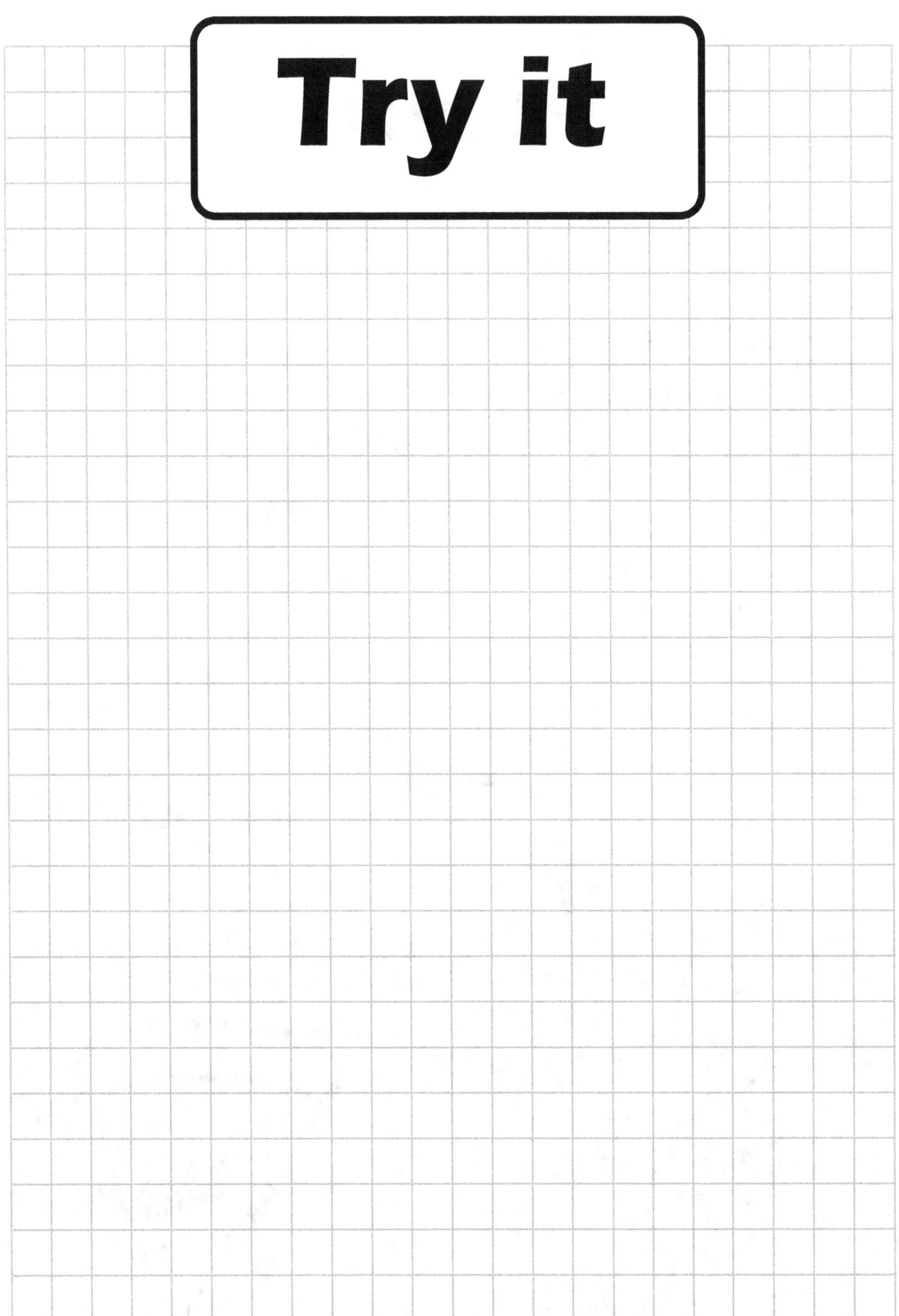

Try it

Pizza

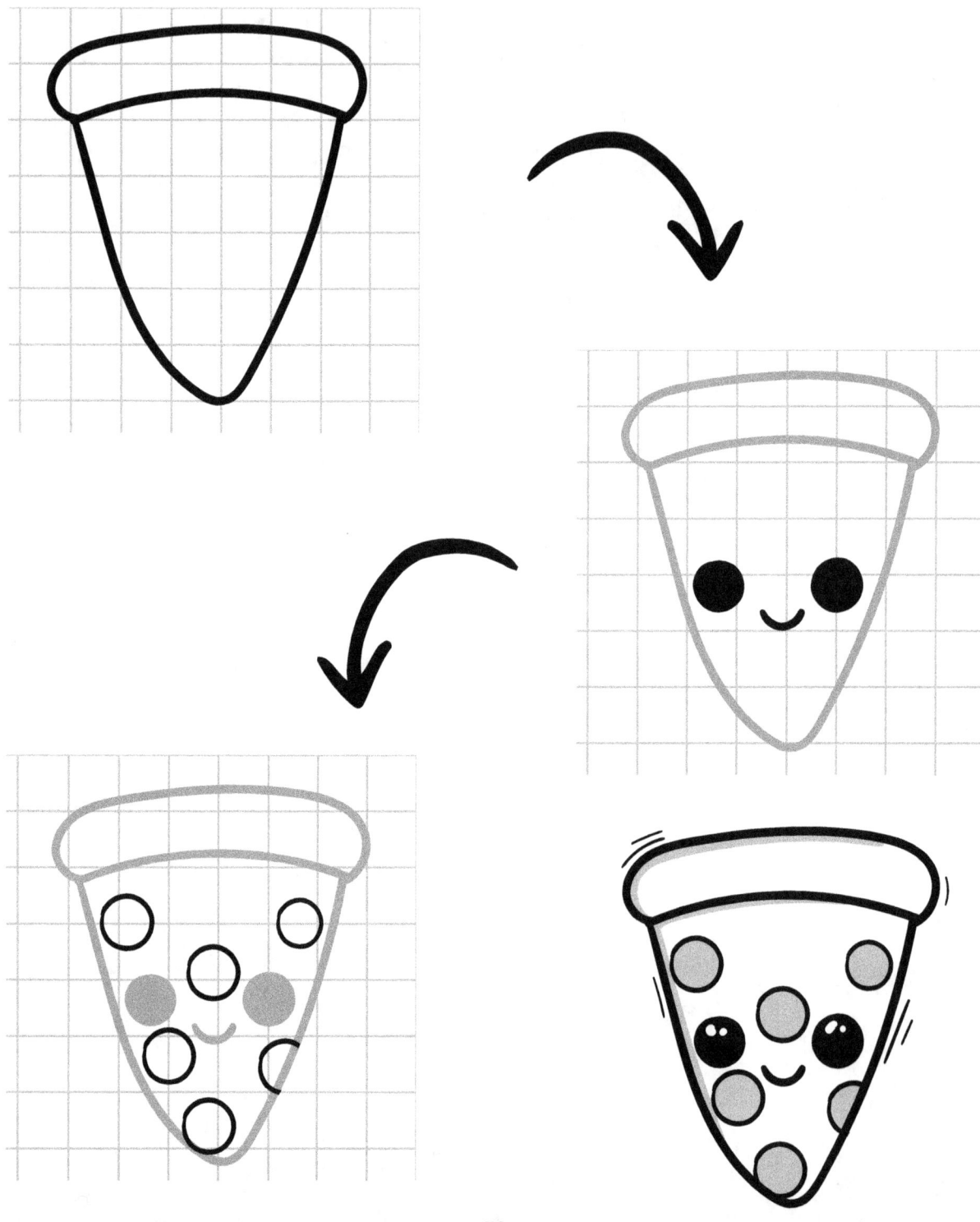

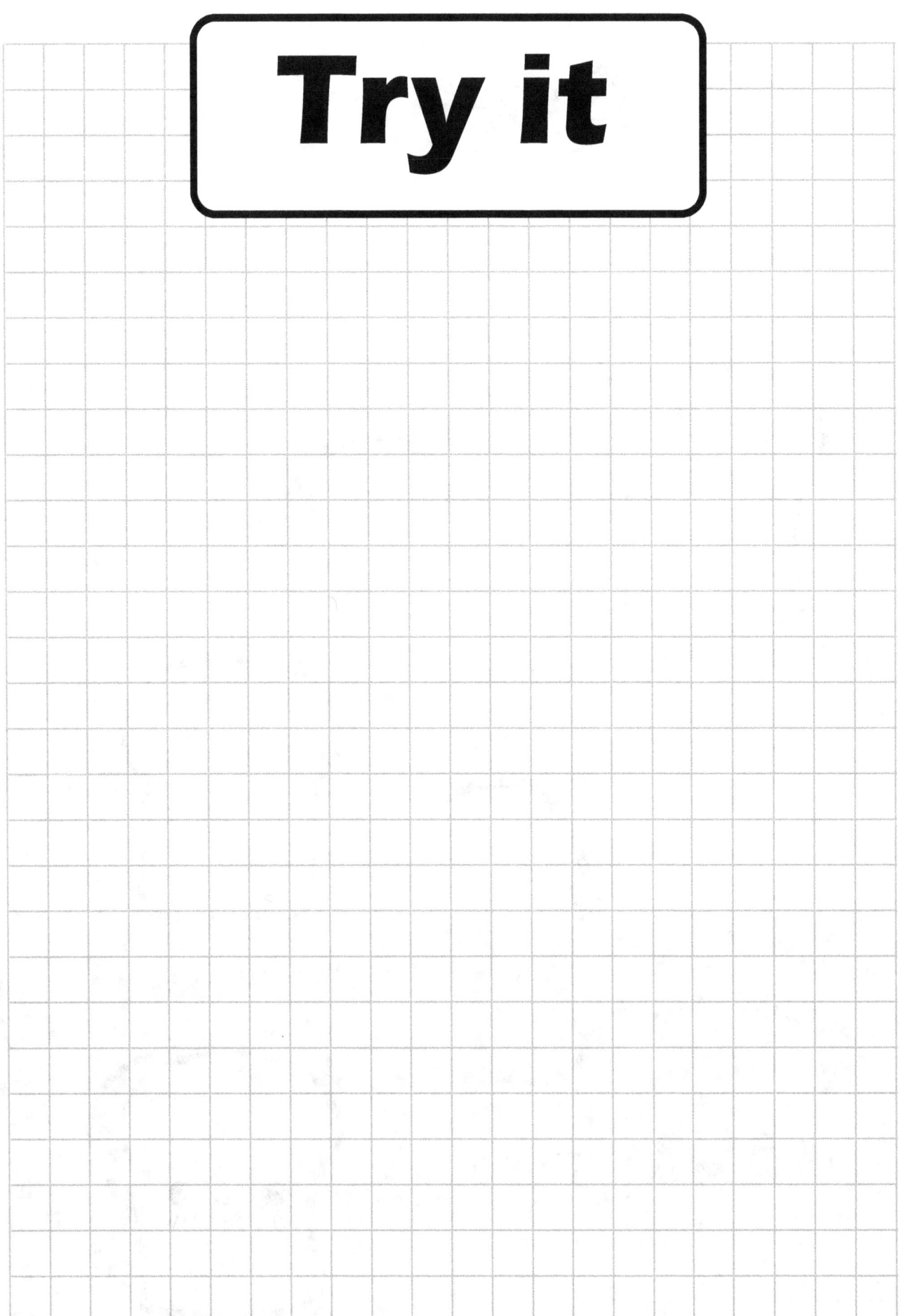

Try it

Bread

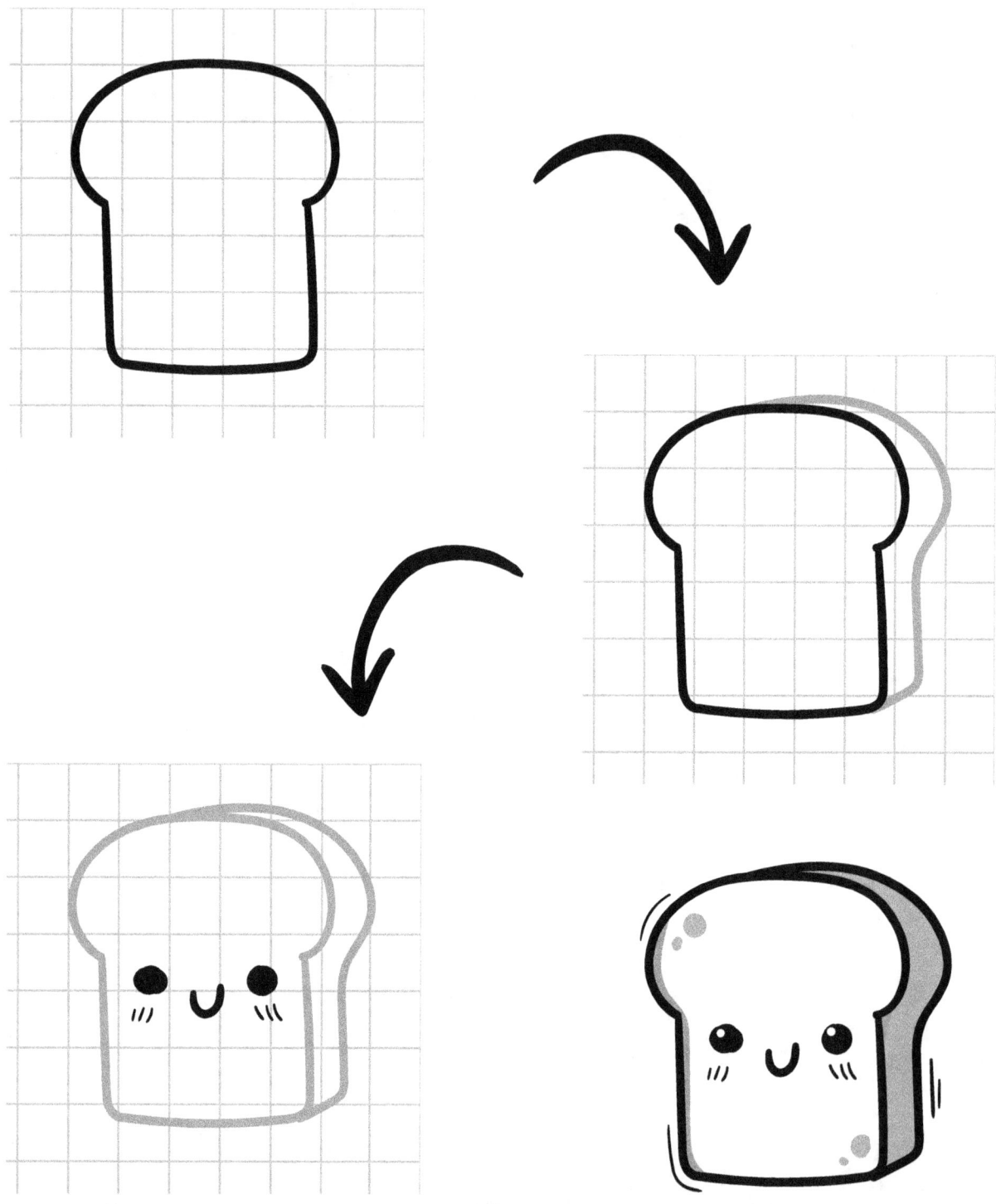

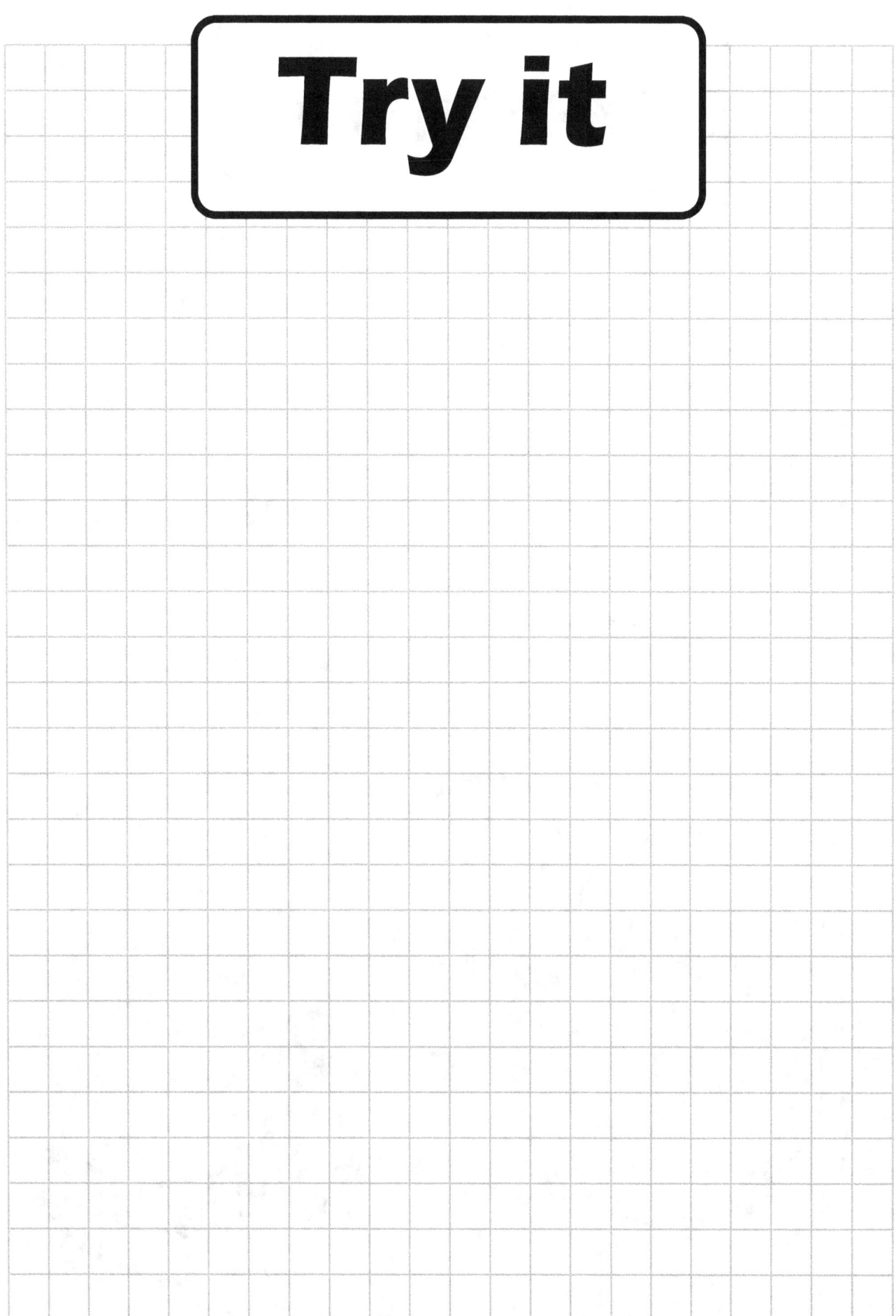

Try it

Banana

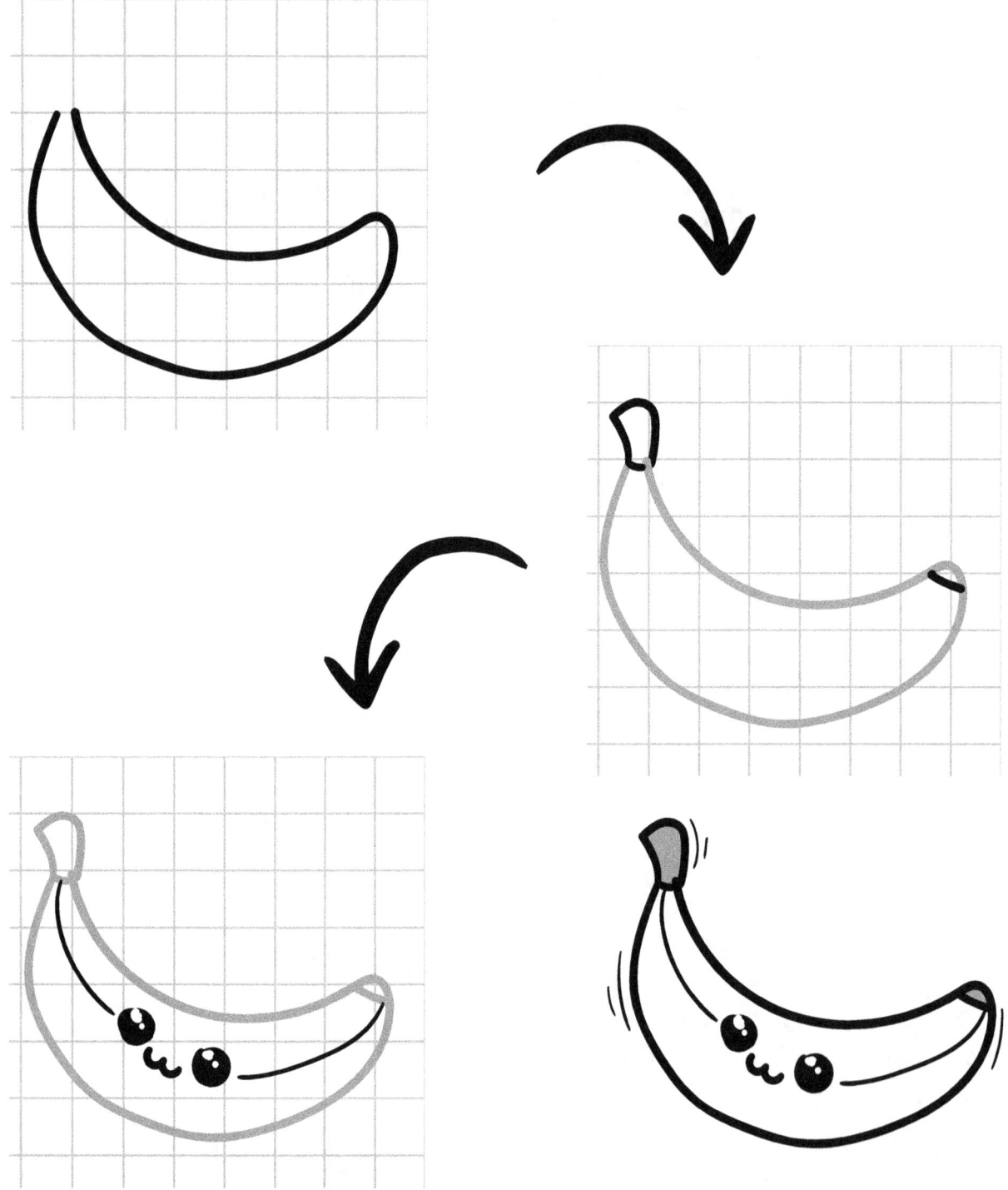

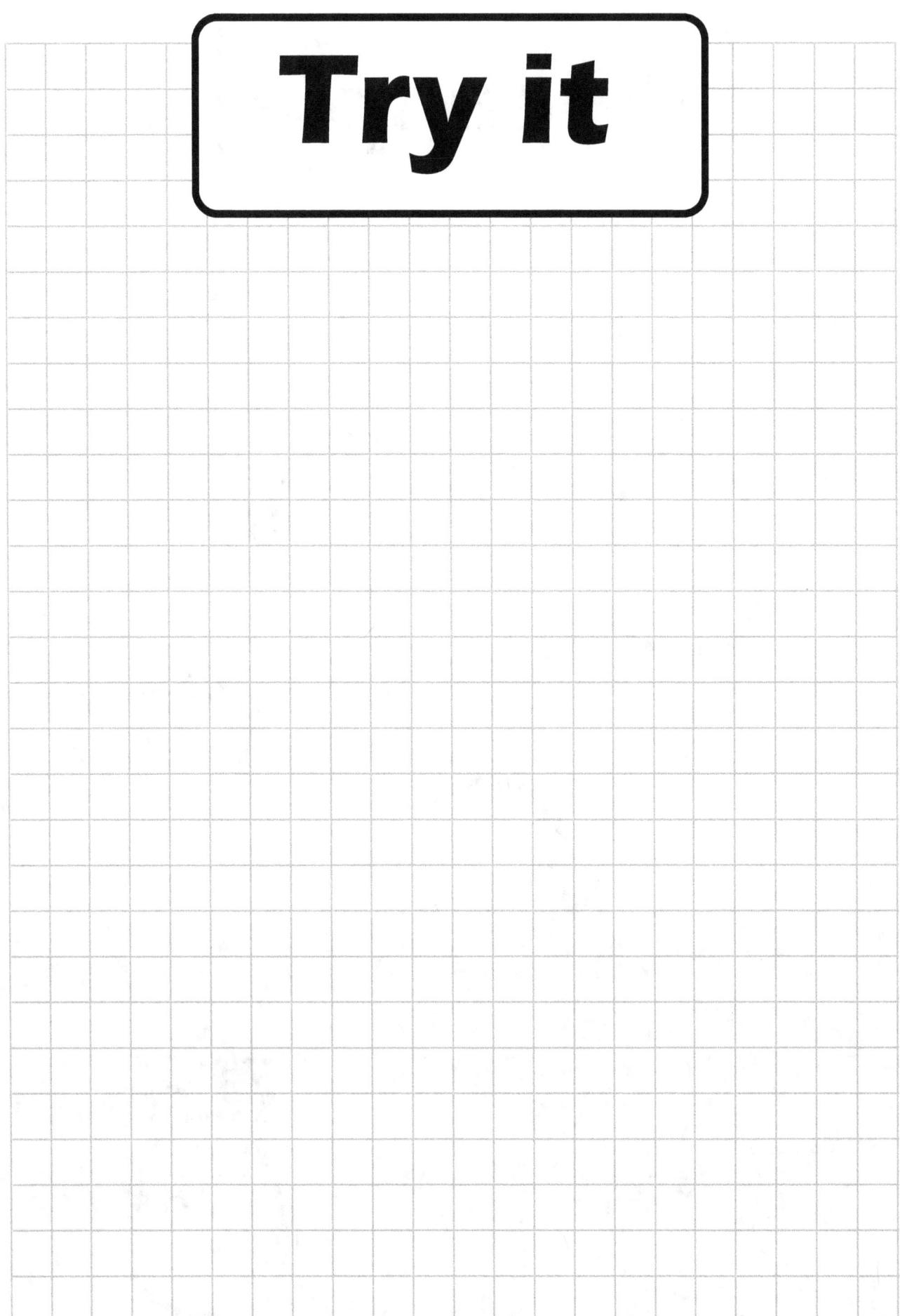

Try it

Pineapple

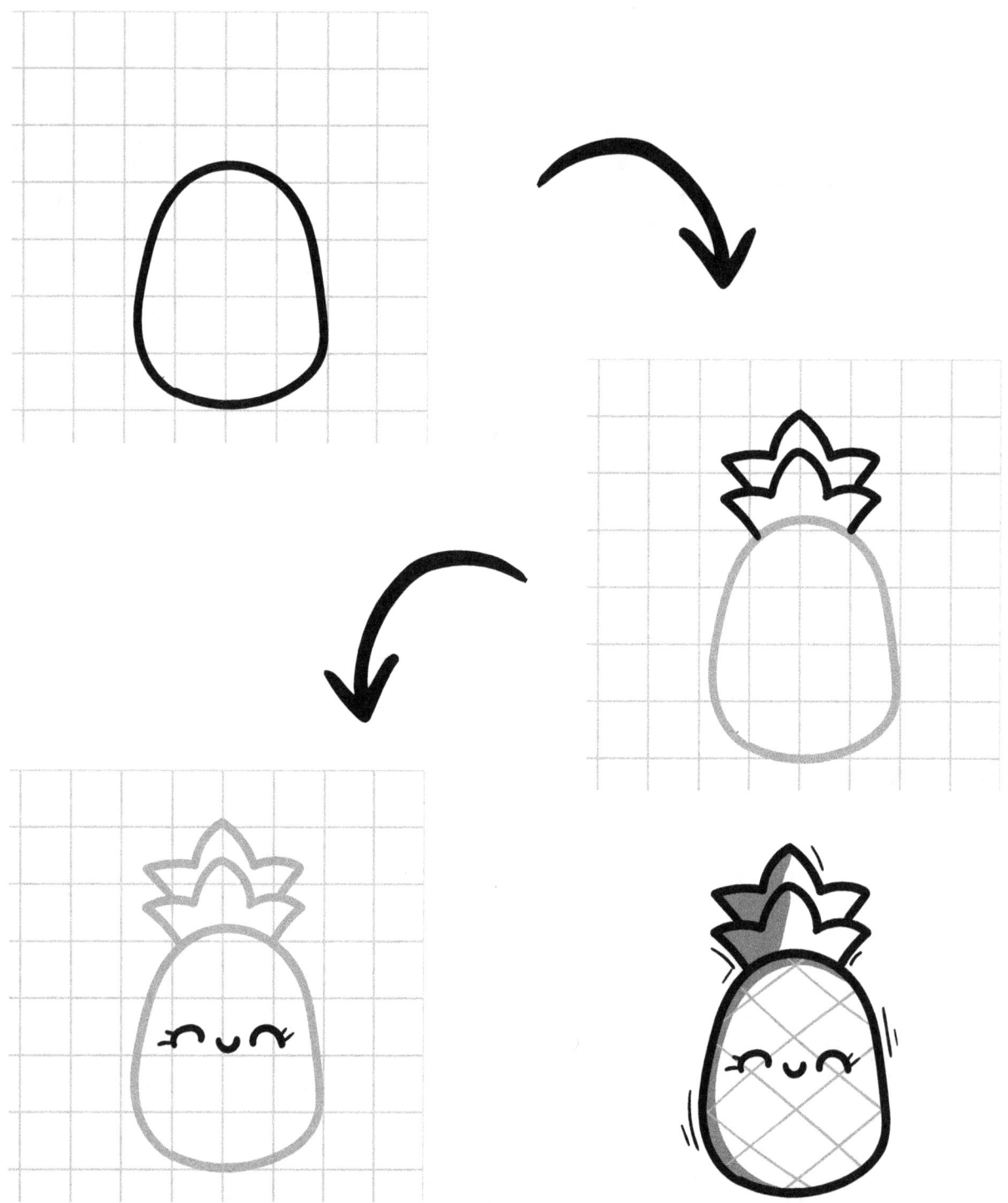

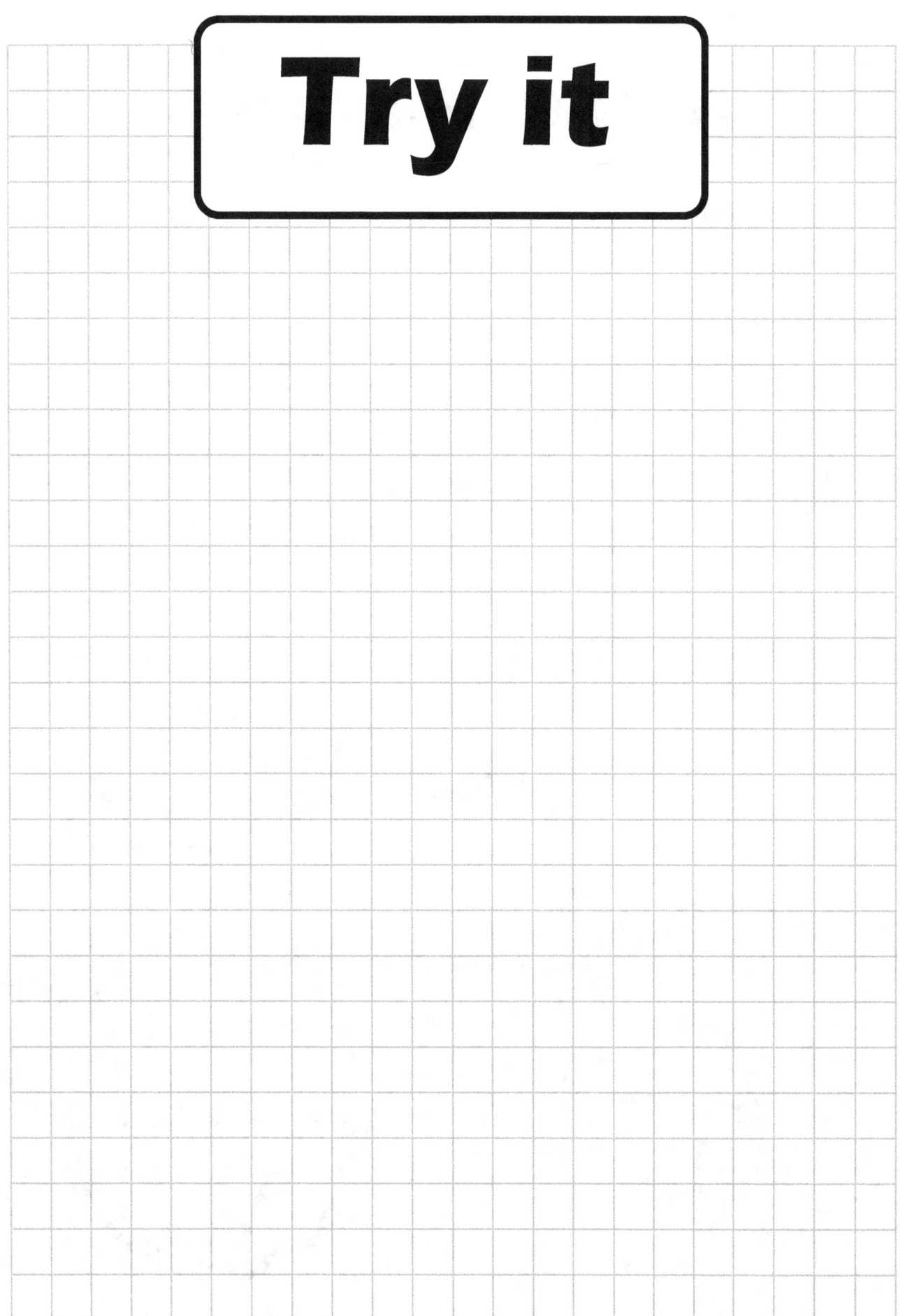

Try it

watermelon

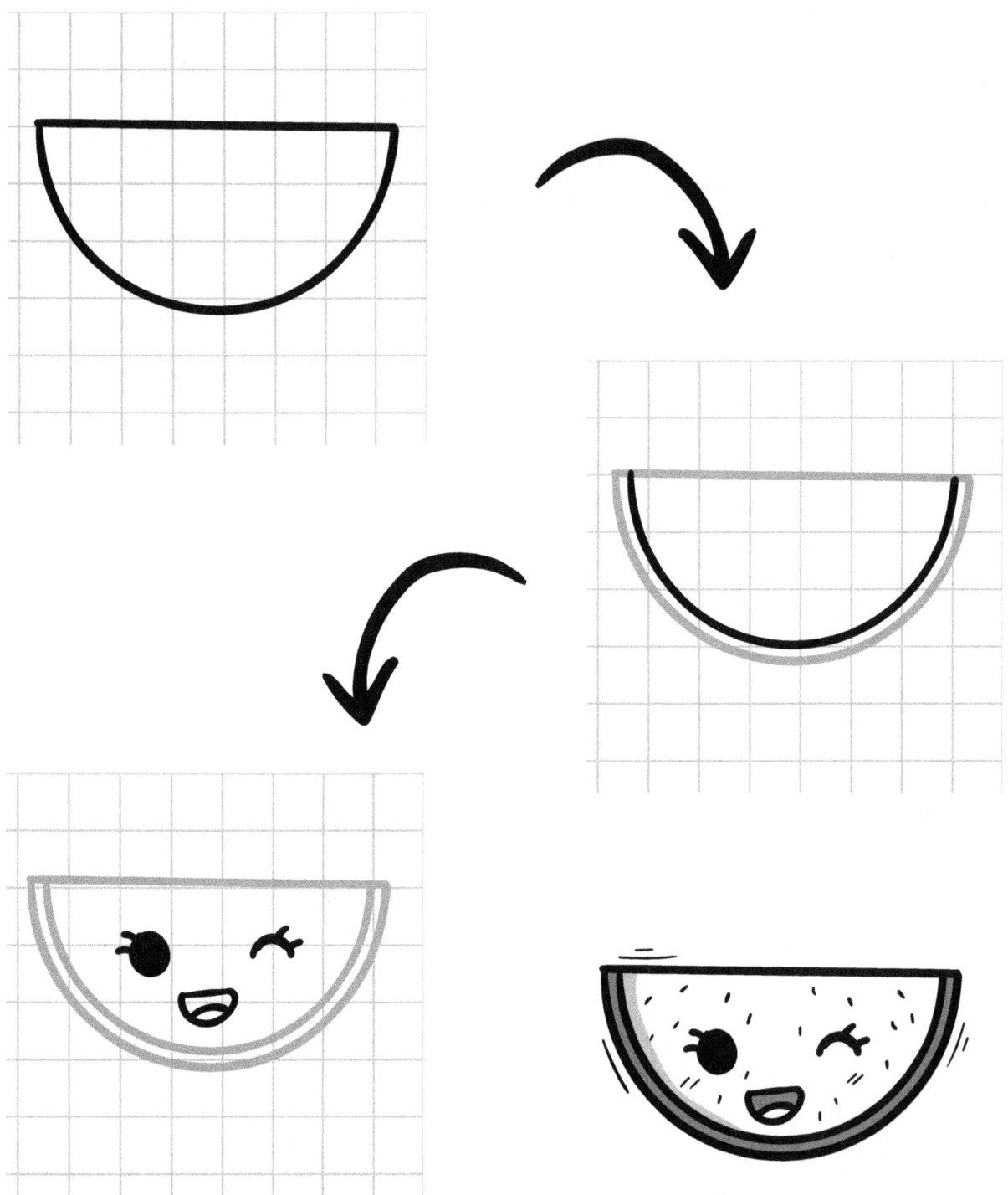

Try it

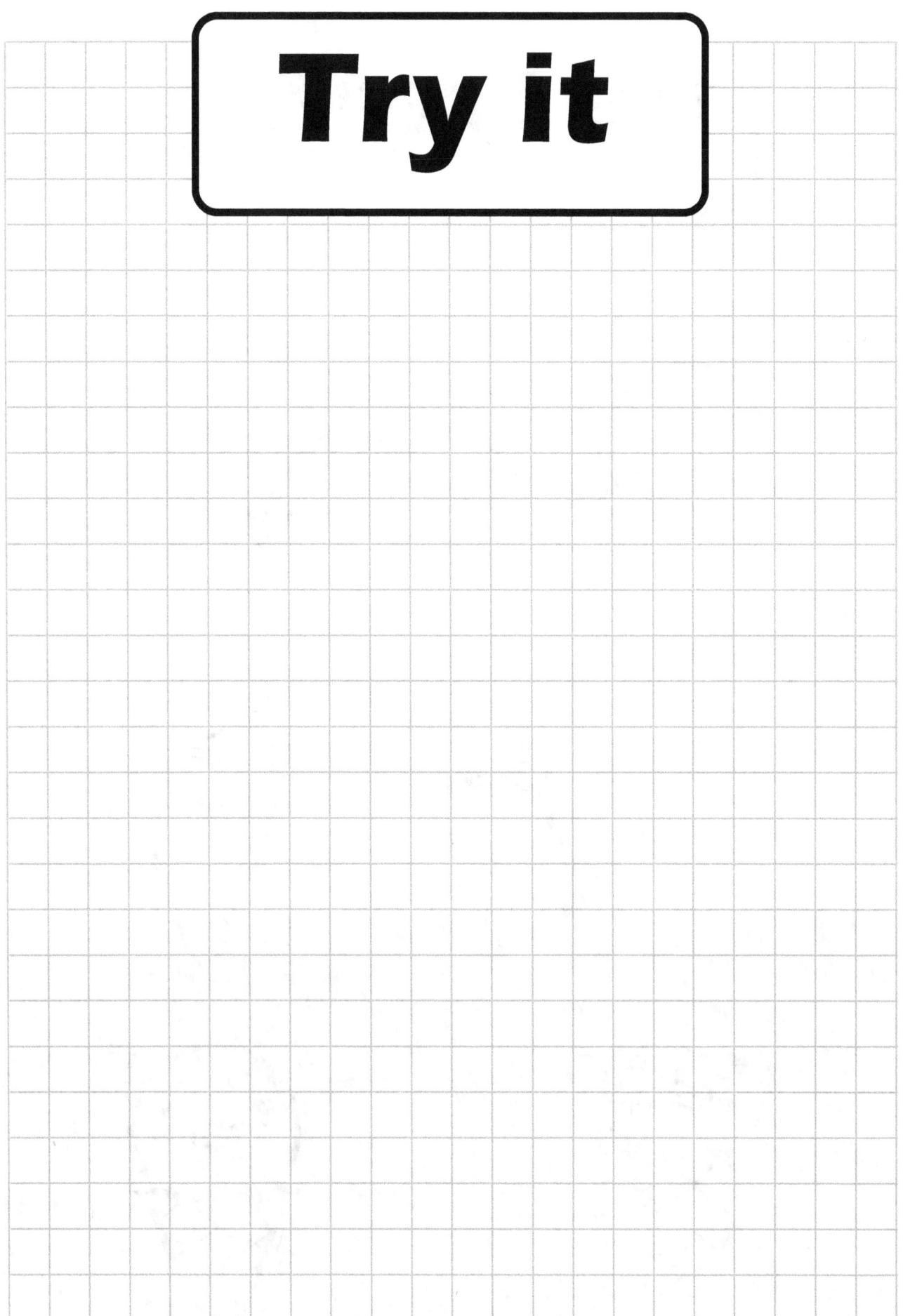

Ice Cream

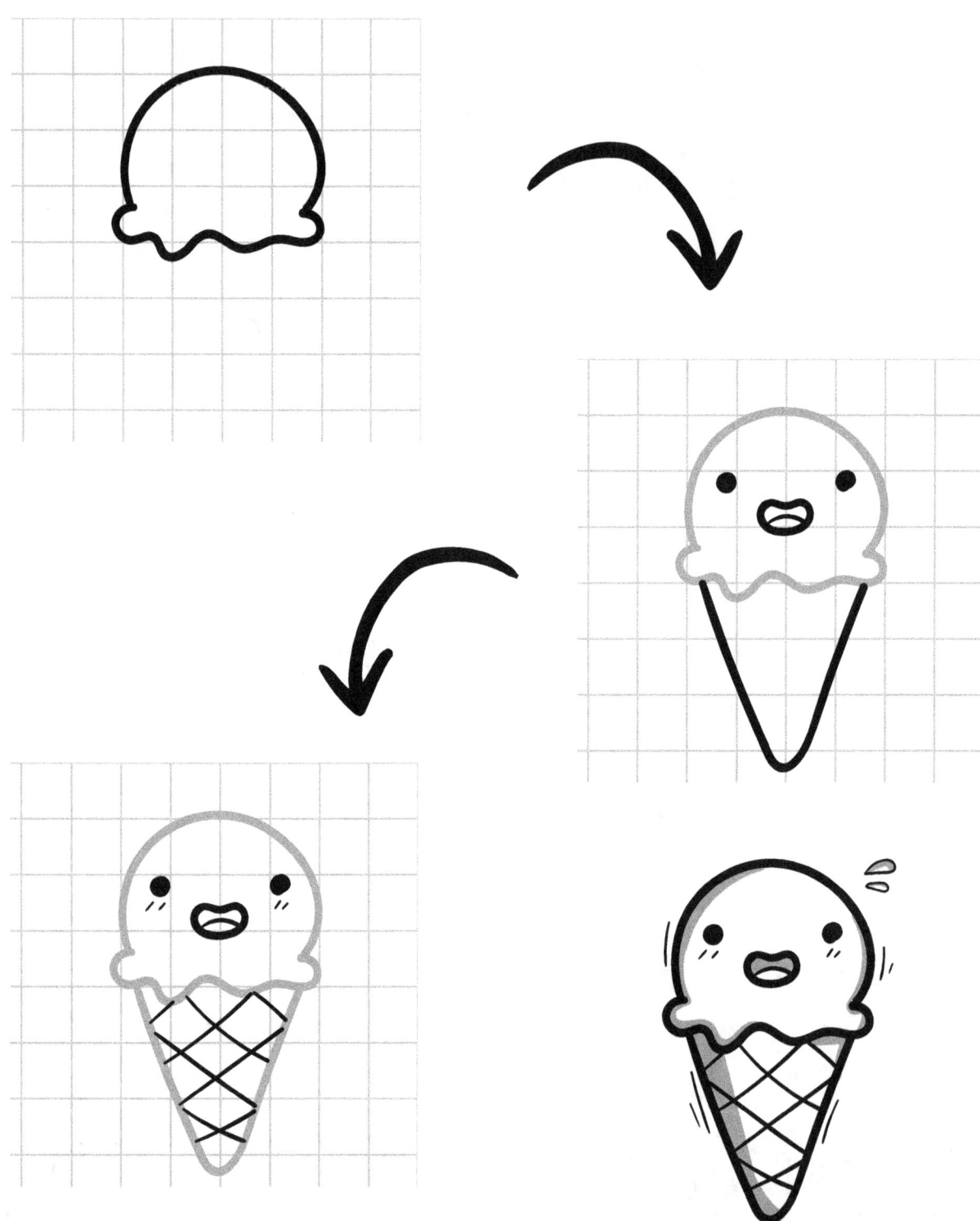

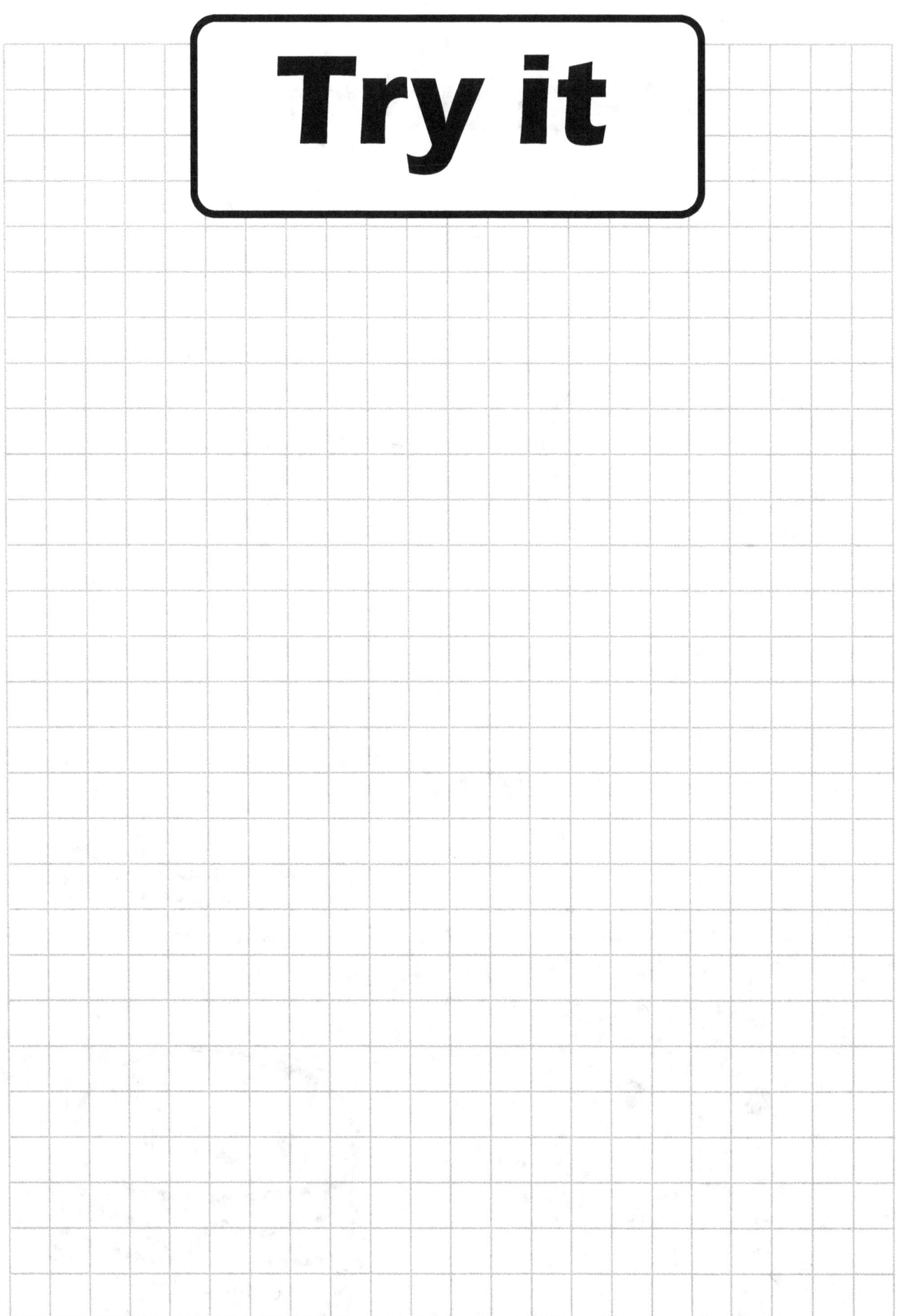

Try it

Hamburger

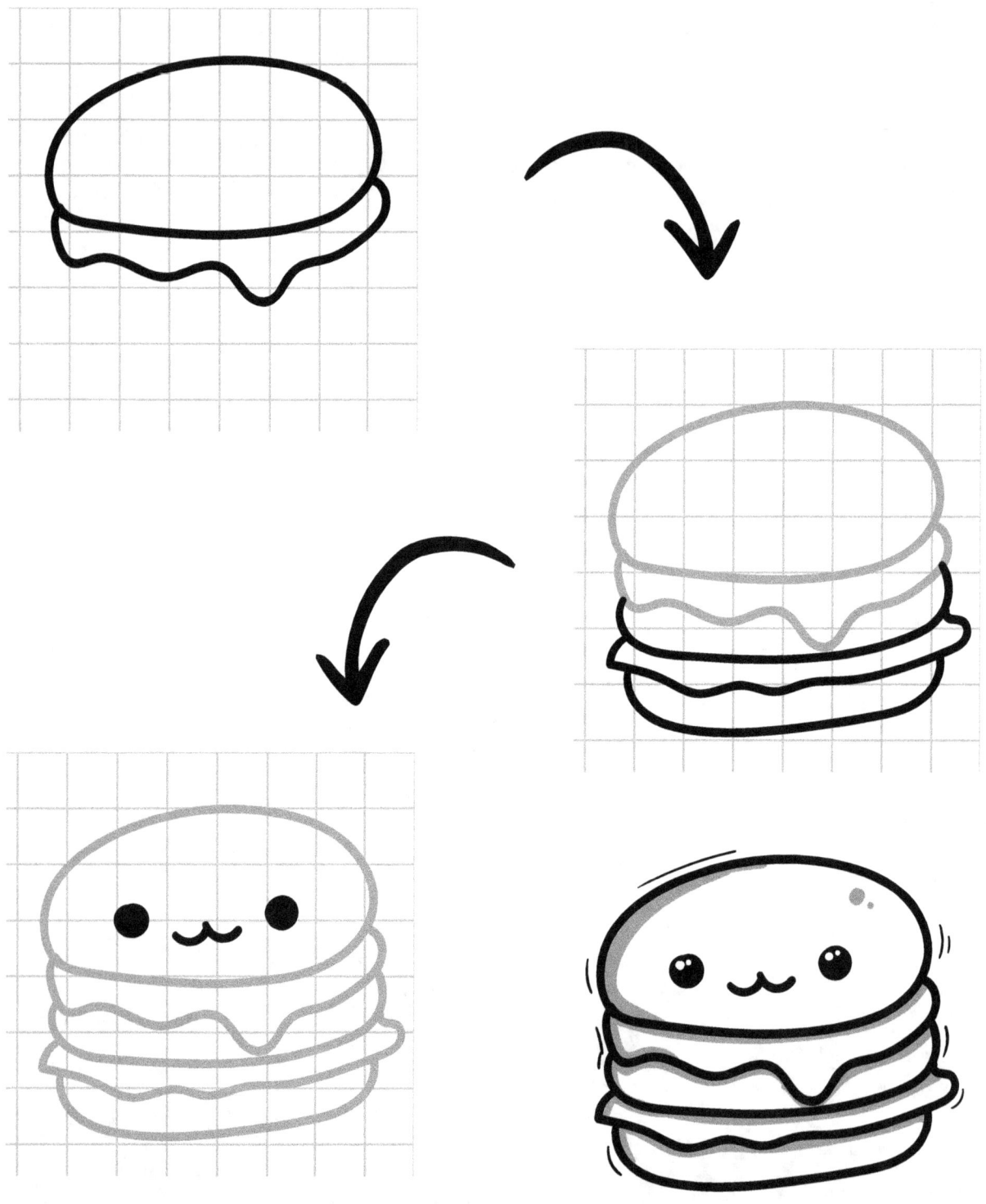

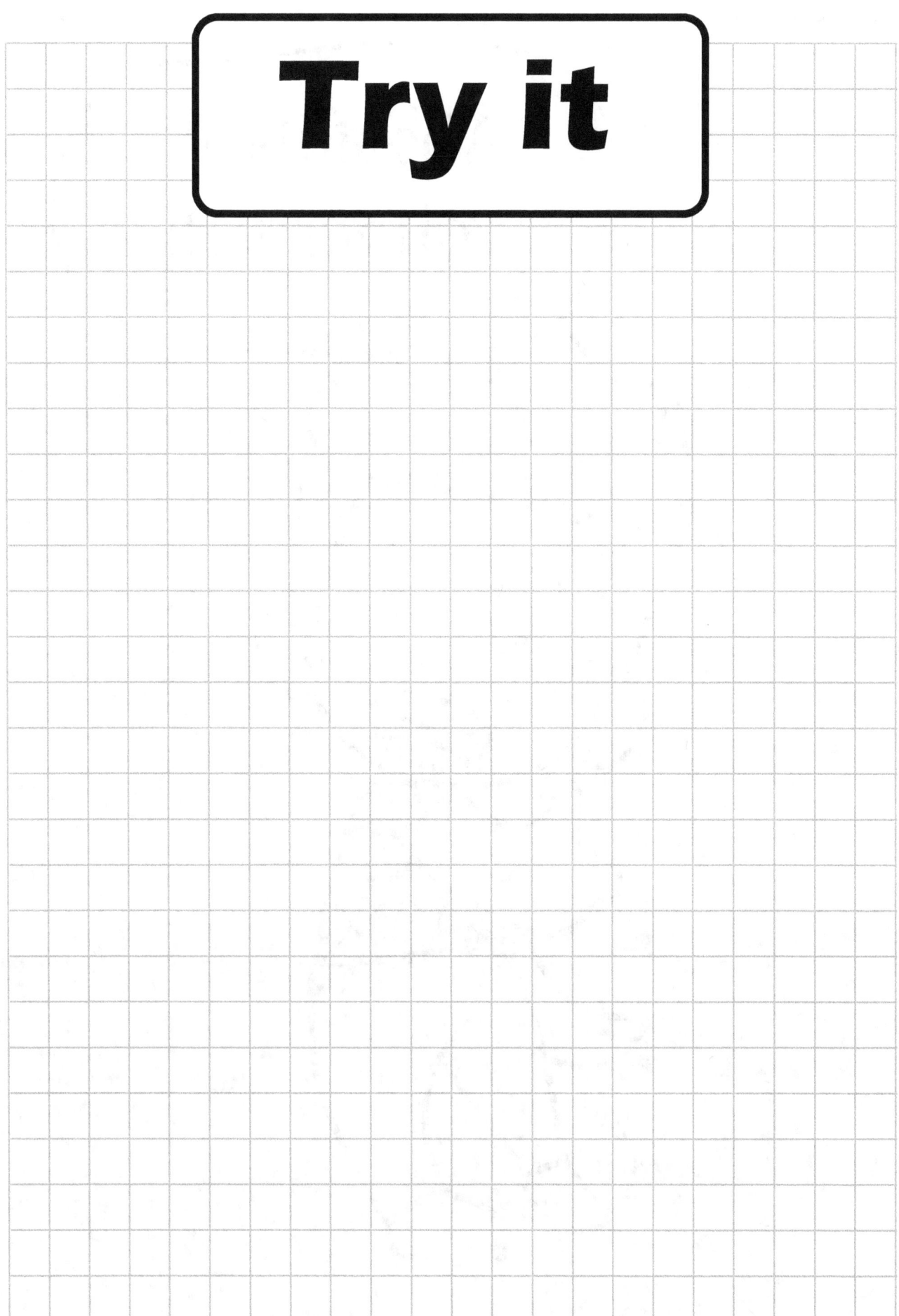

Try it

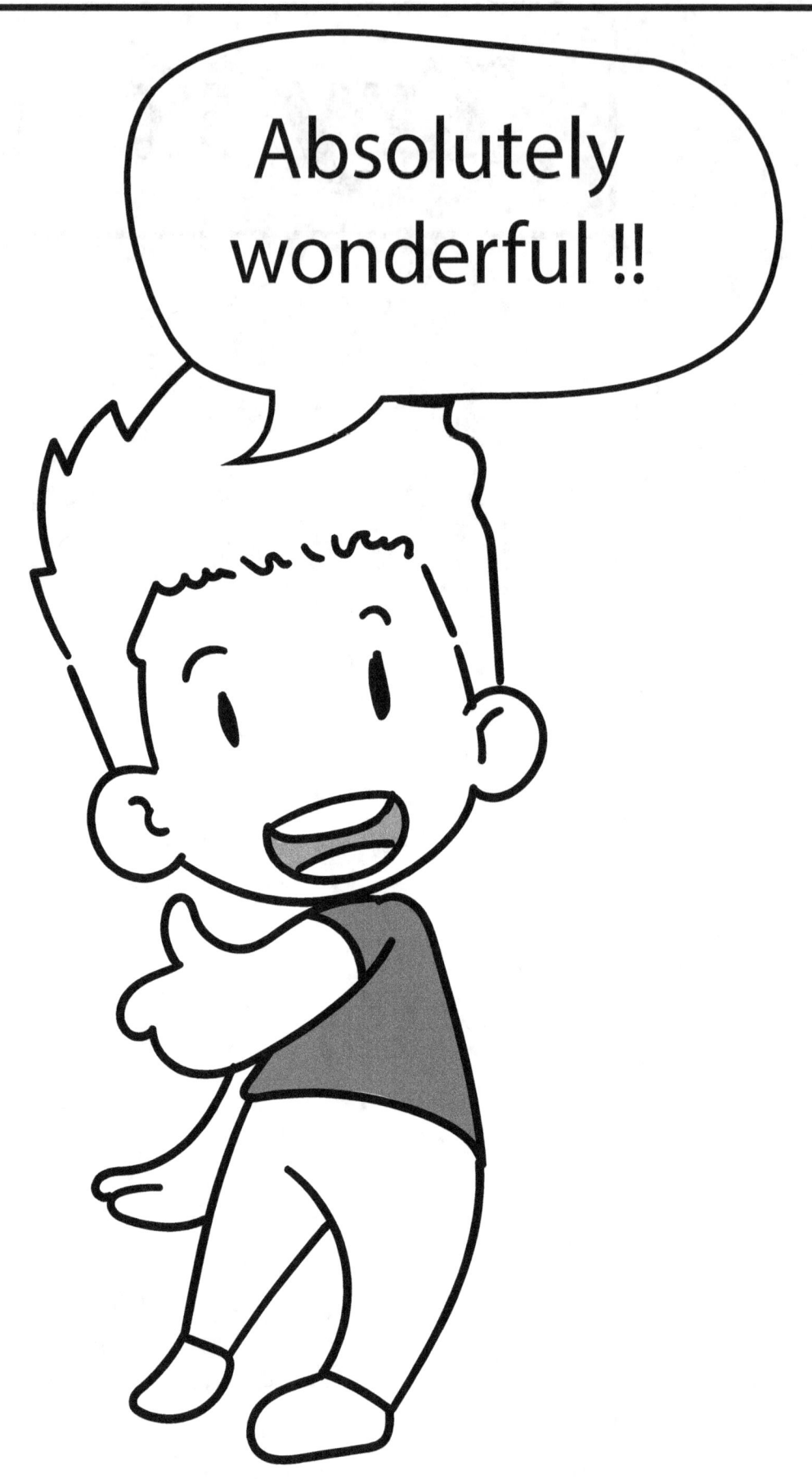

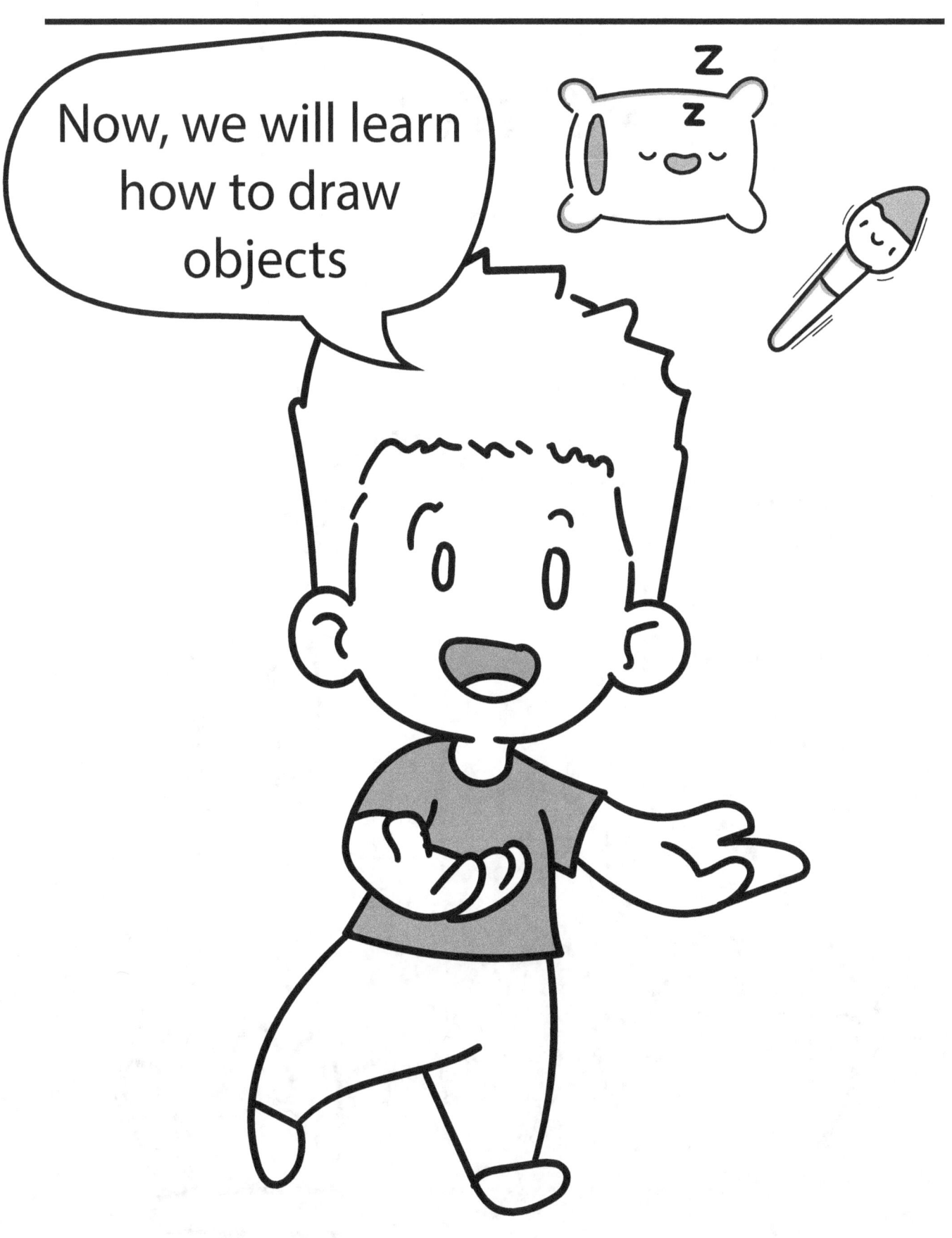

Plant

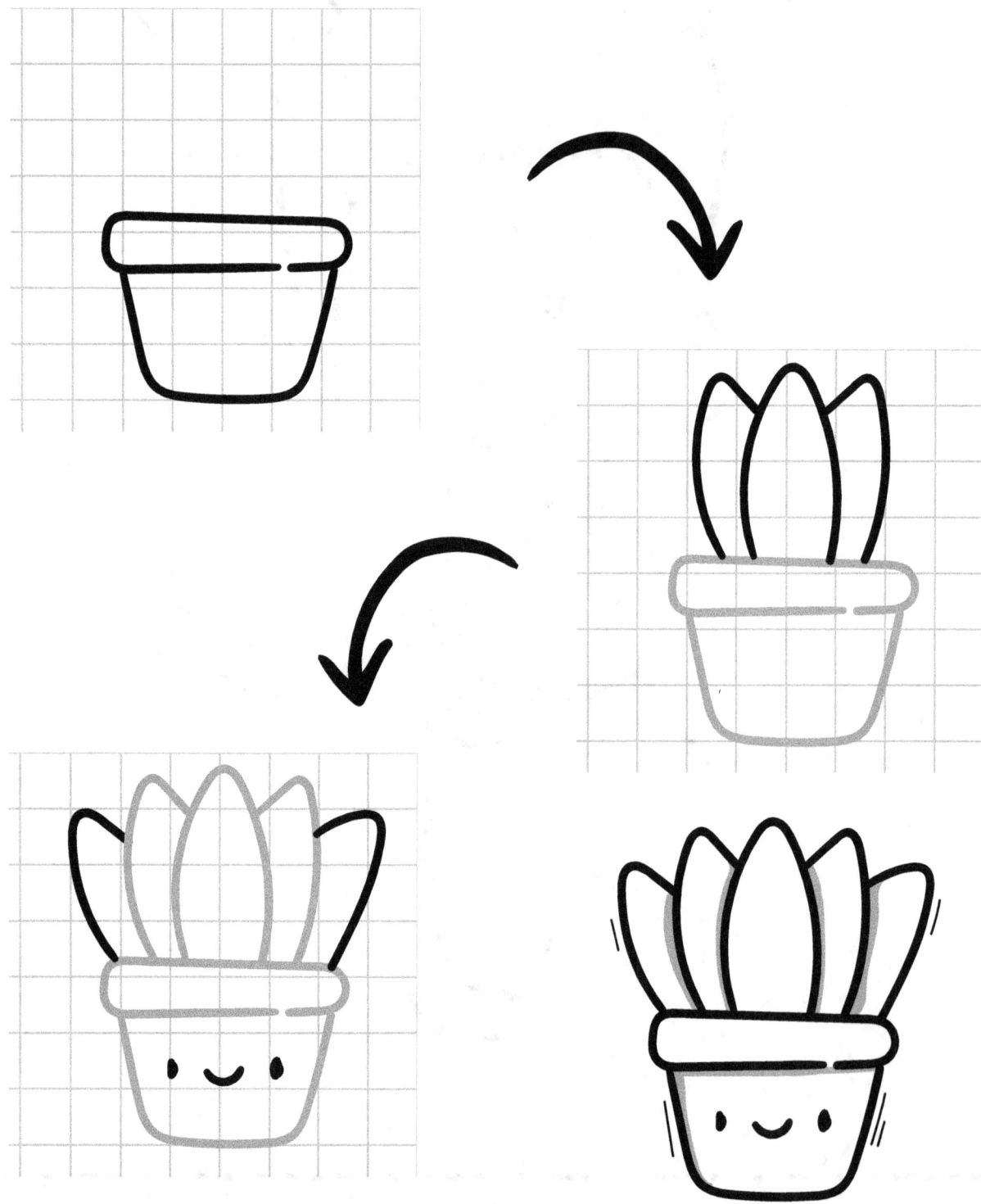

Try it

More than once

Cup

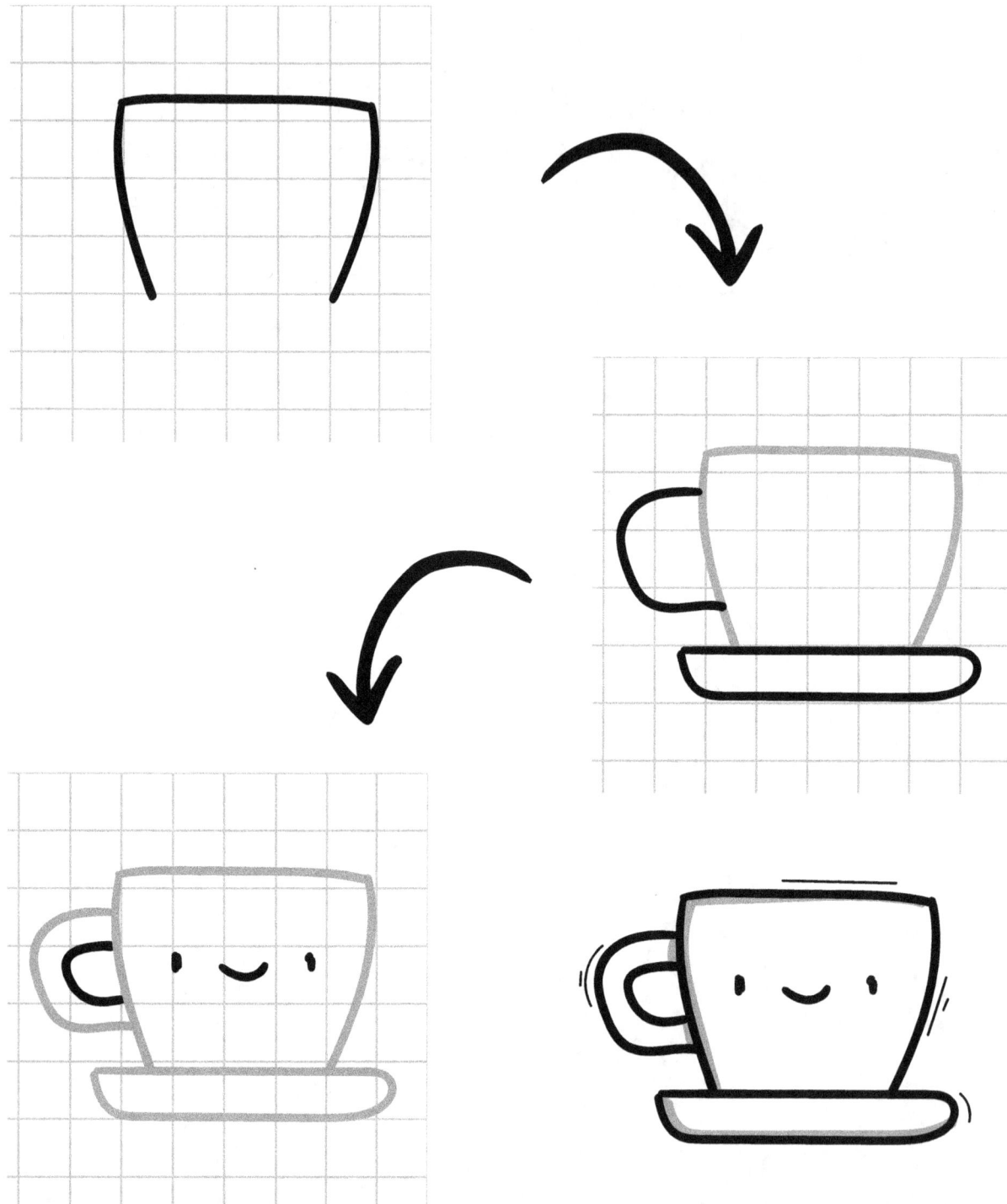

Try it

Lamp

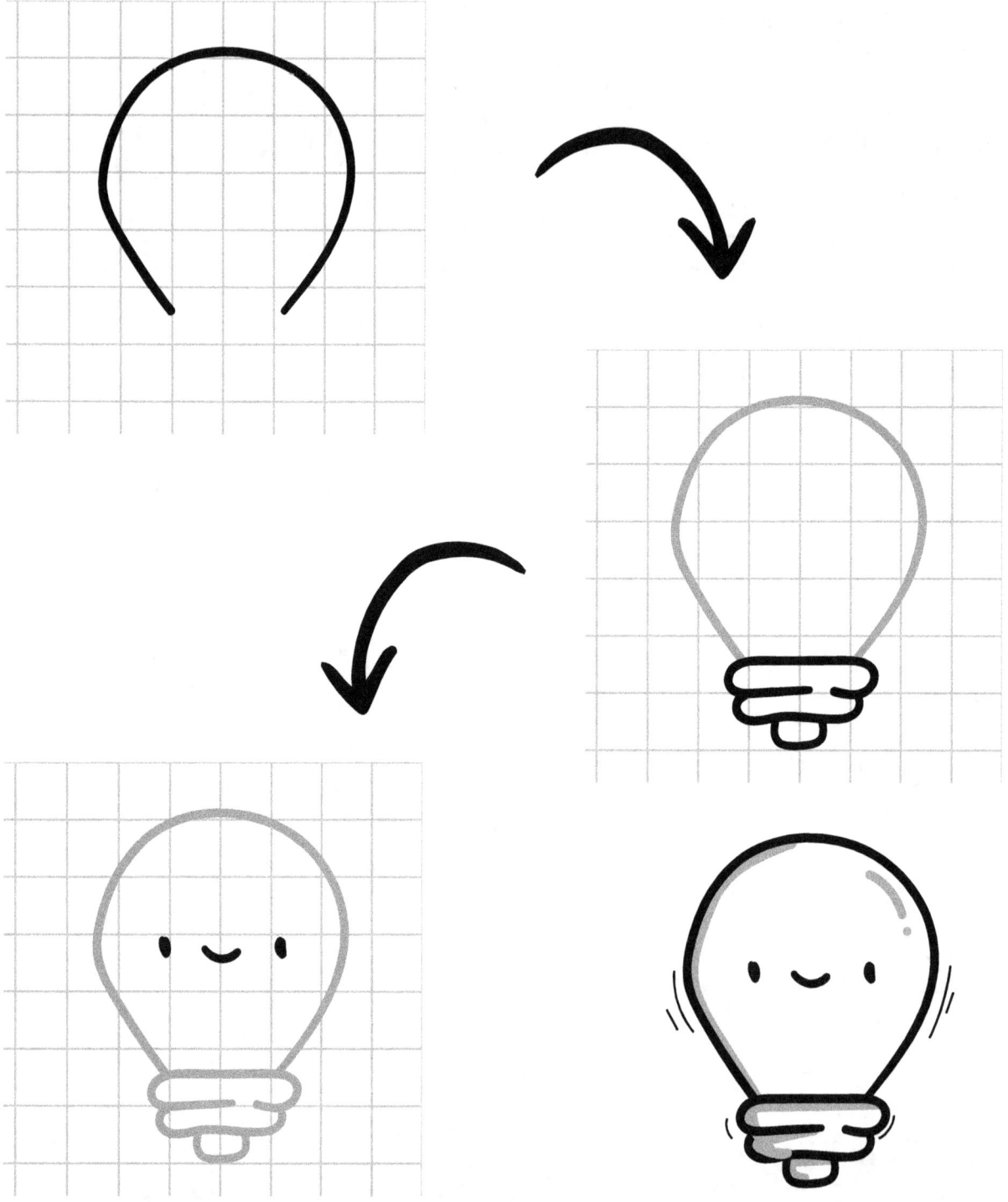

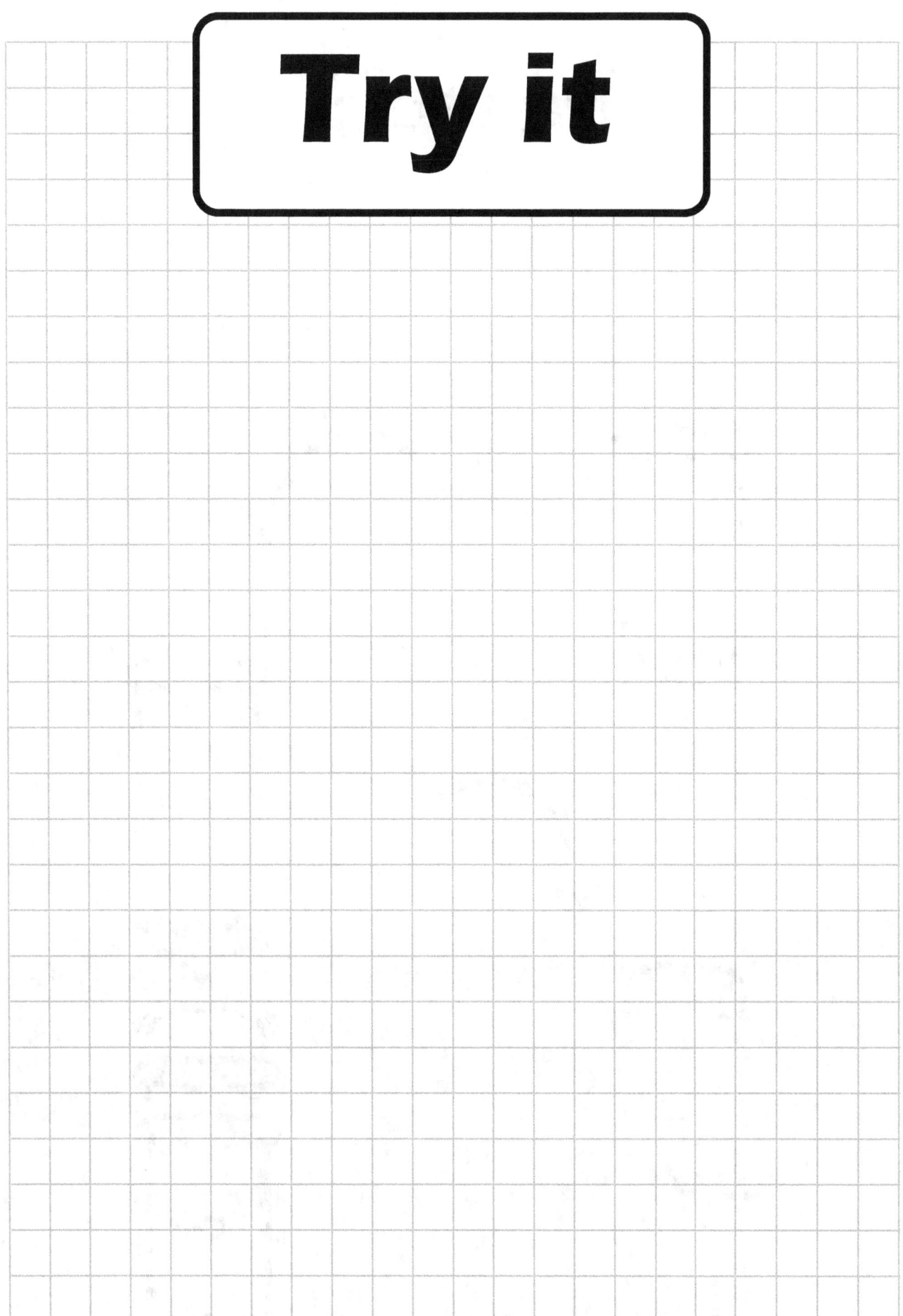

Try it

Pencil

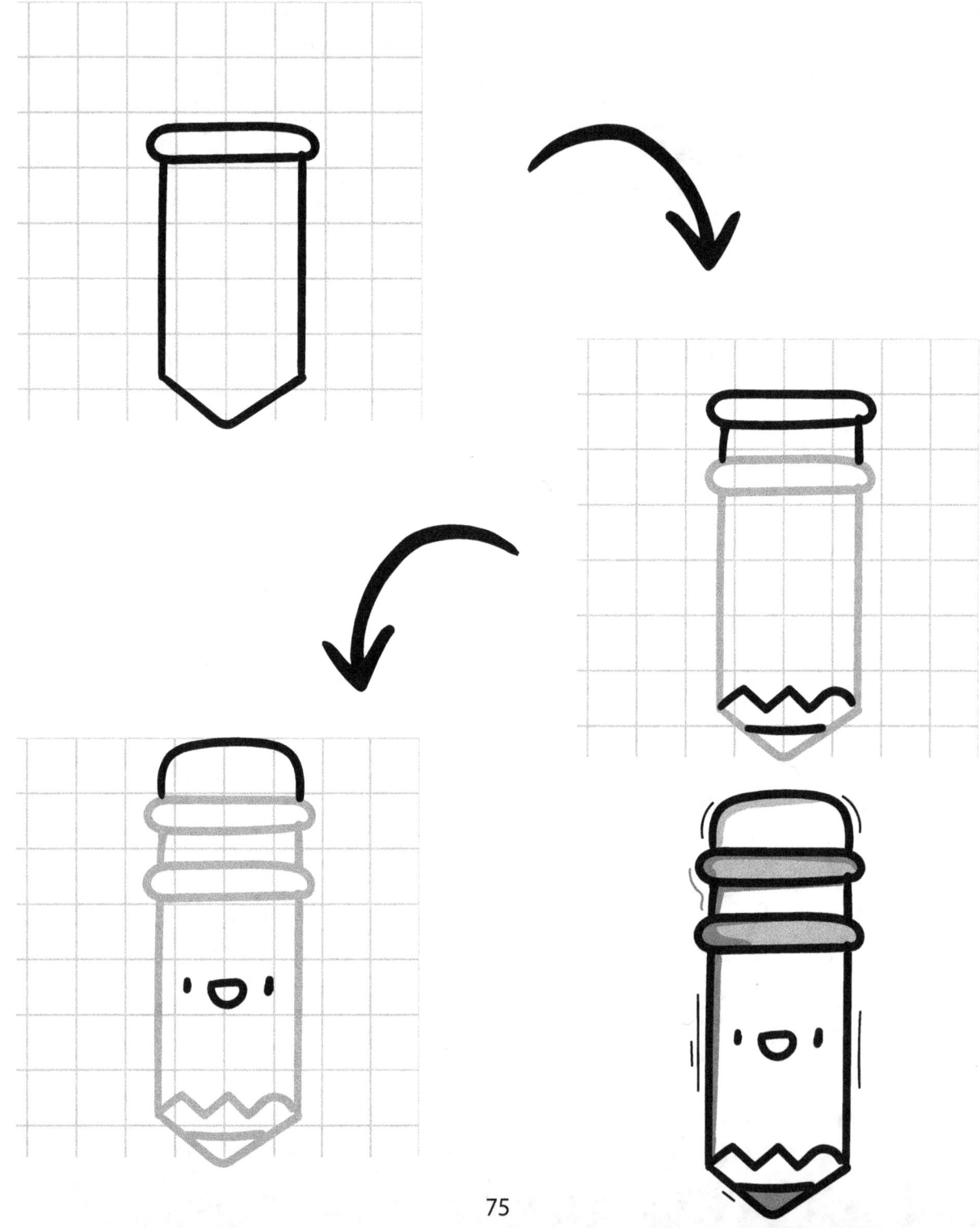

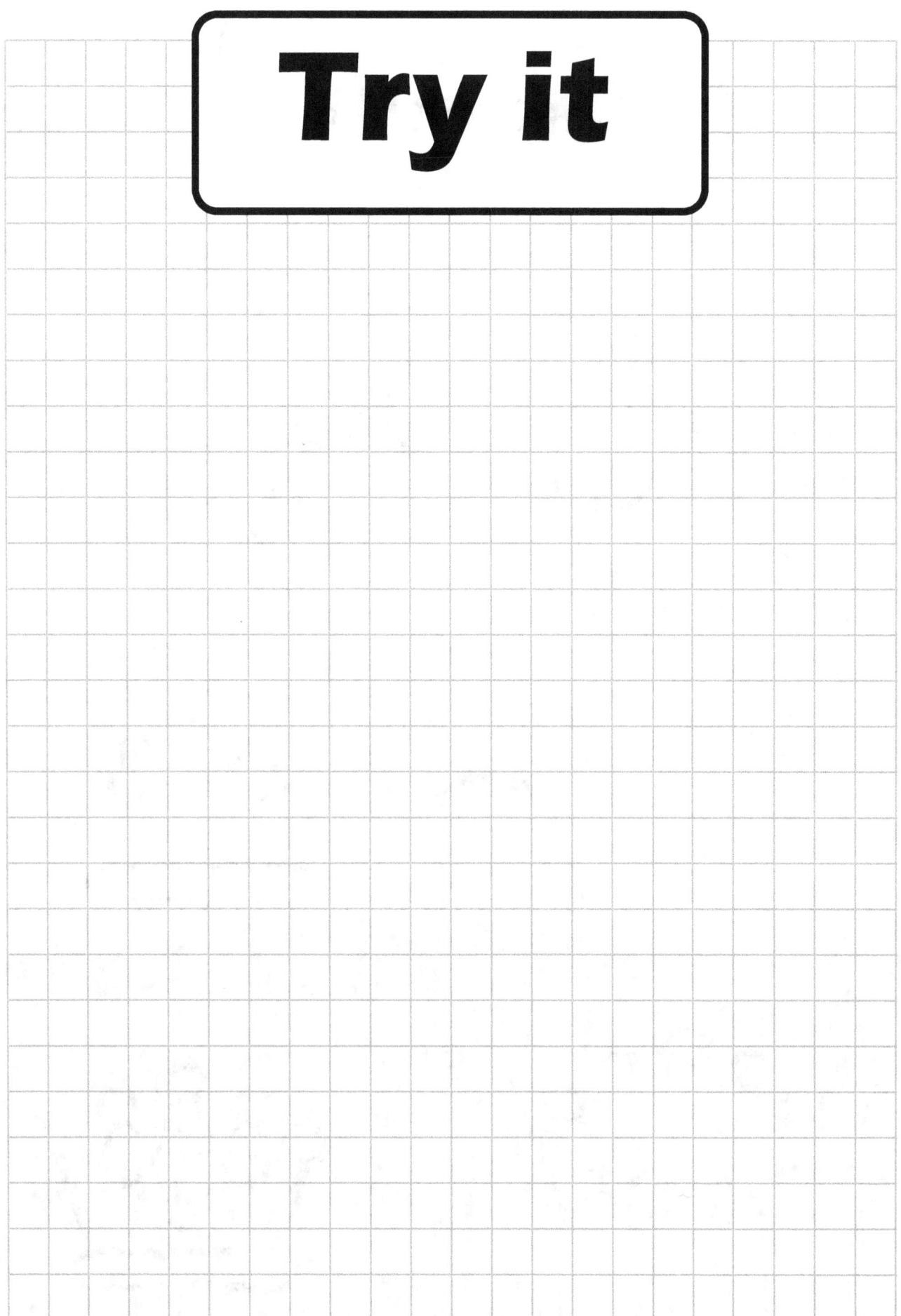

Try it

Crown

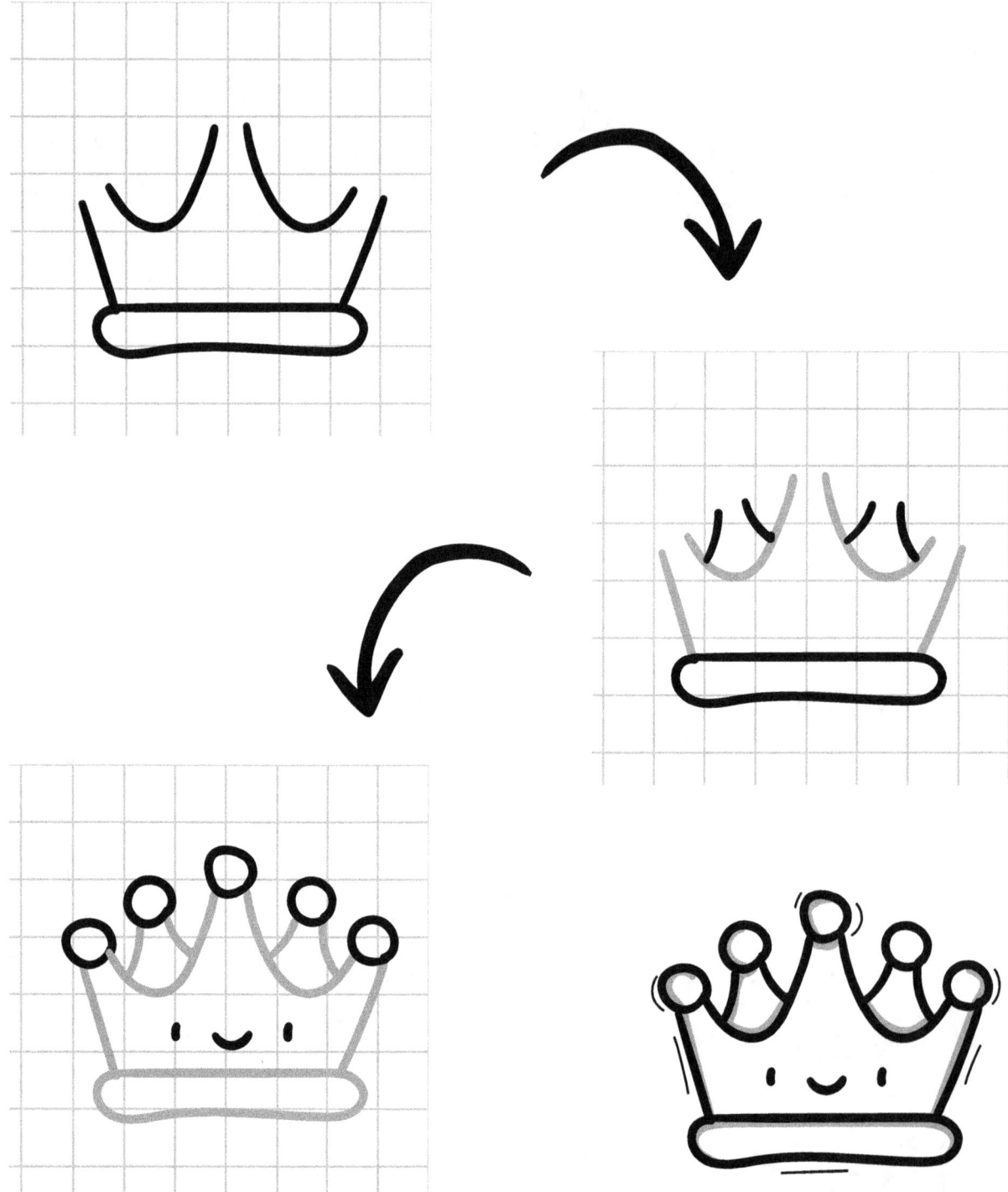

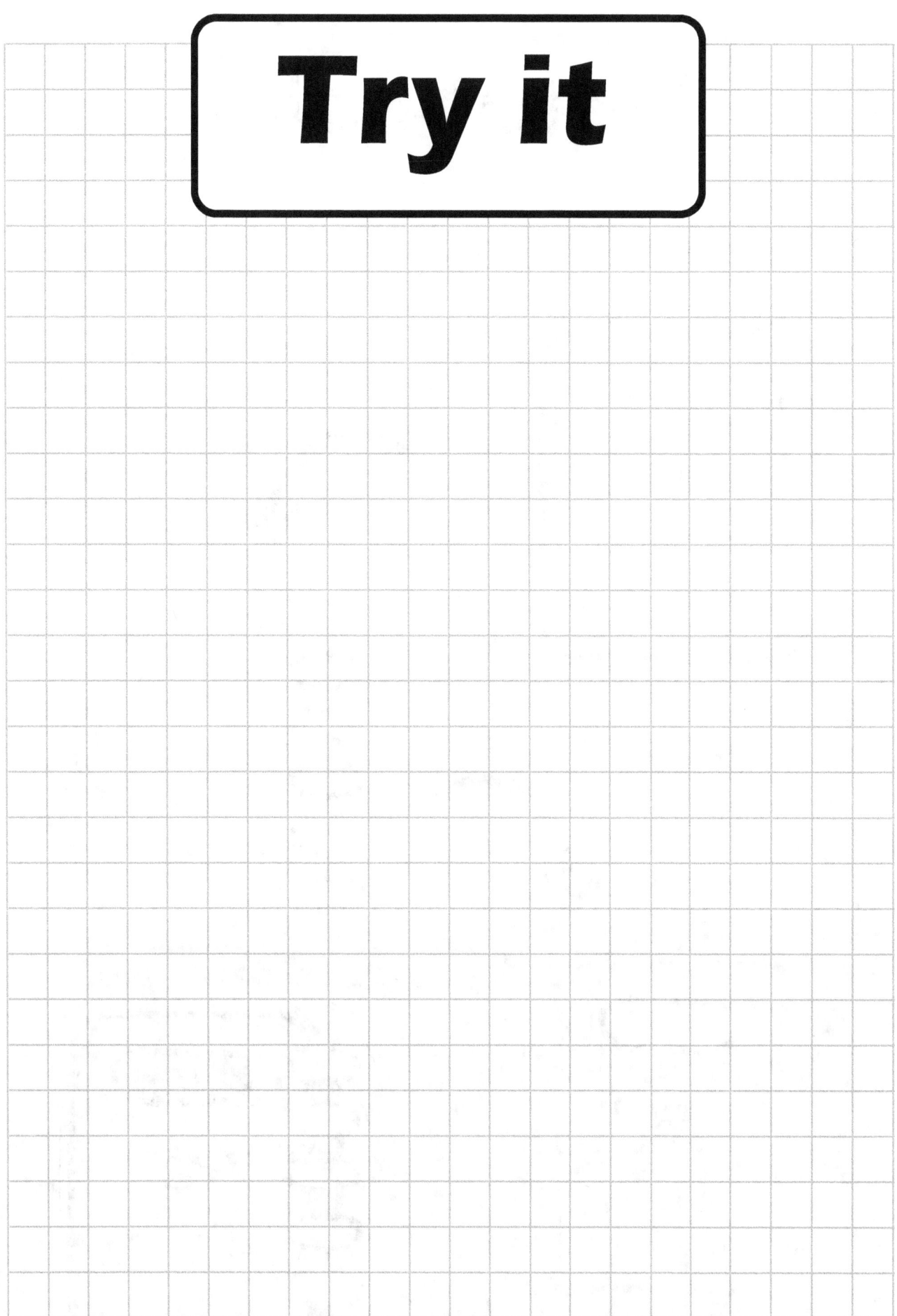

Try it

Notebook

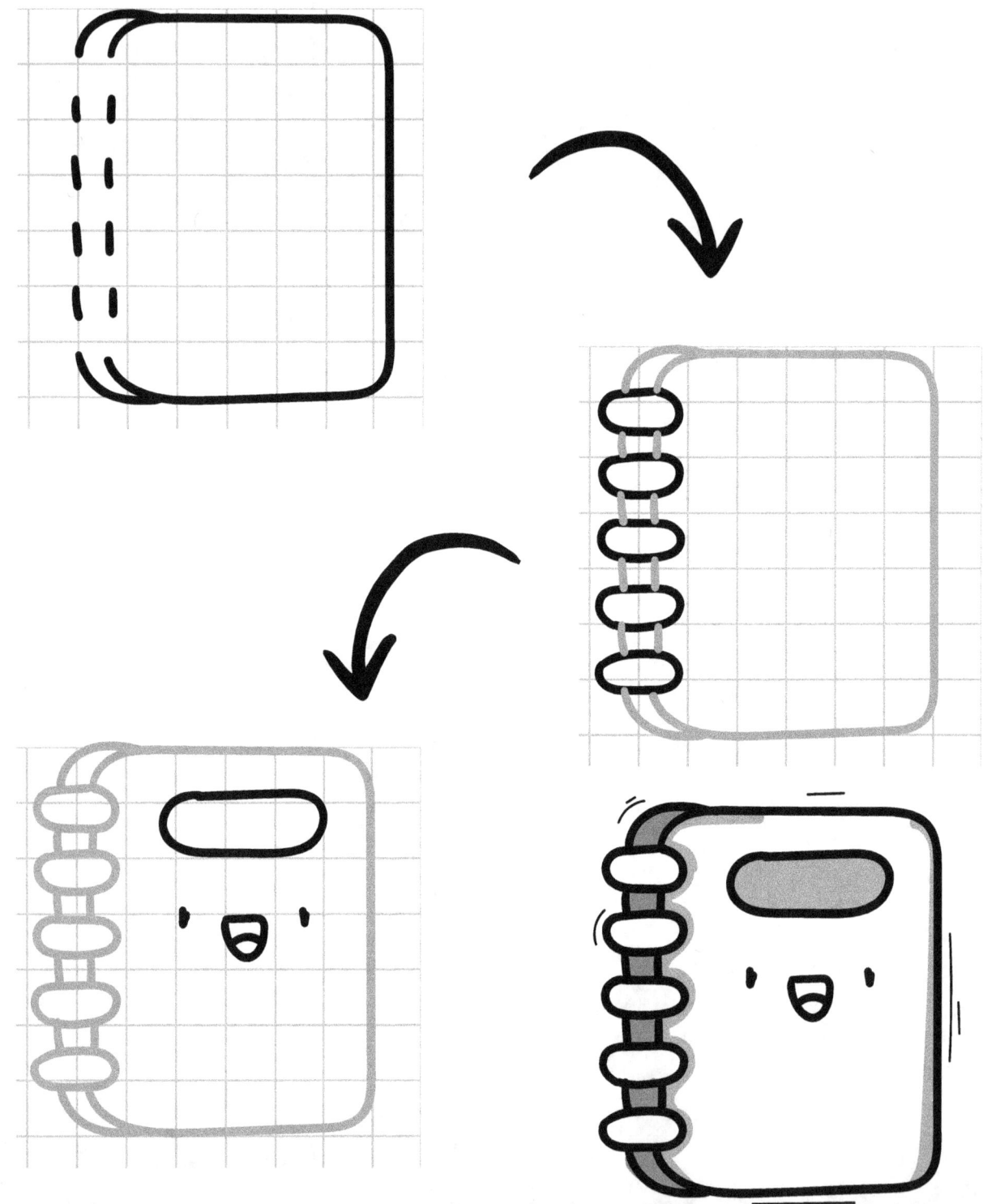

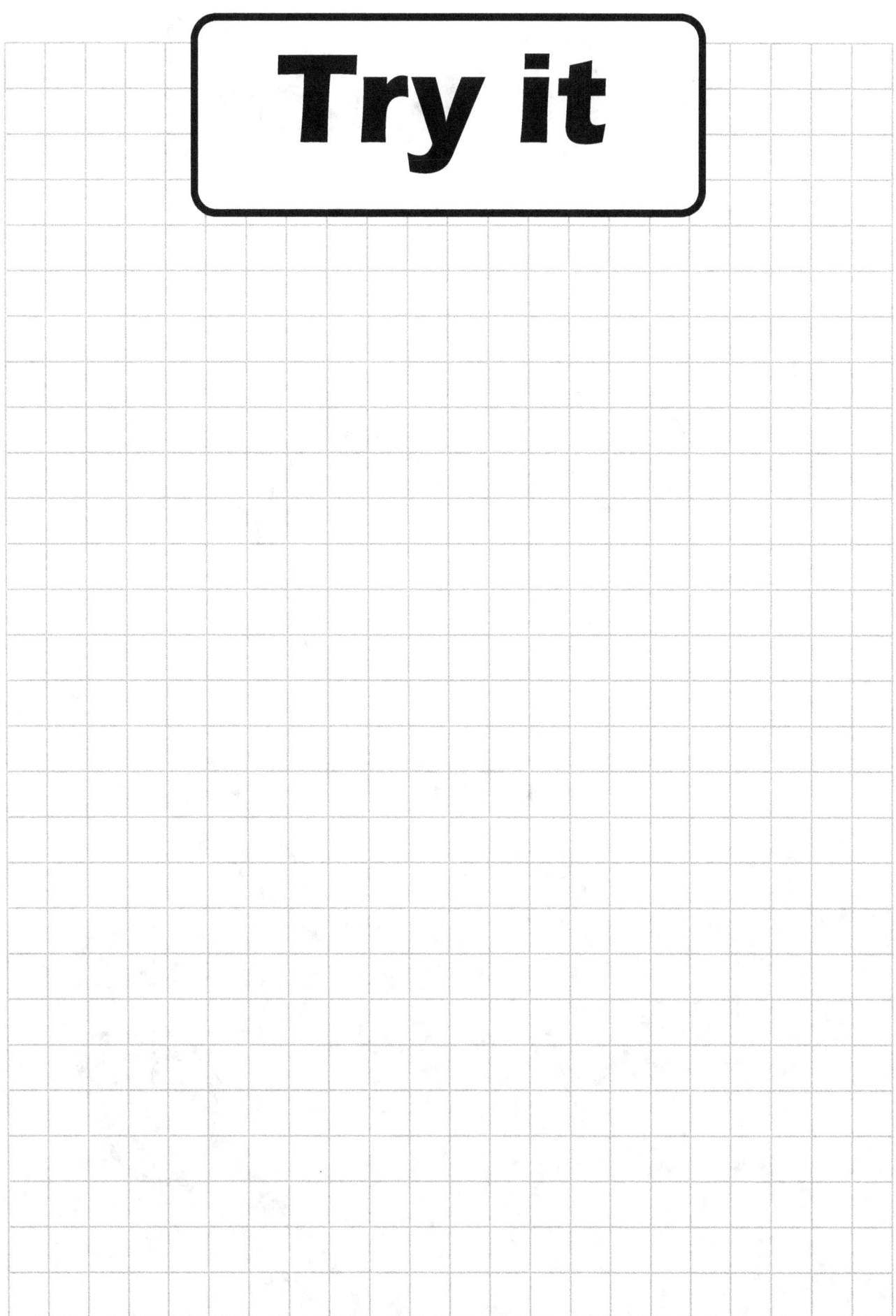

Try it

Paint brush

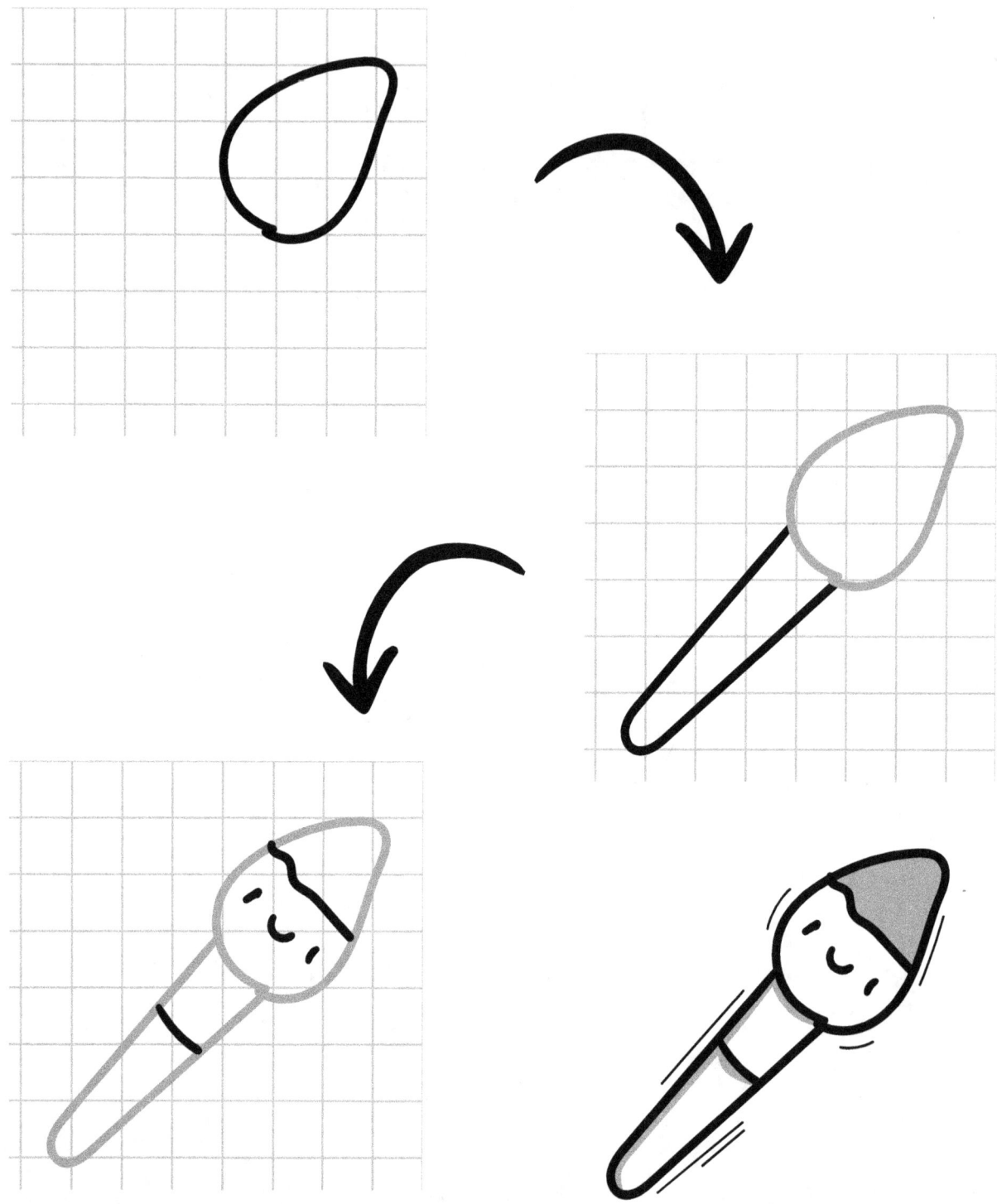

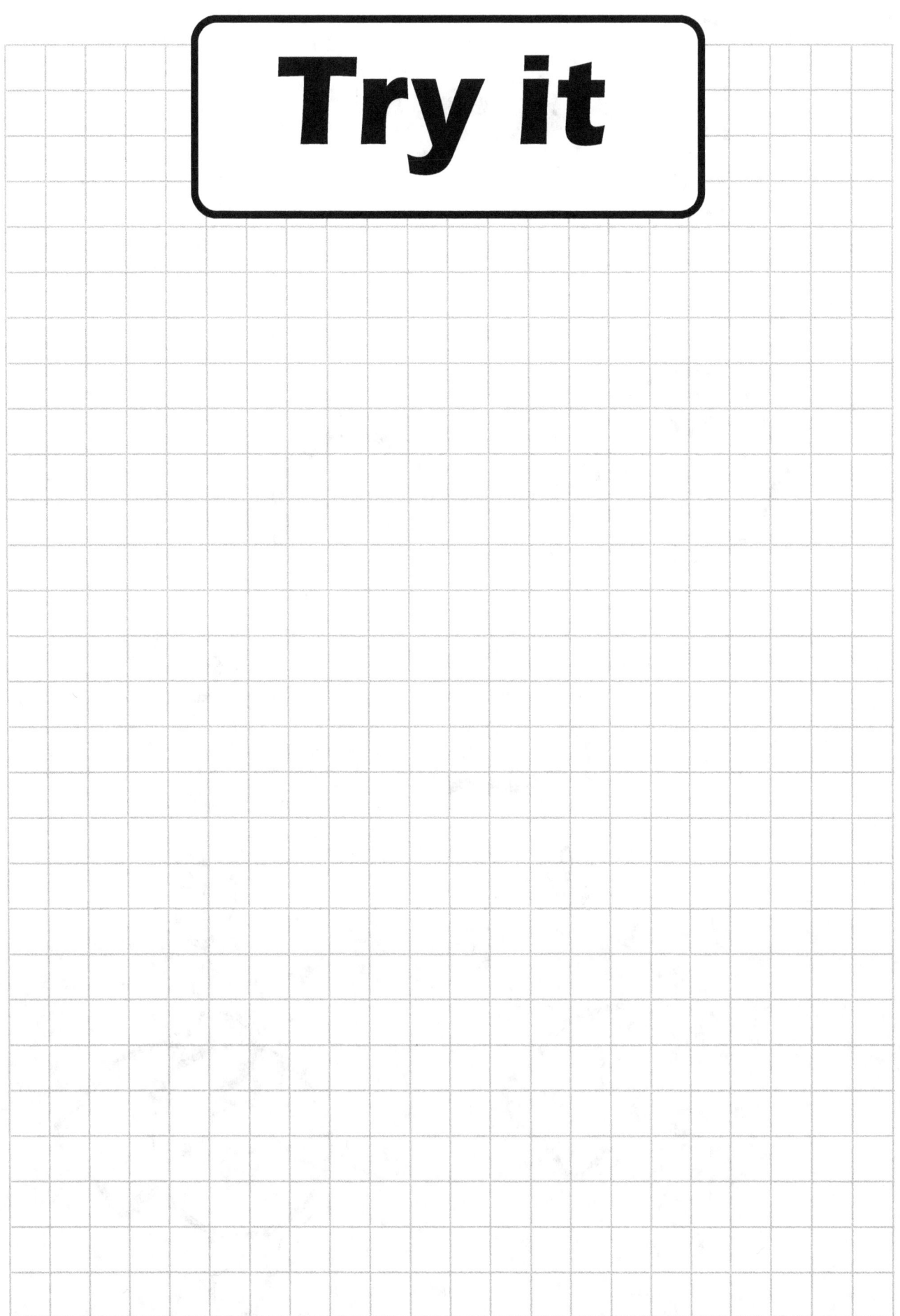

Try it

Key

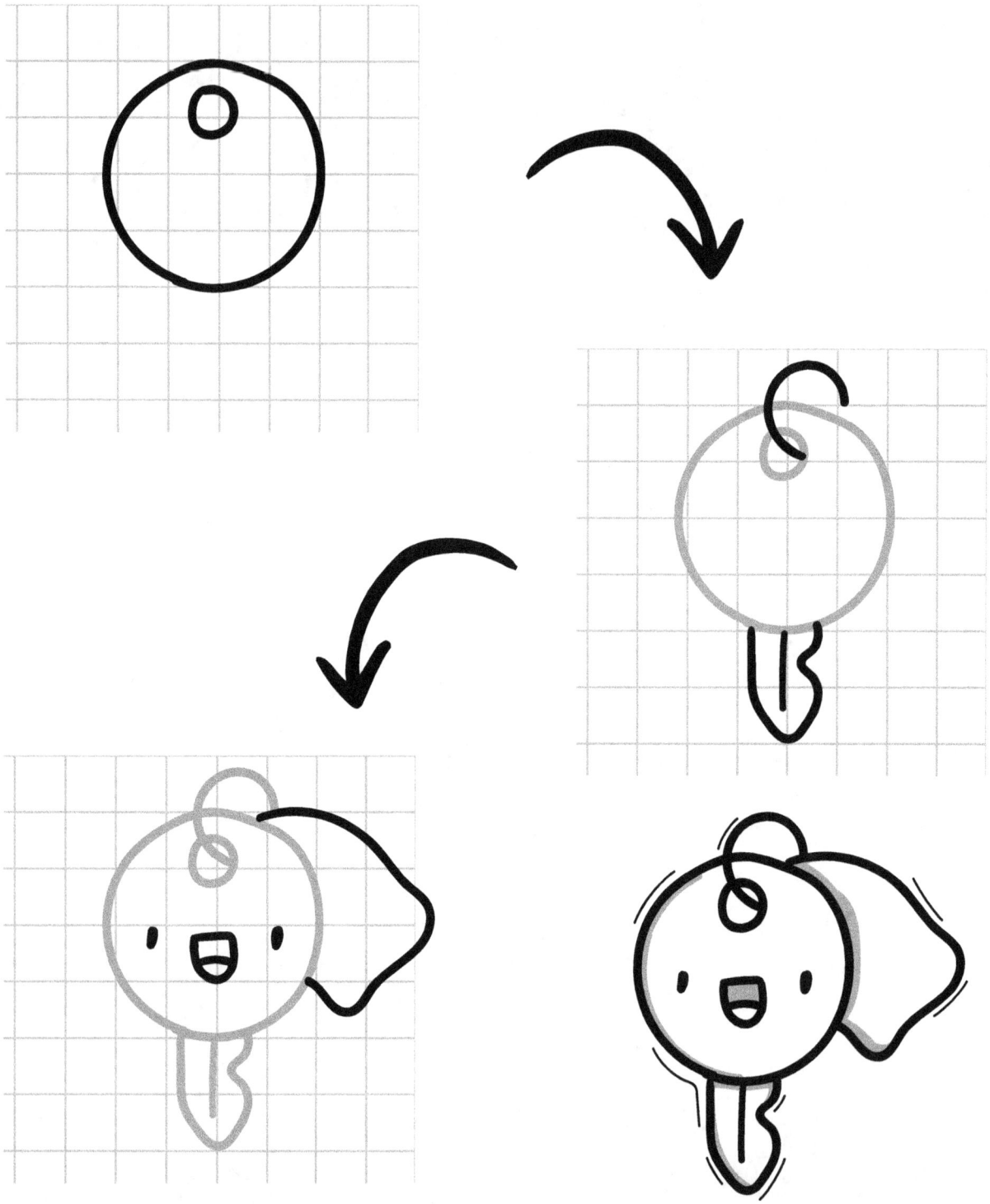

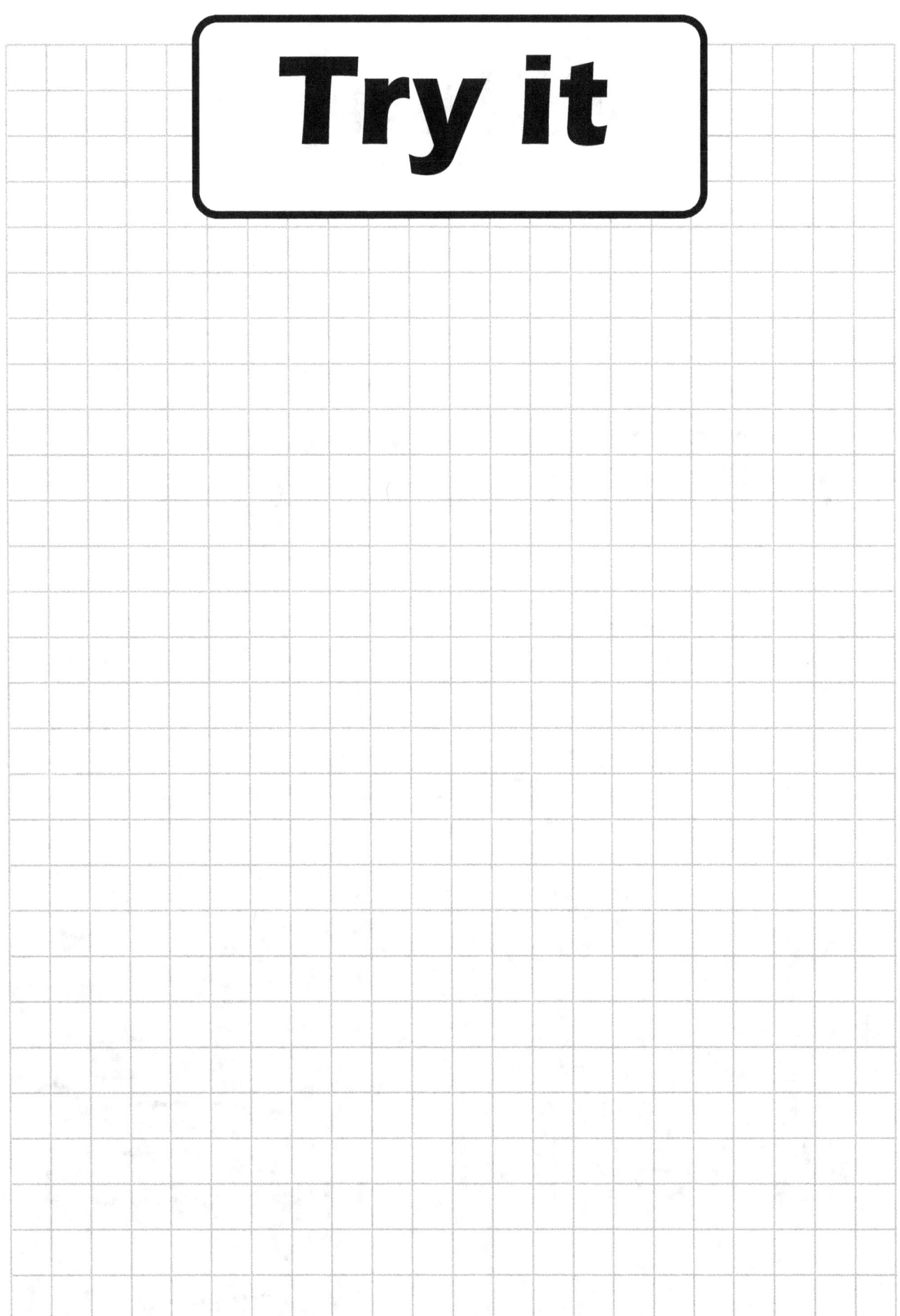

Try it

Pillow

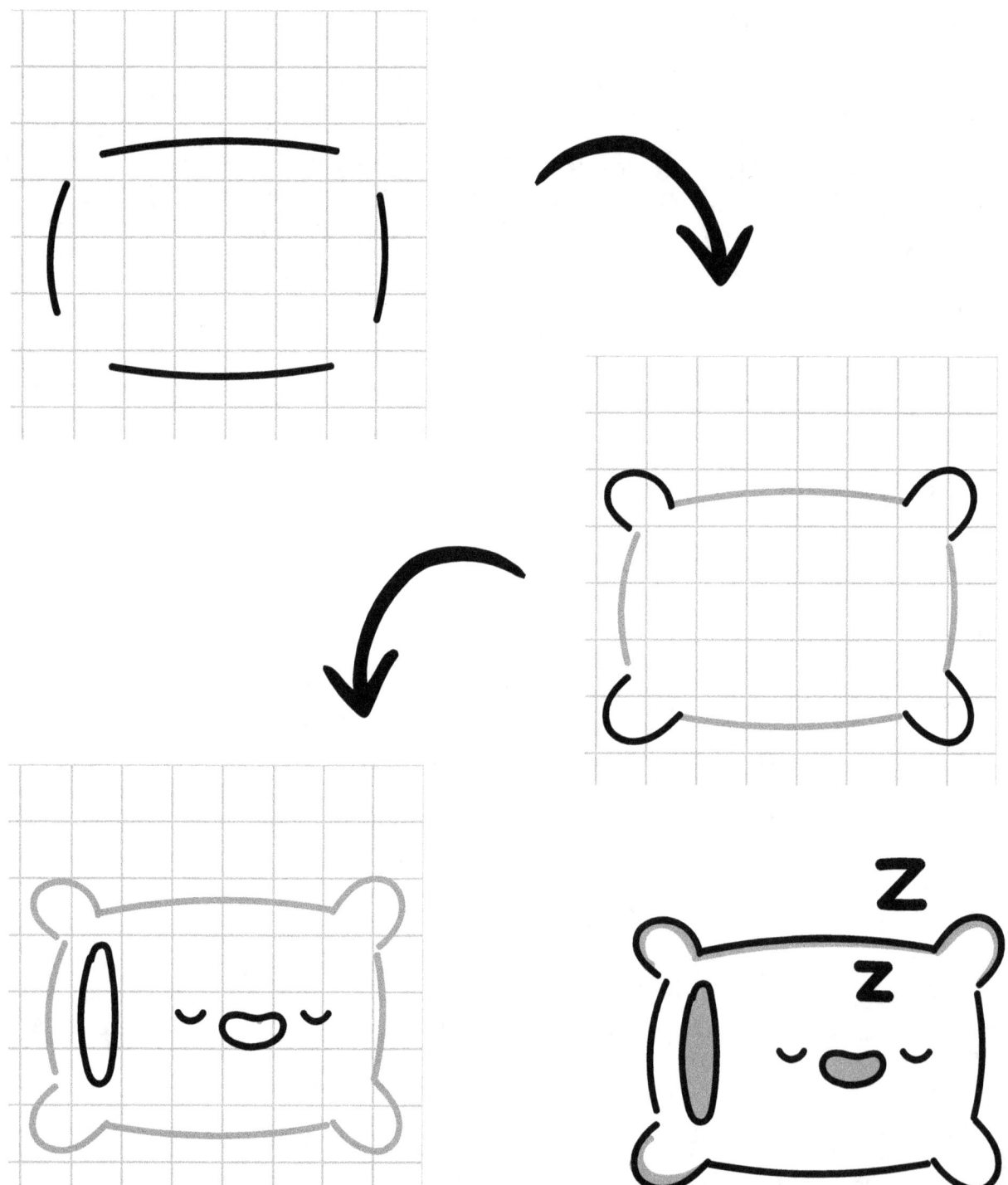

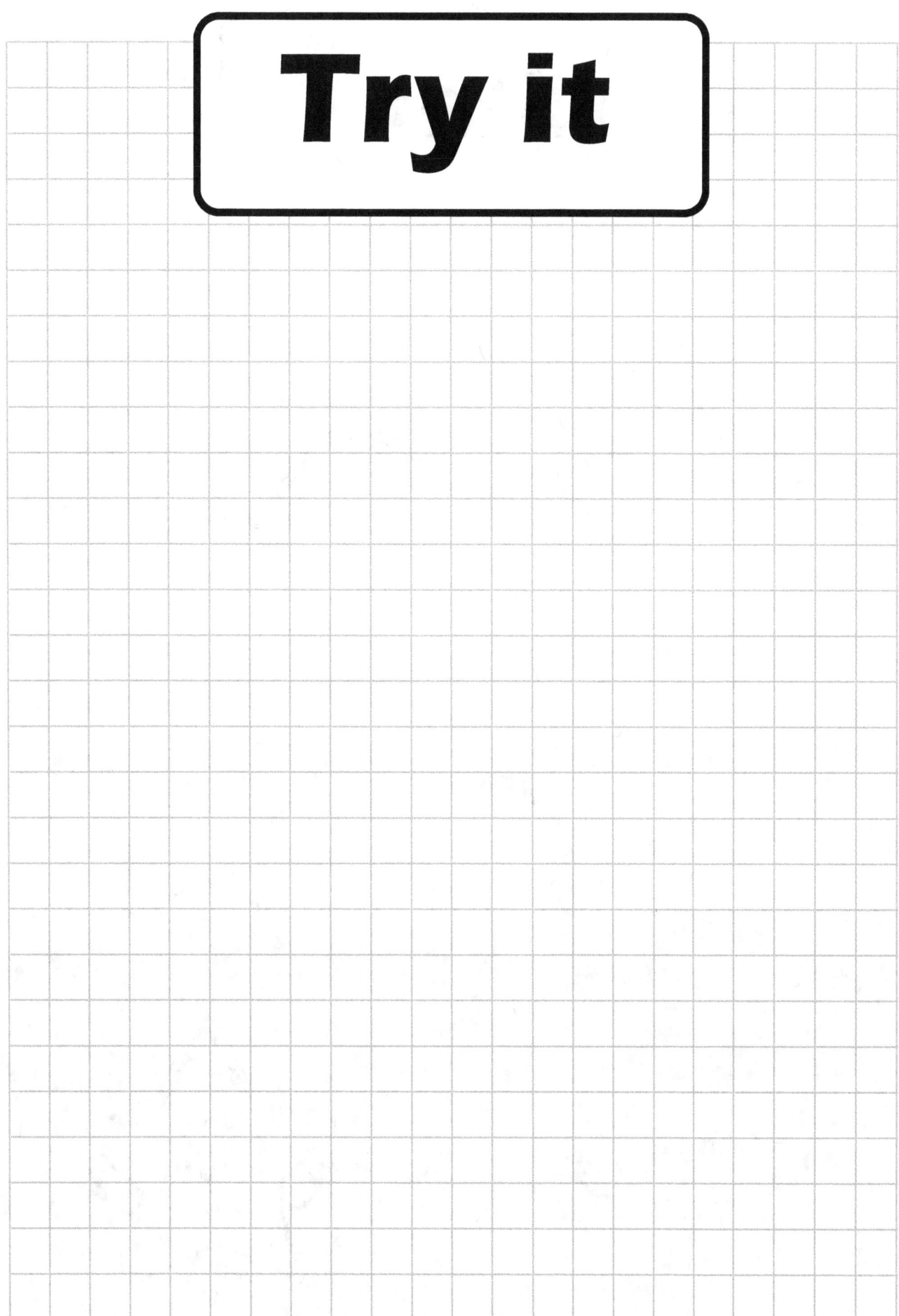

Try it

Star

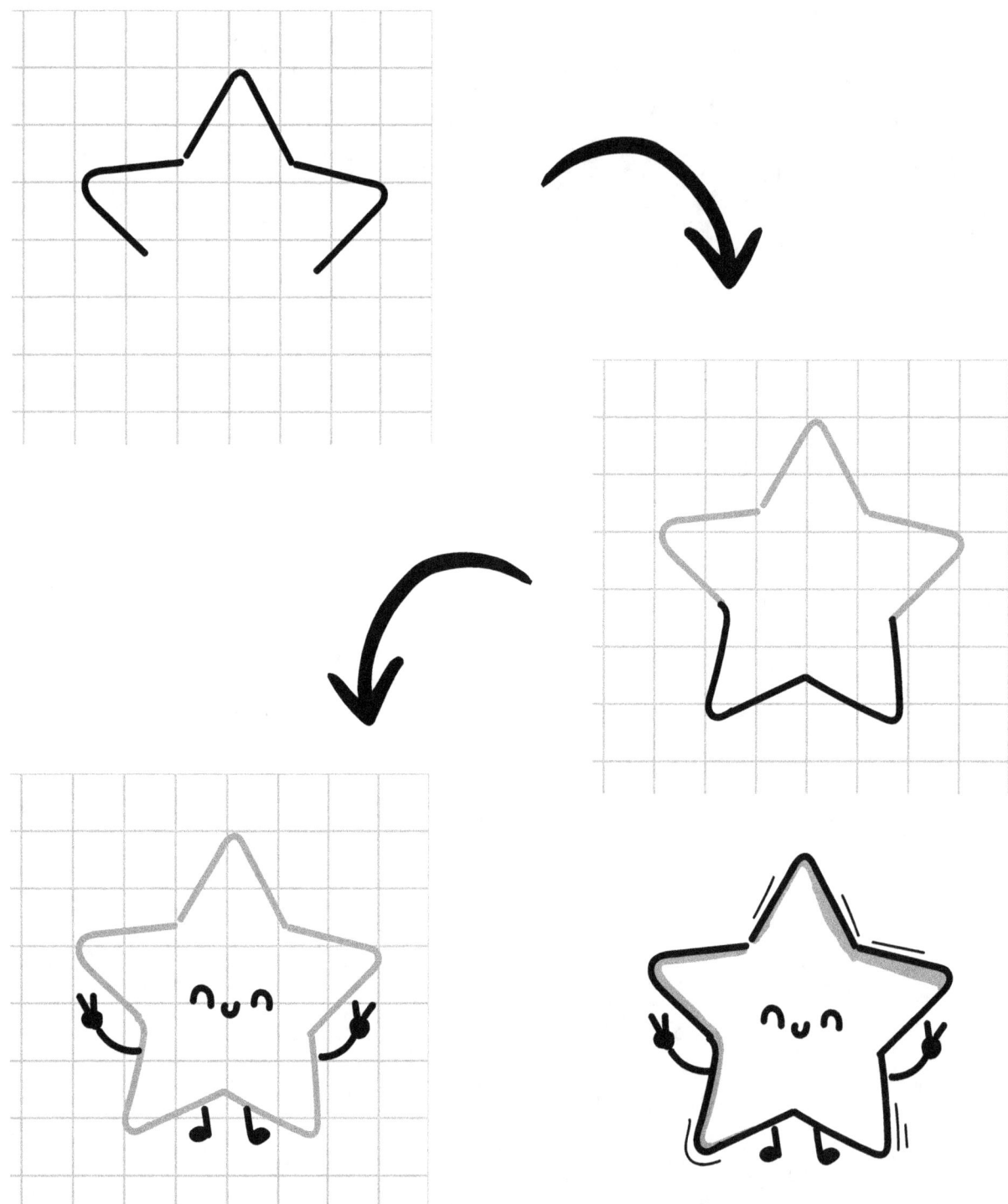

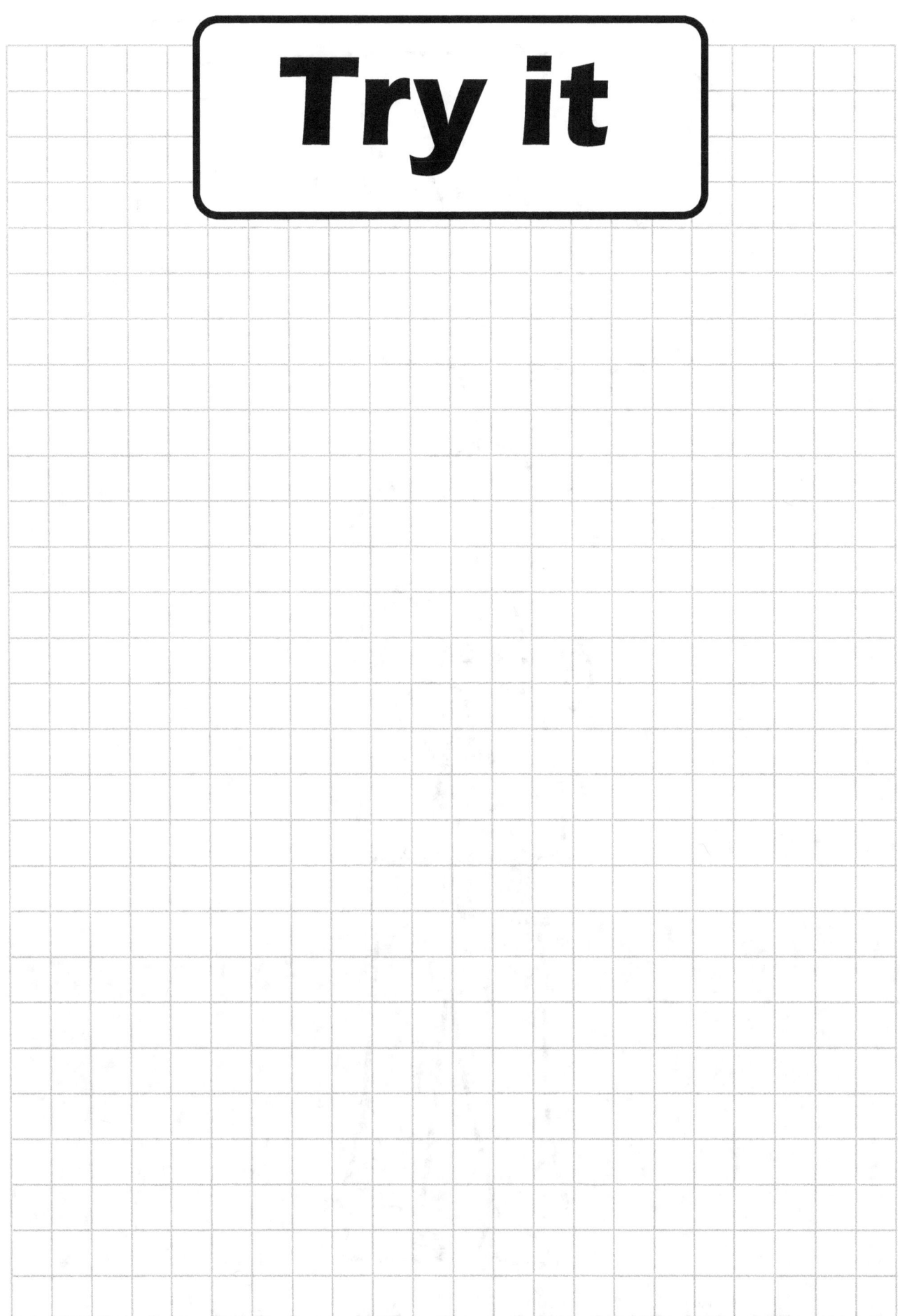

Try it

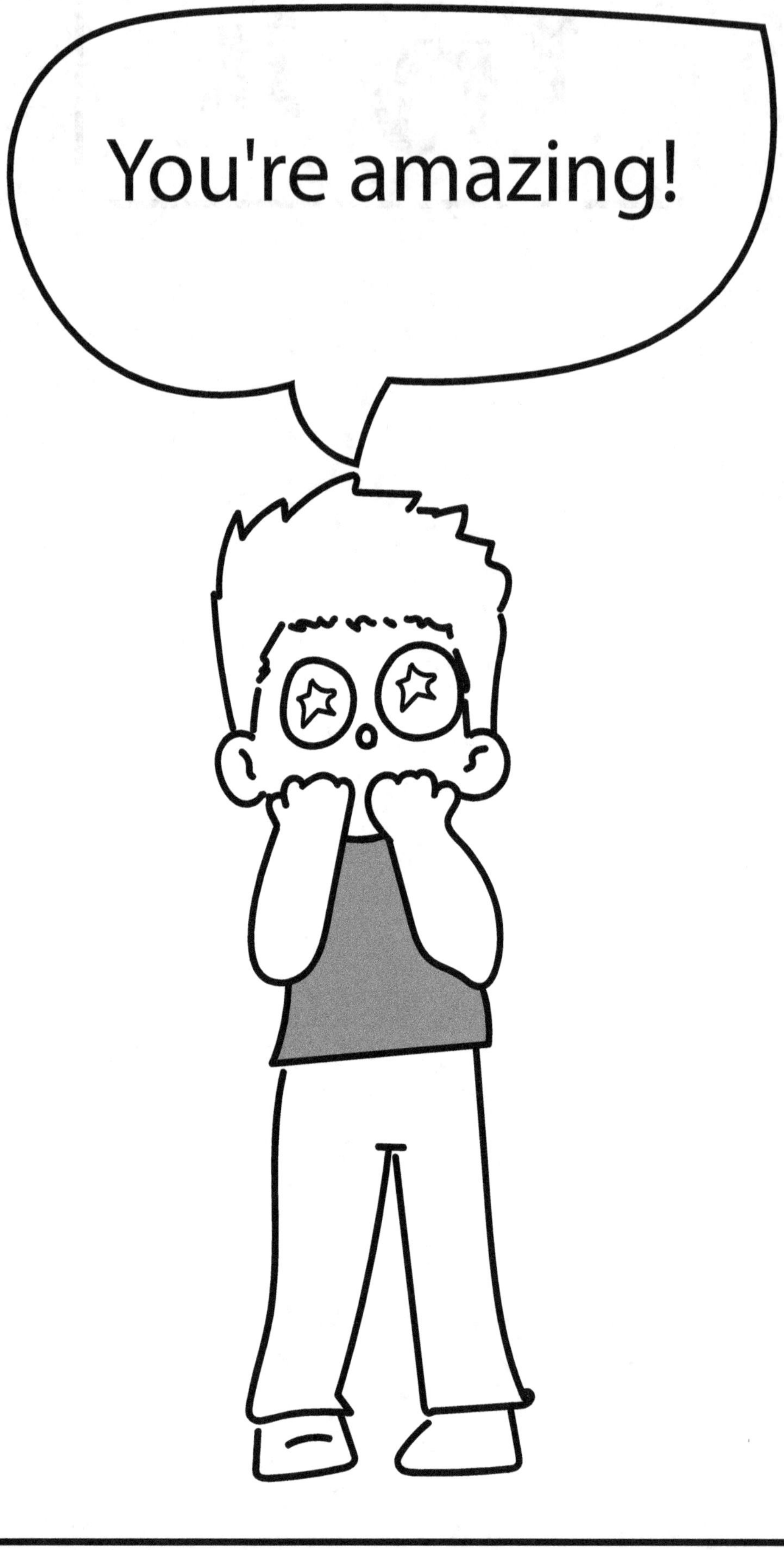
You're amazing!

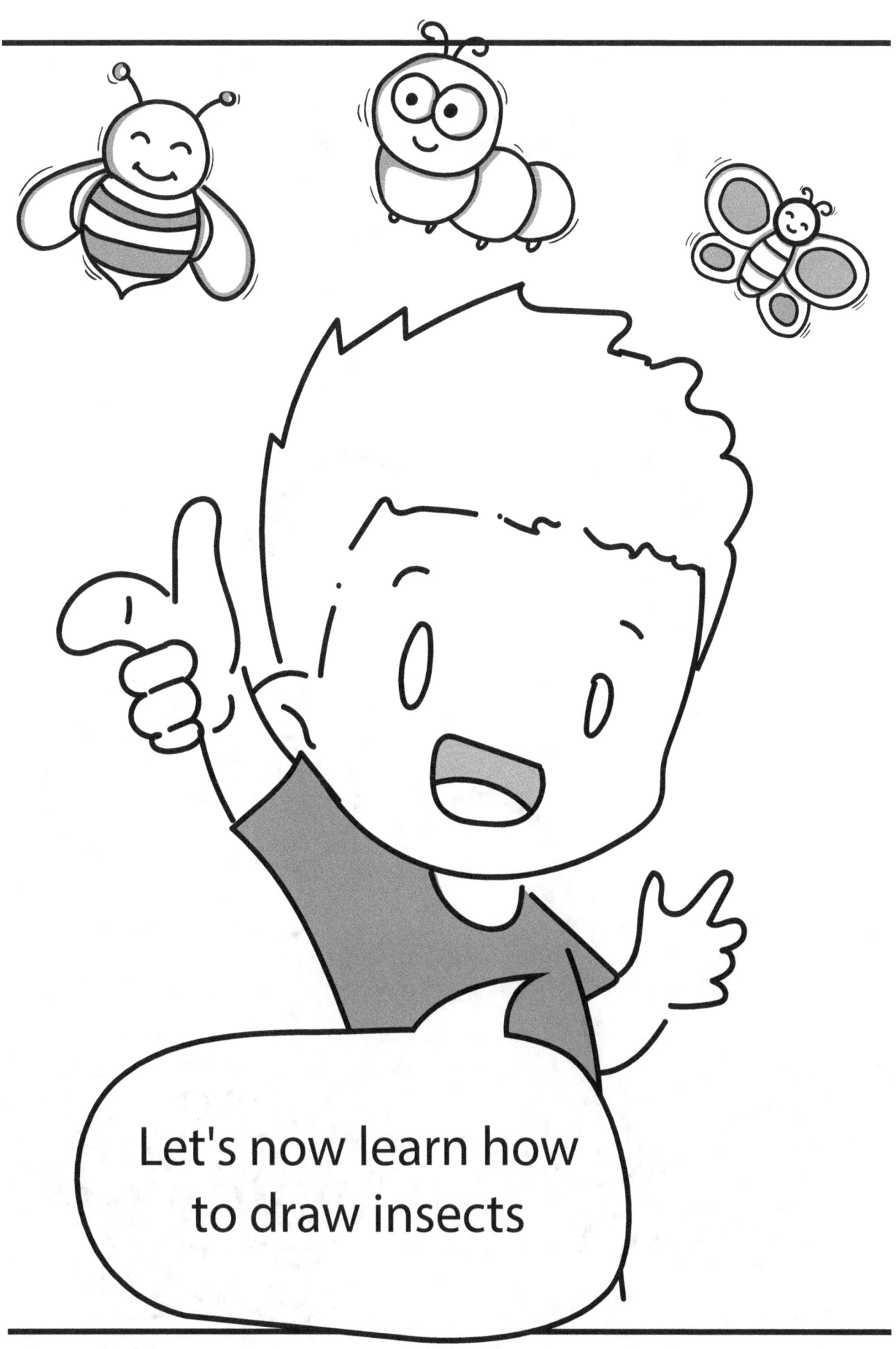

Let's now learn how to draw insects

Butterfly

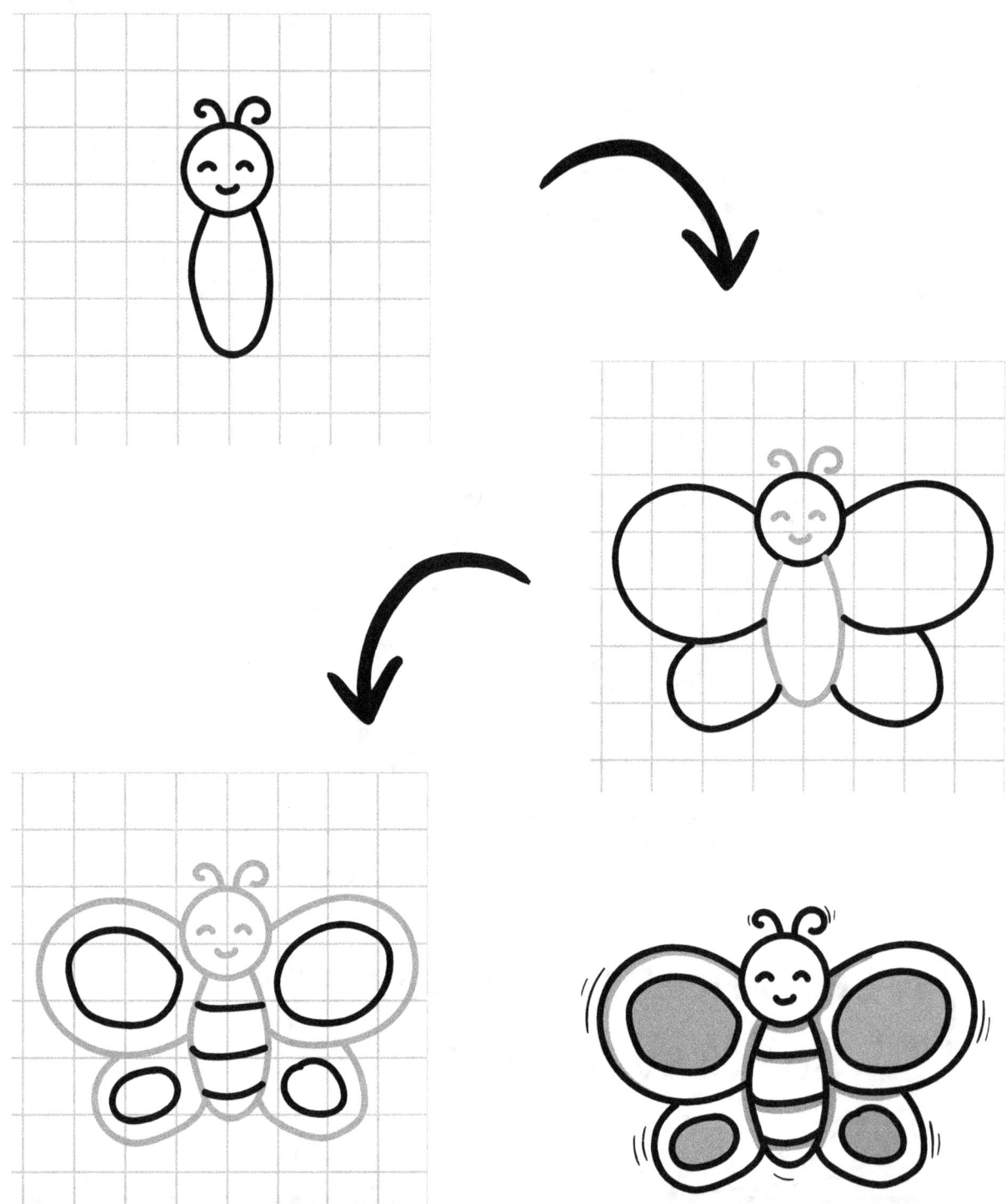

Try it

More than once

Worm

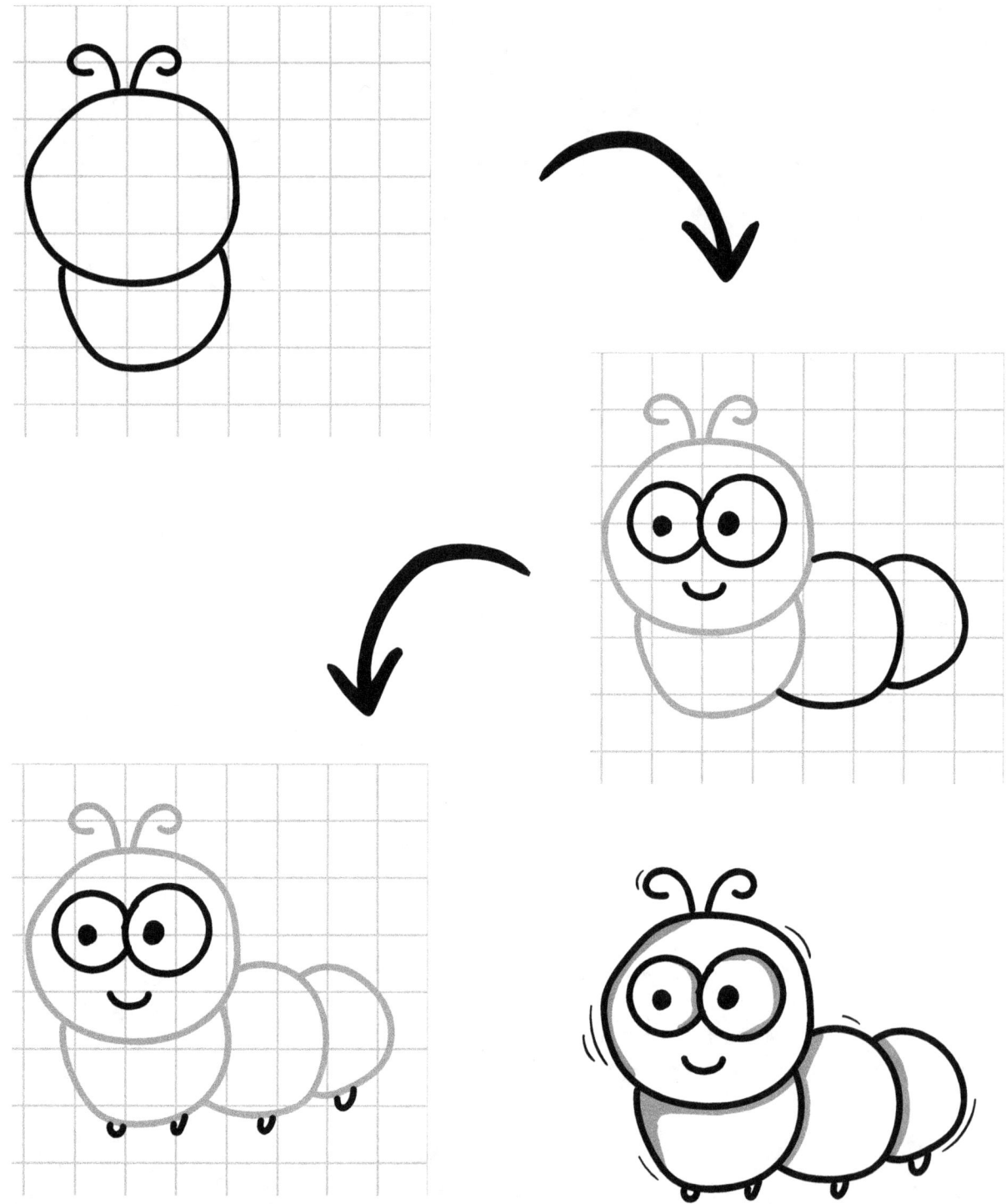

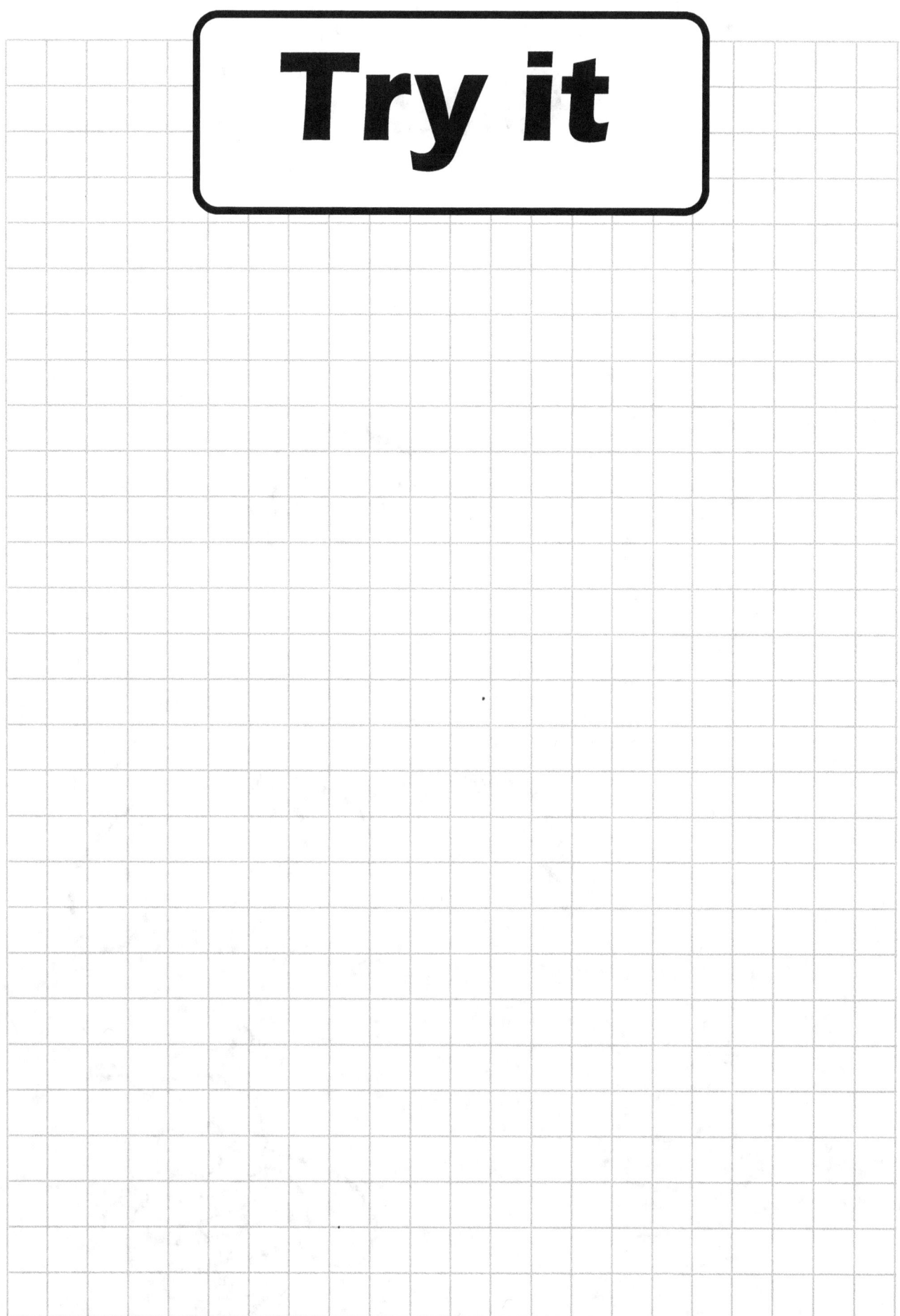

Try it

Bee

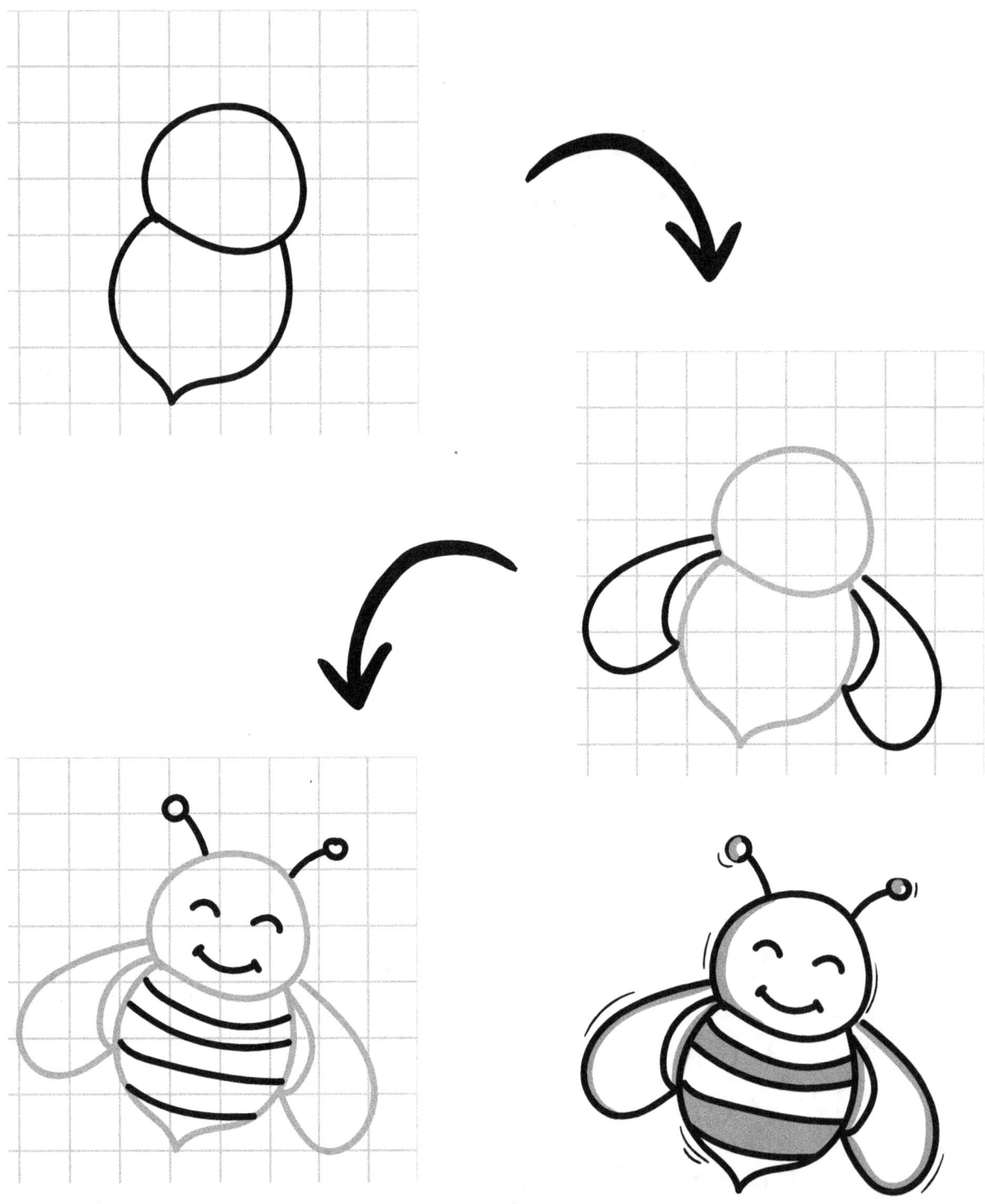

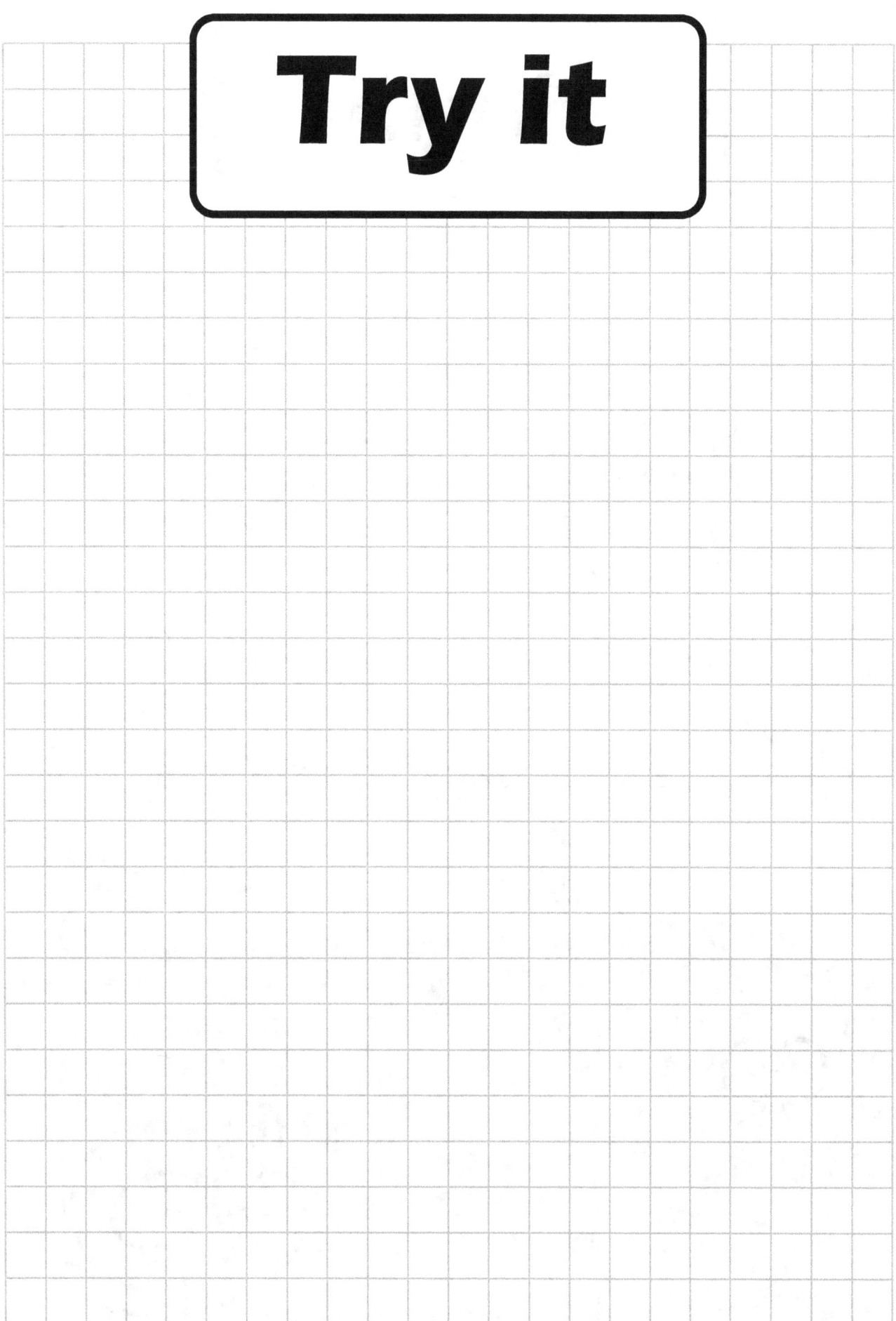

Try it

Snail

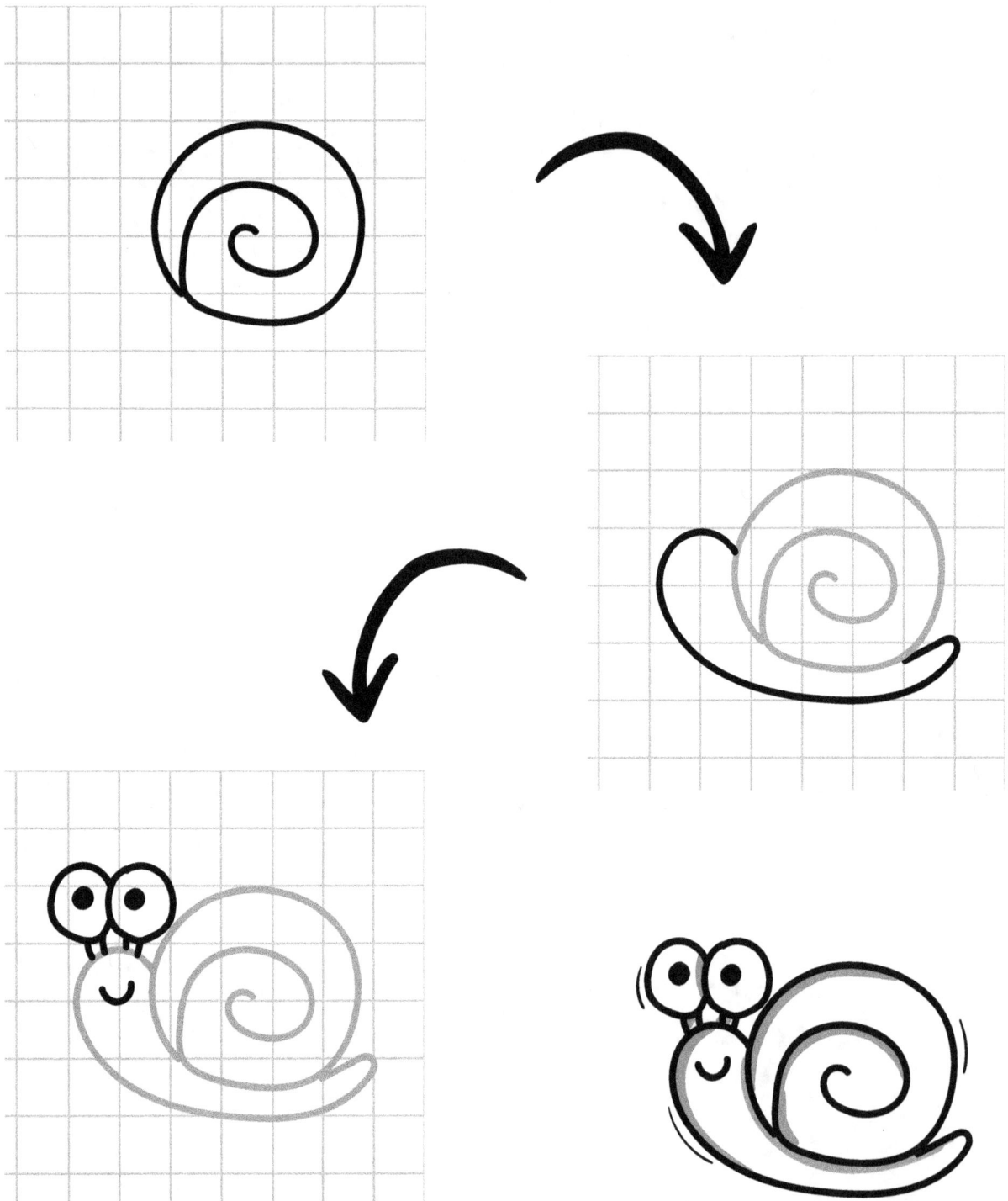

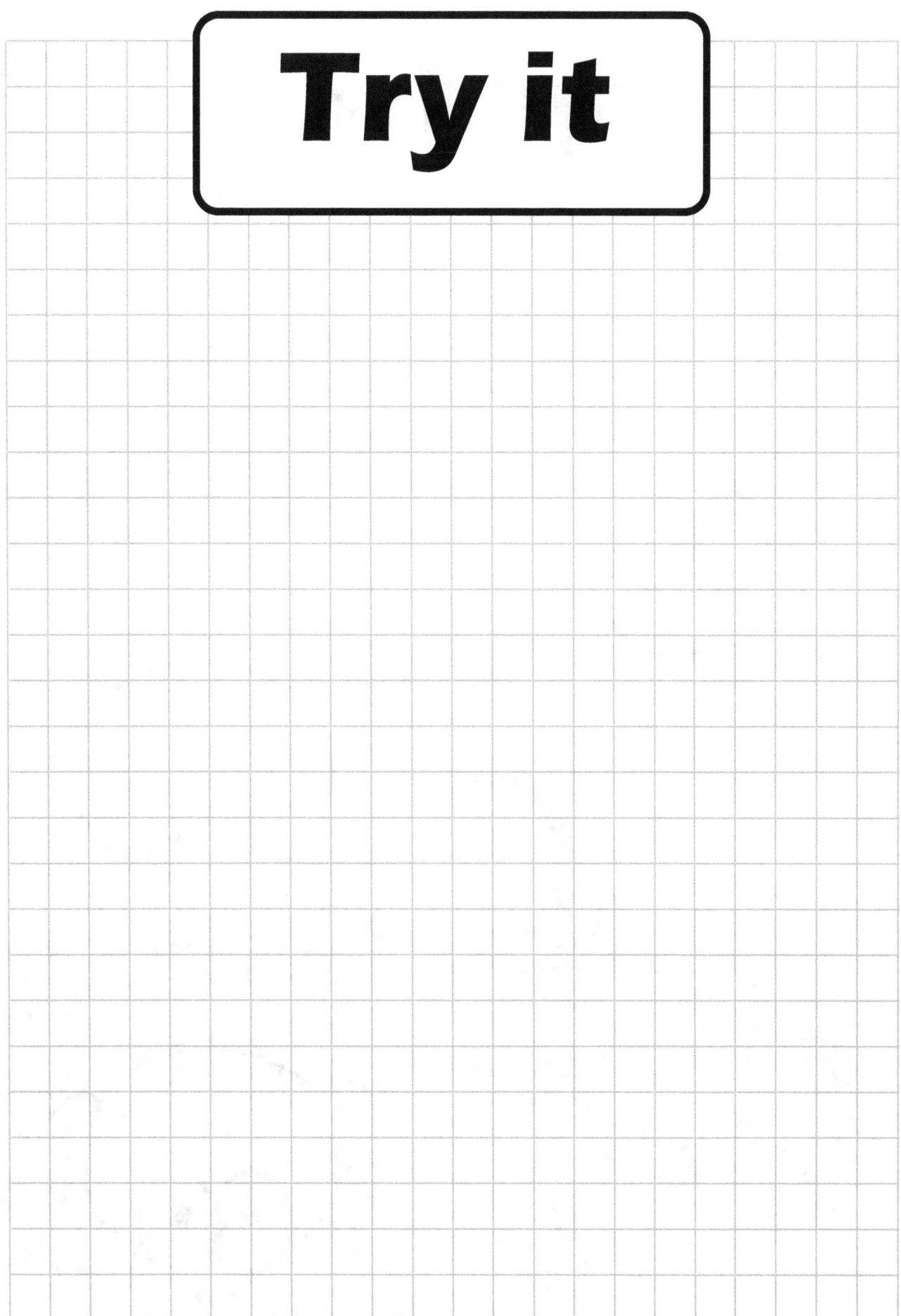

Try it

Spider

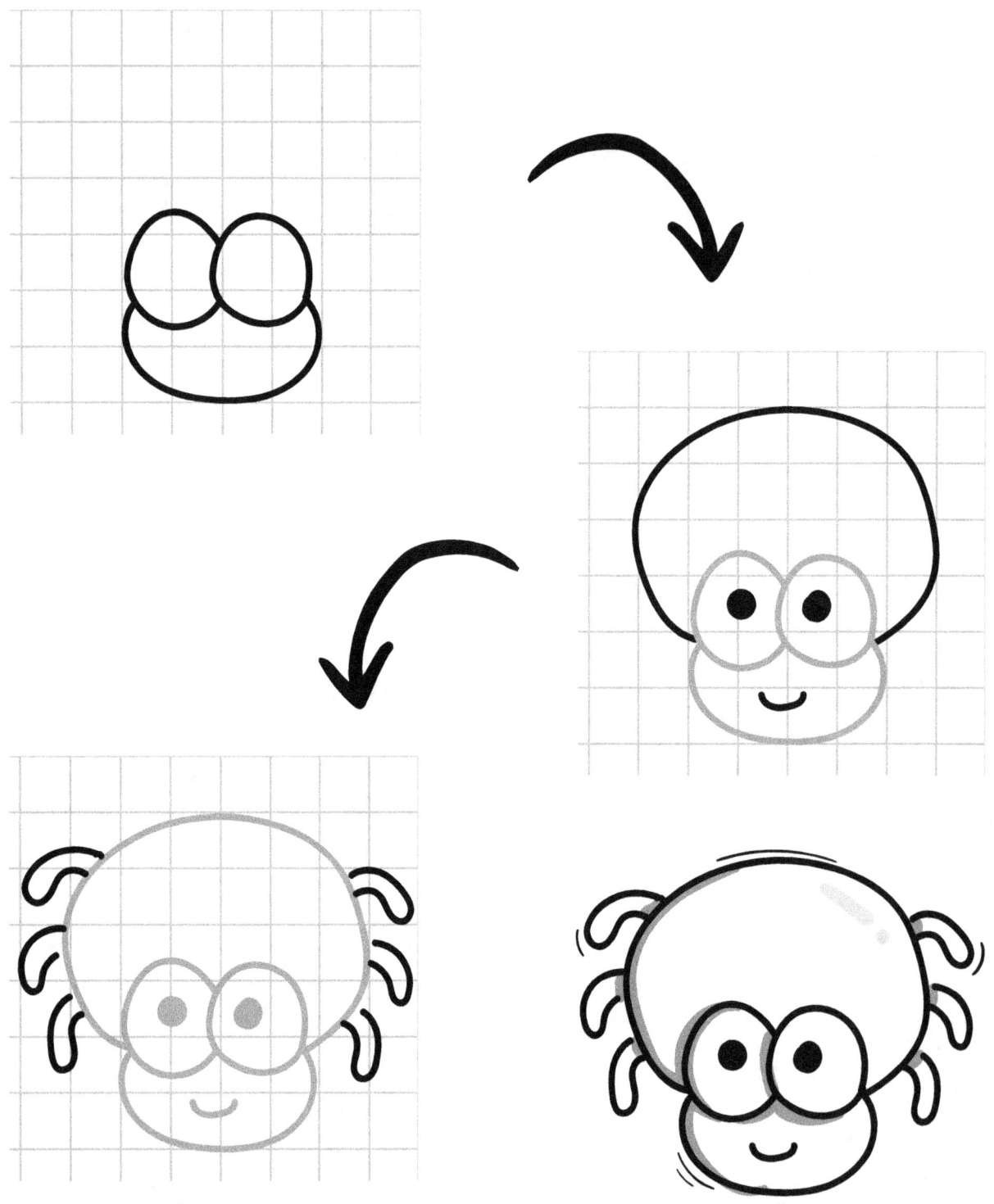

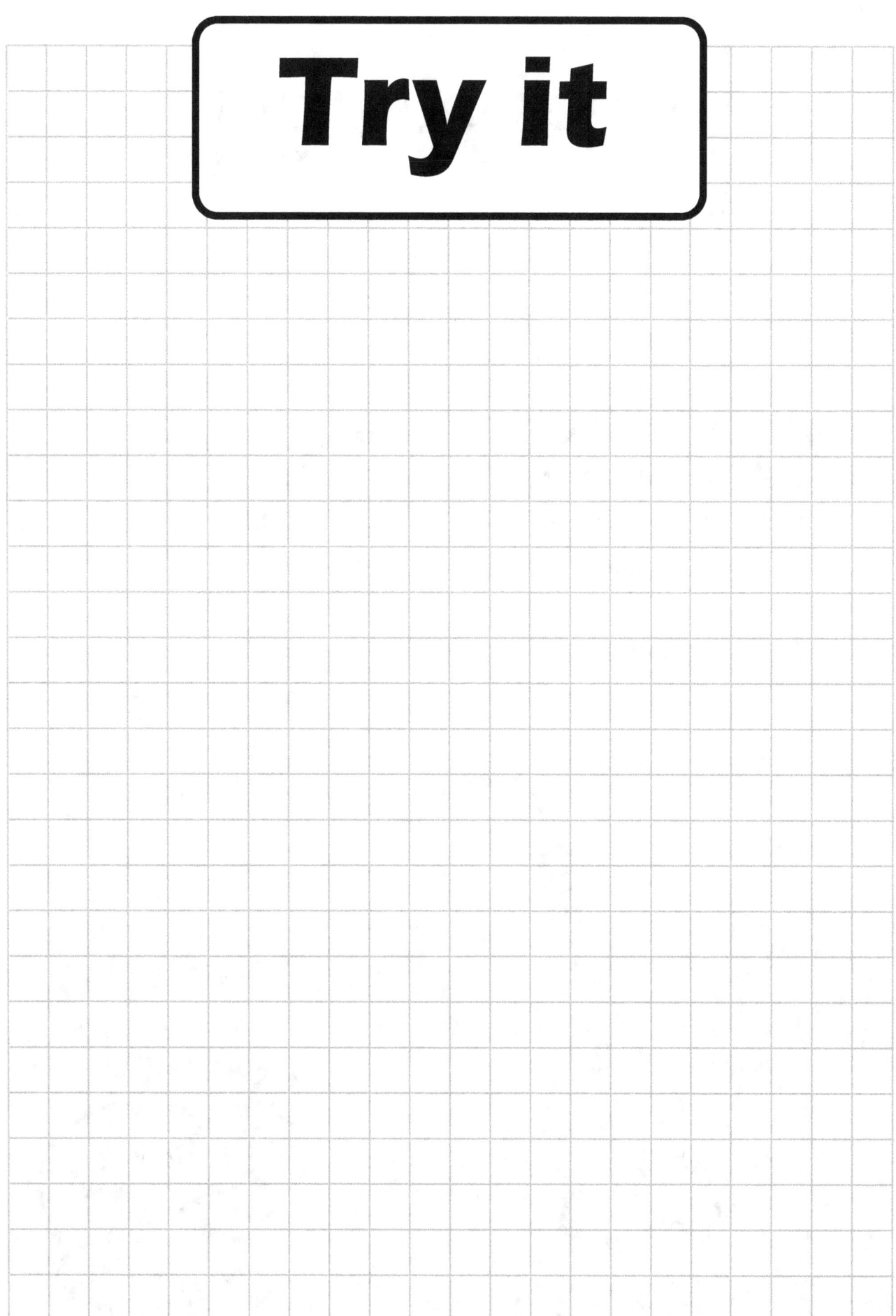

Try it

Ladybug

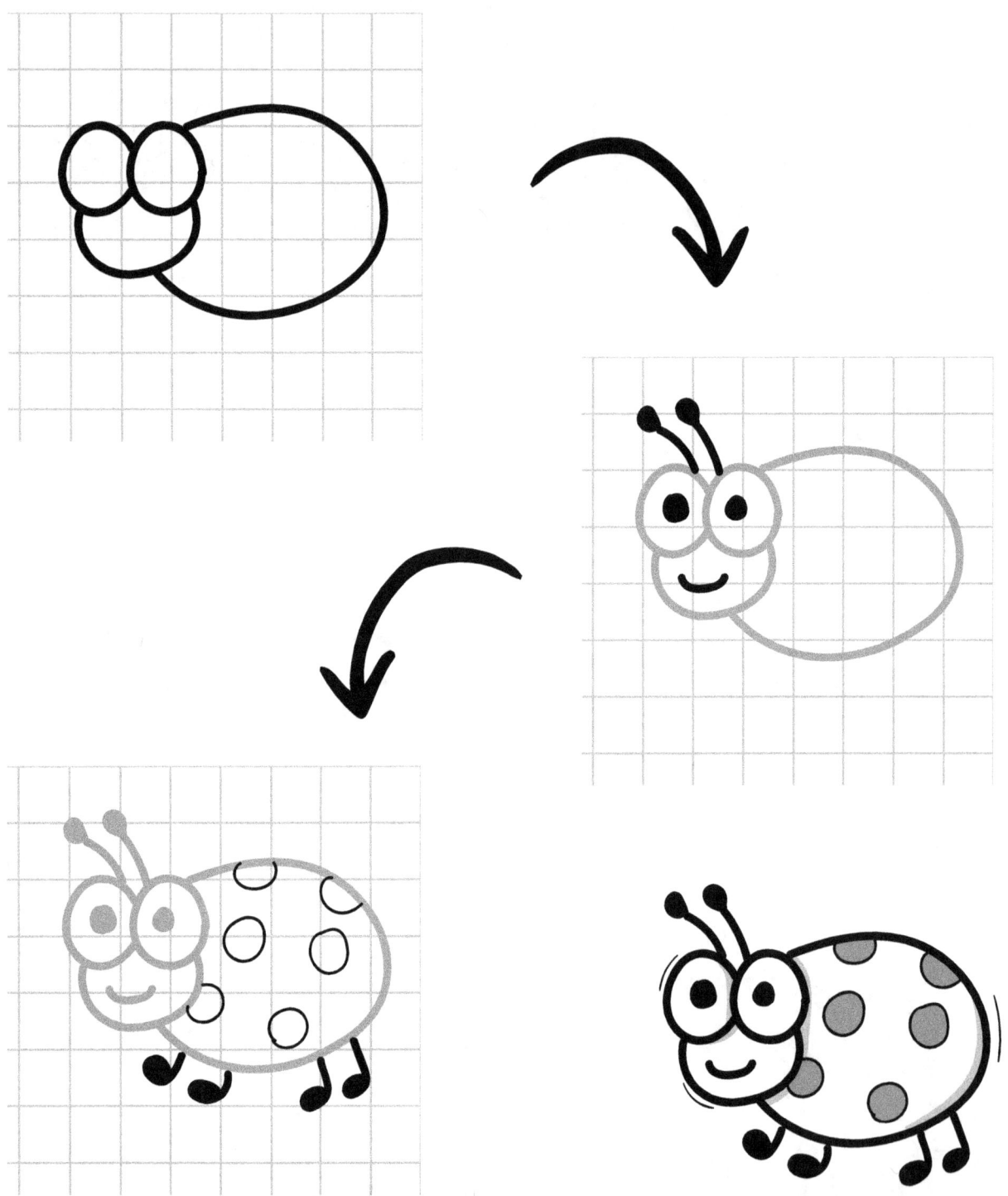

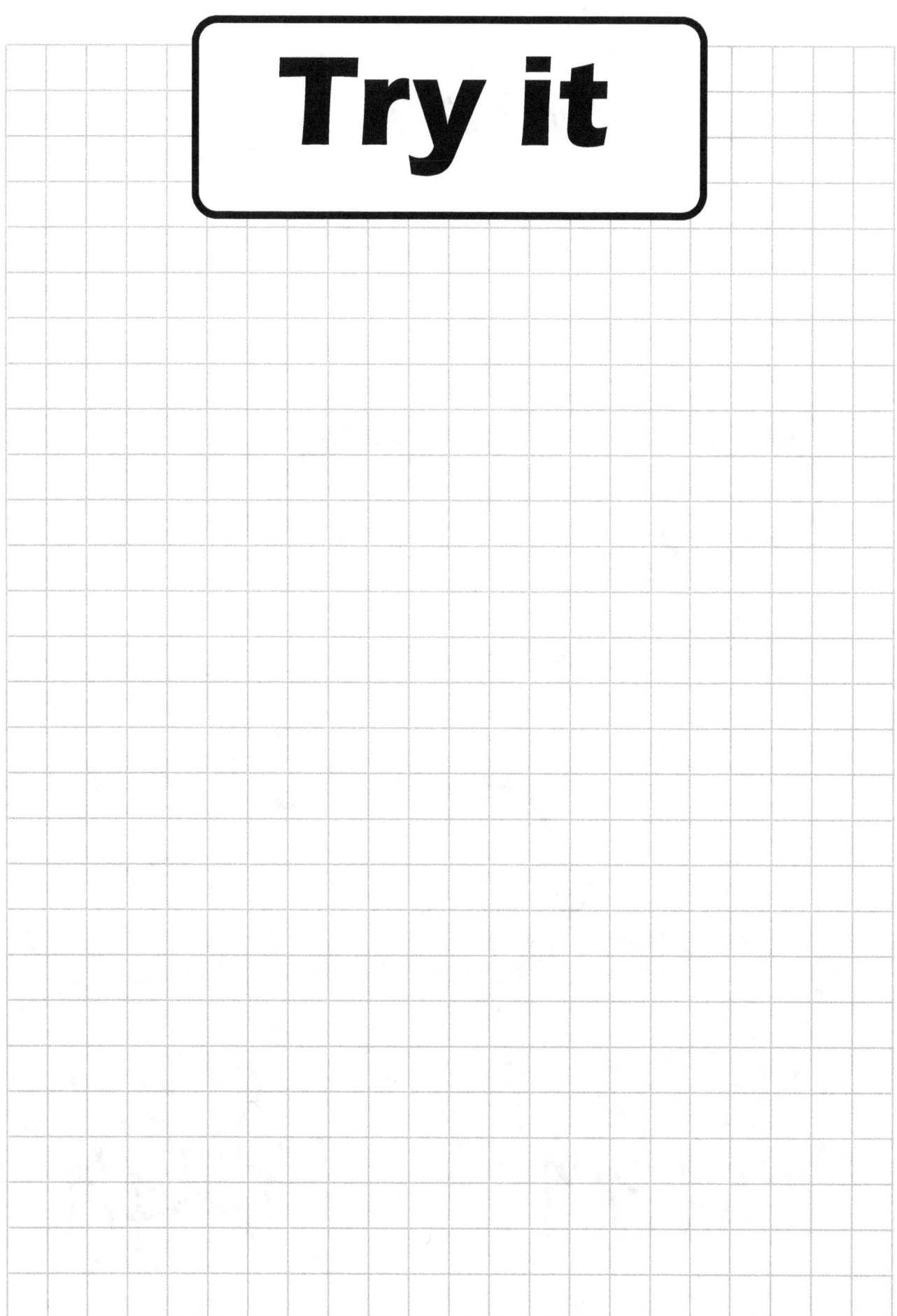

Try it

Ant

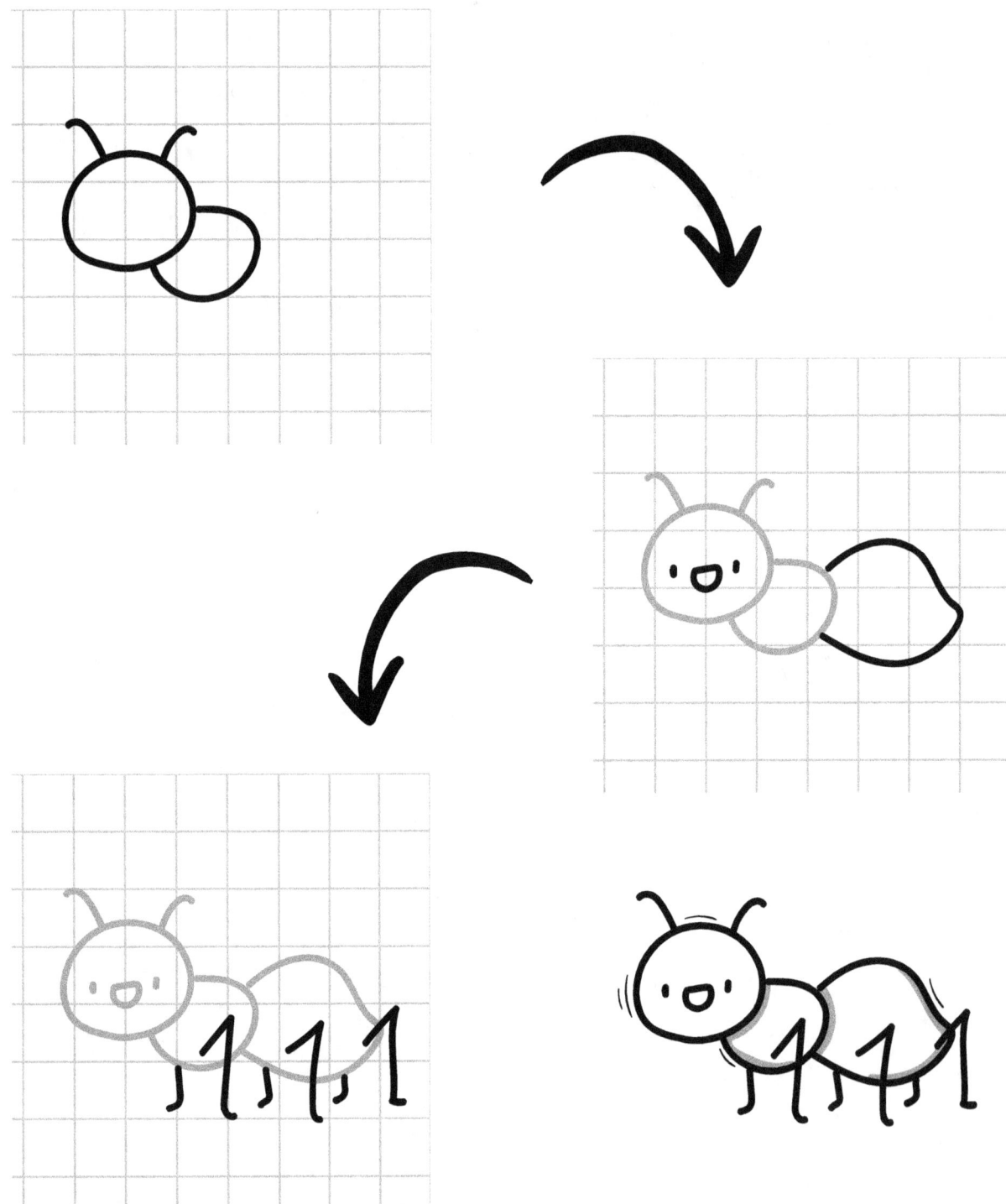

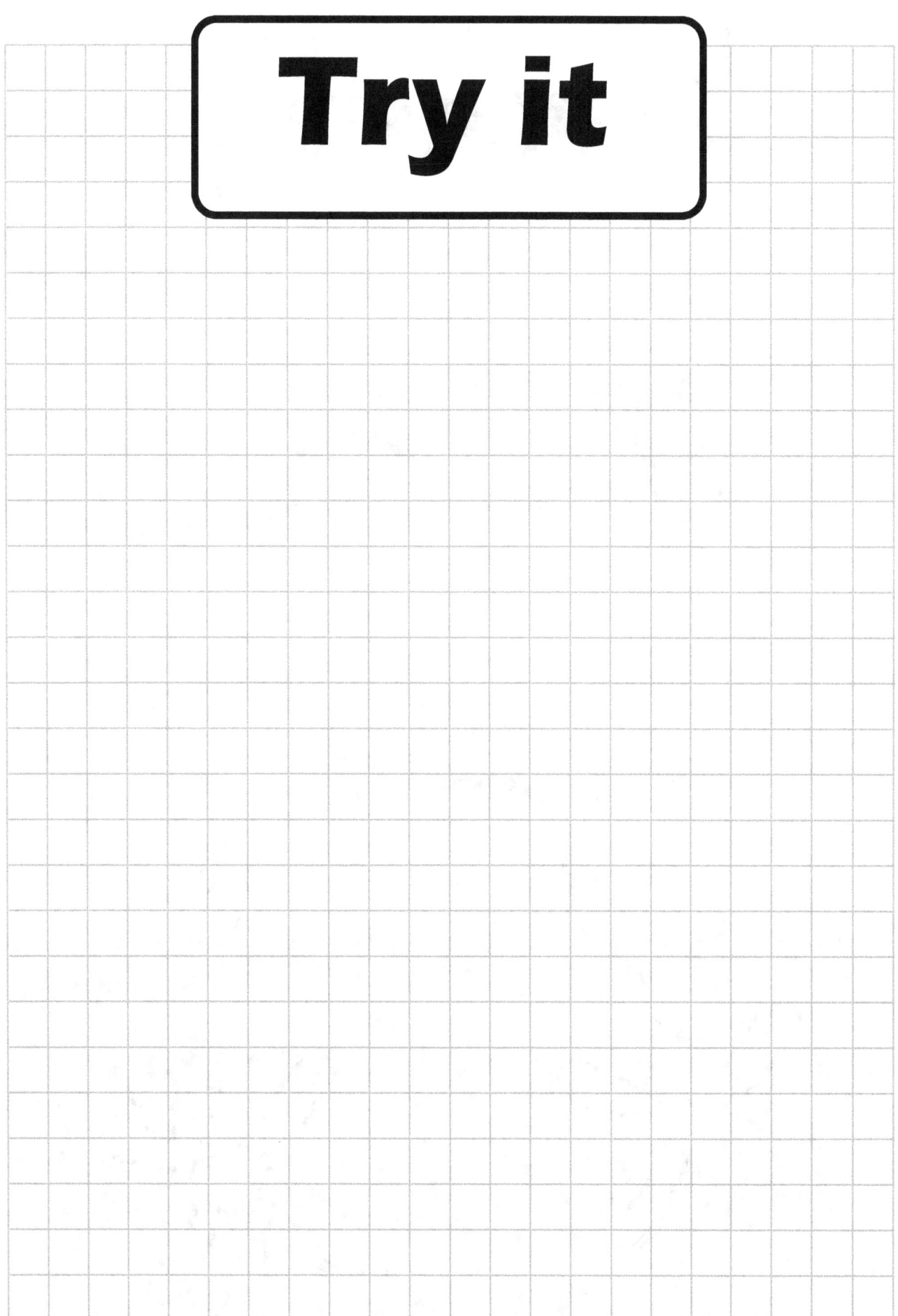

Try it

Dragonfly

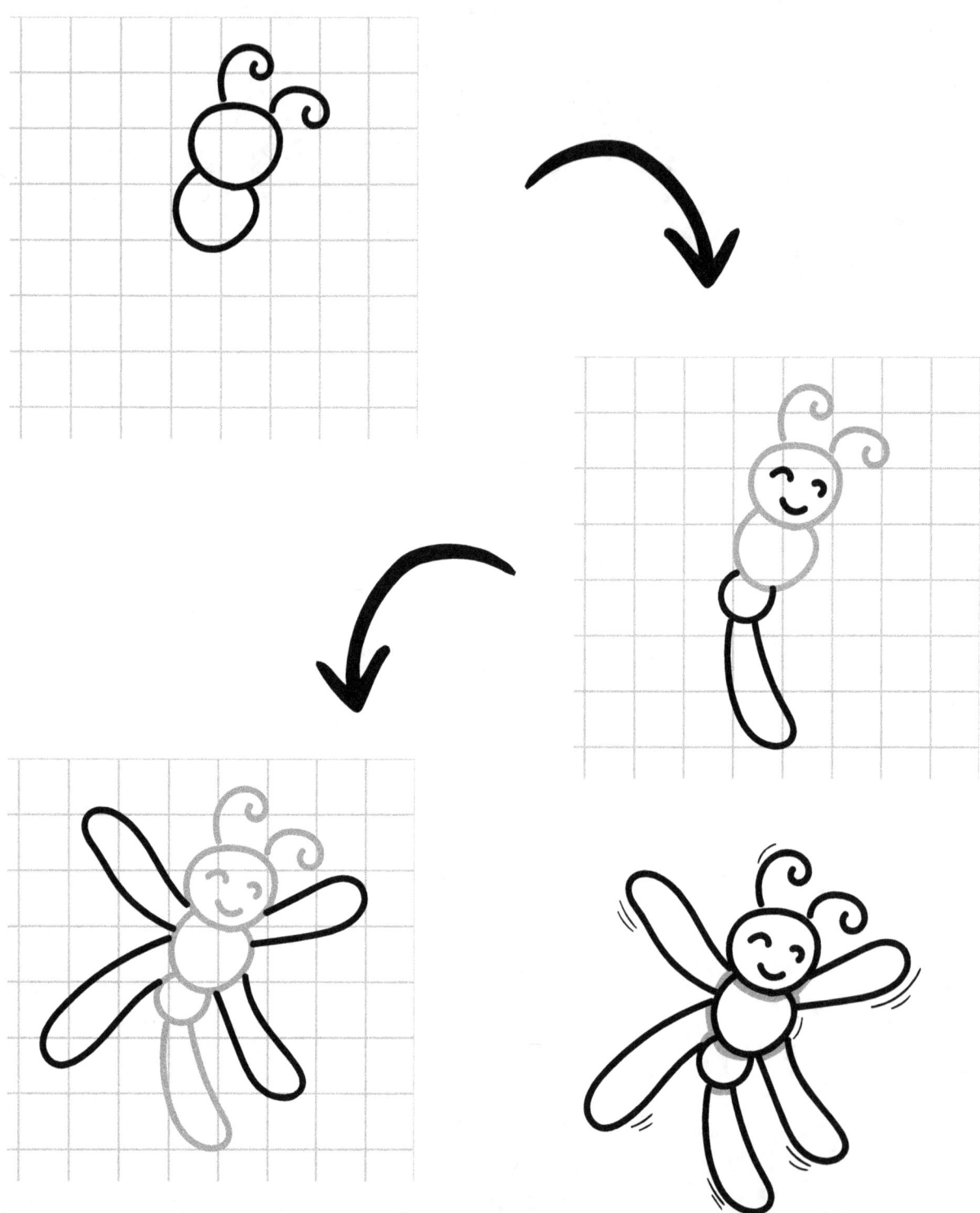

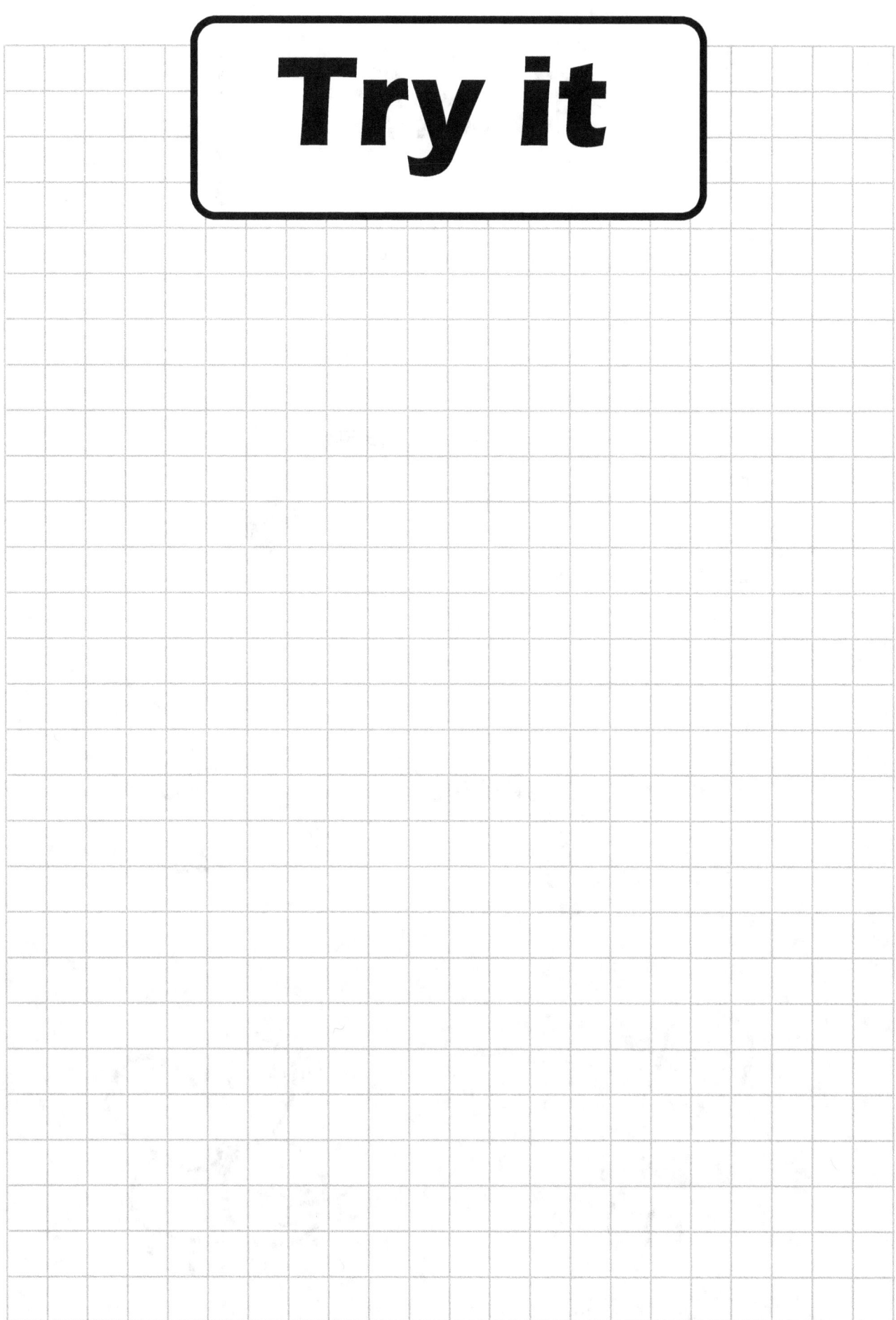

Try it

Tank

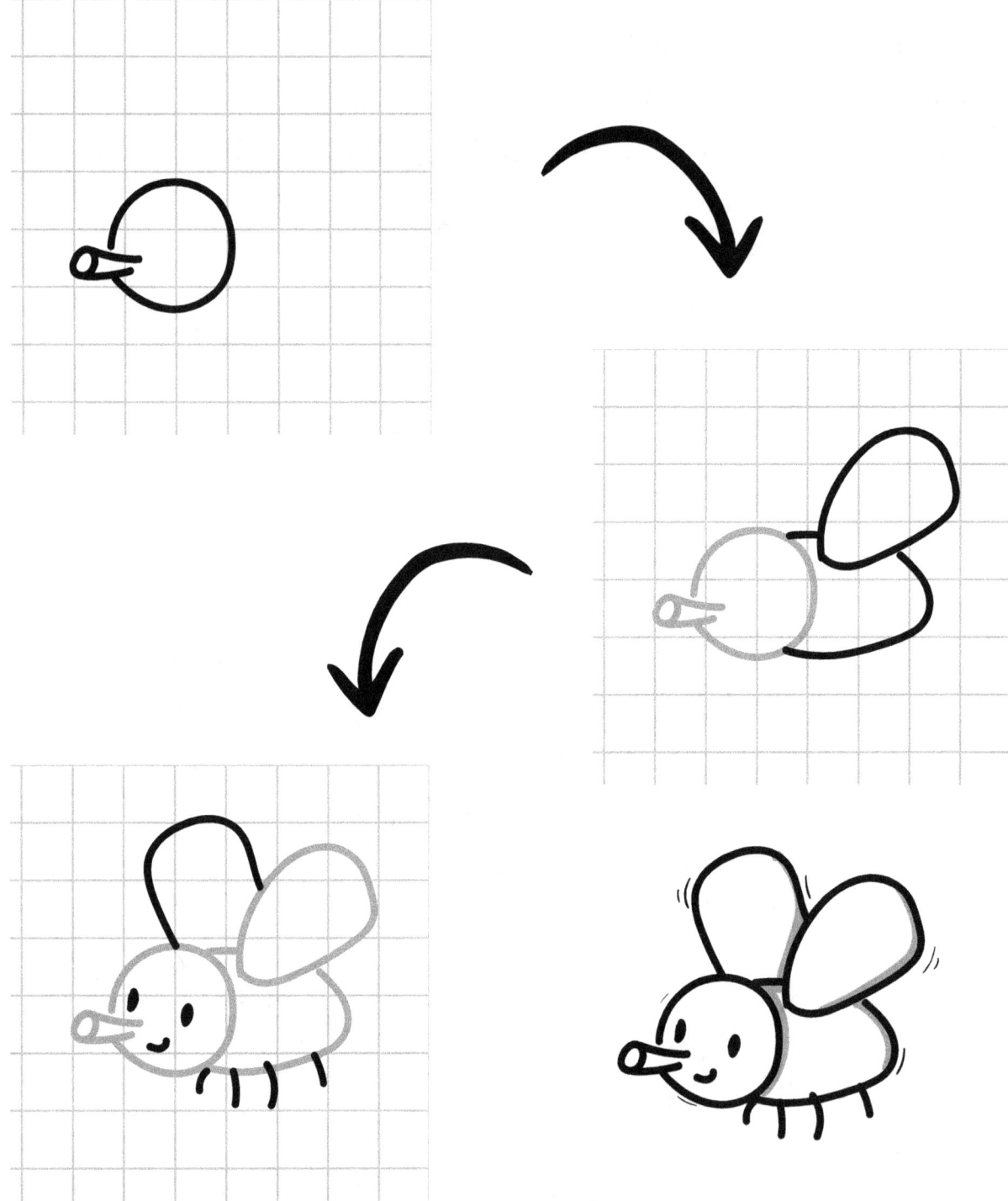

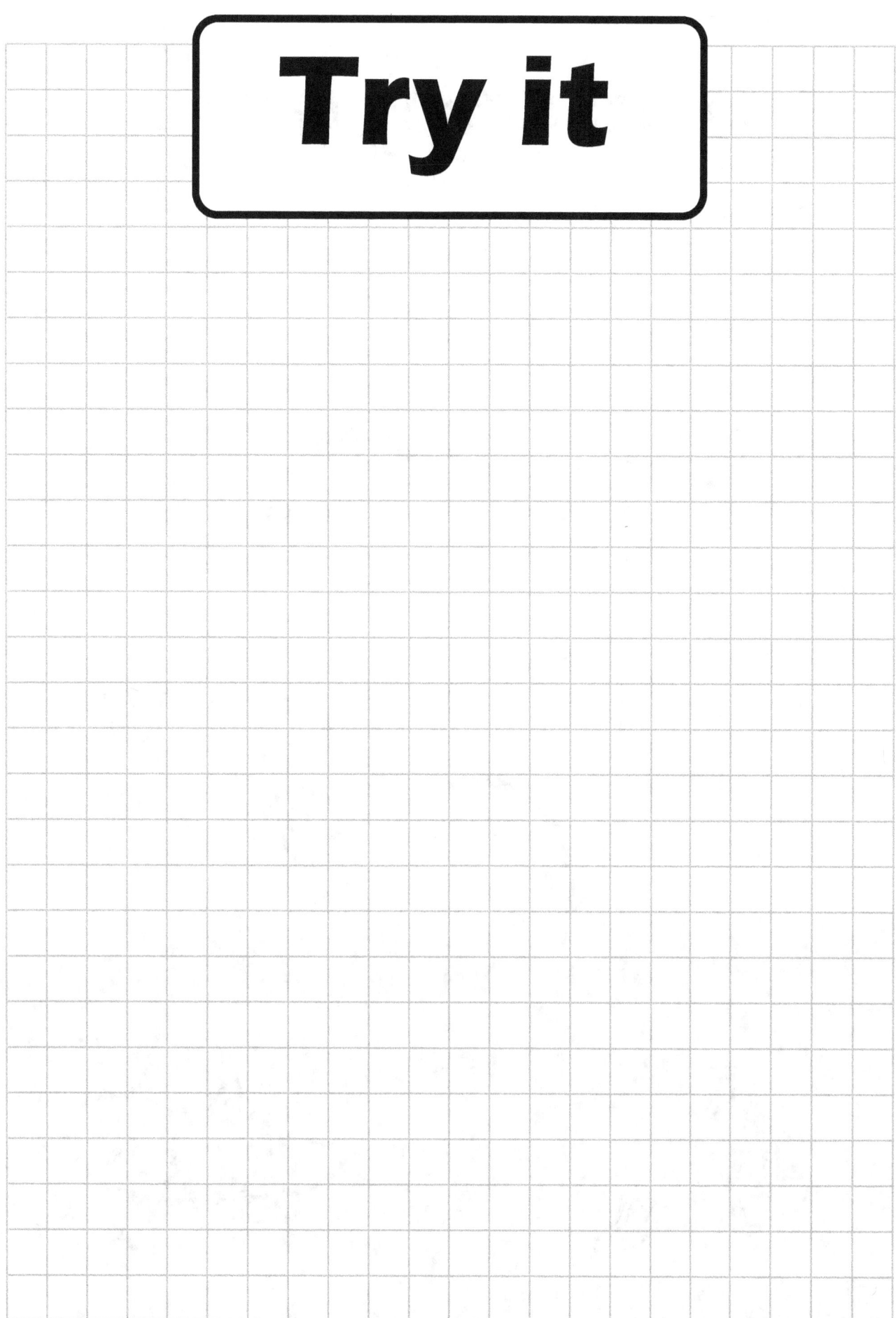

Try it

Grasshopper

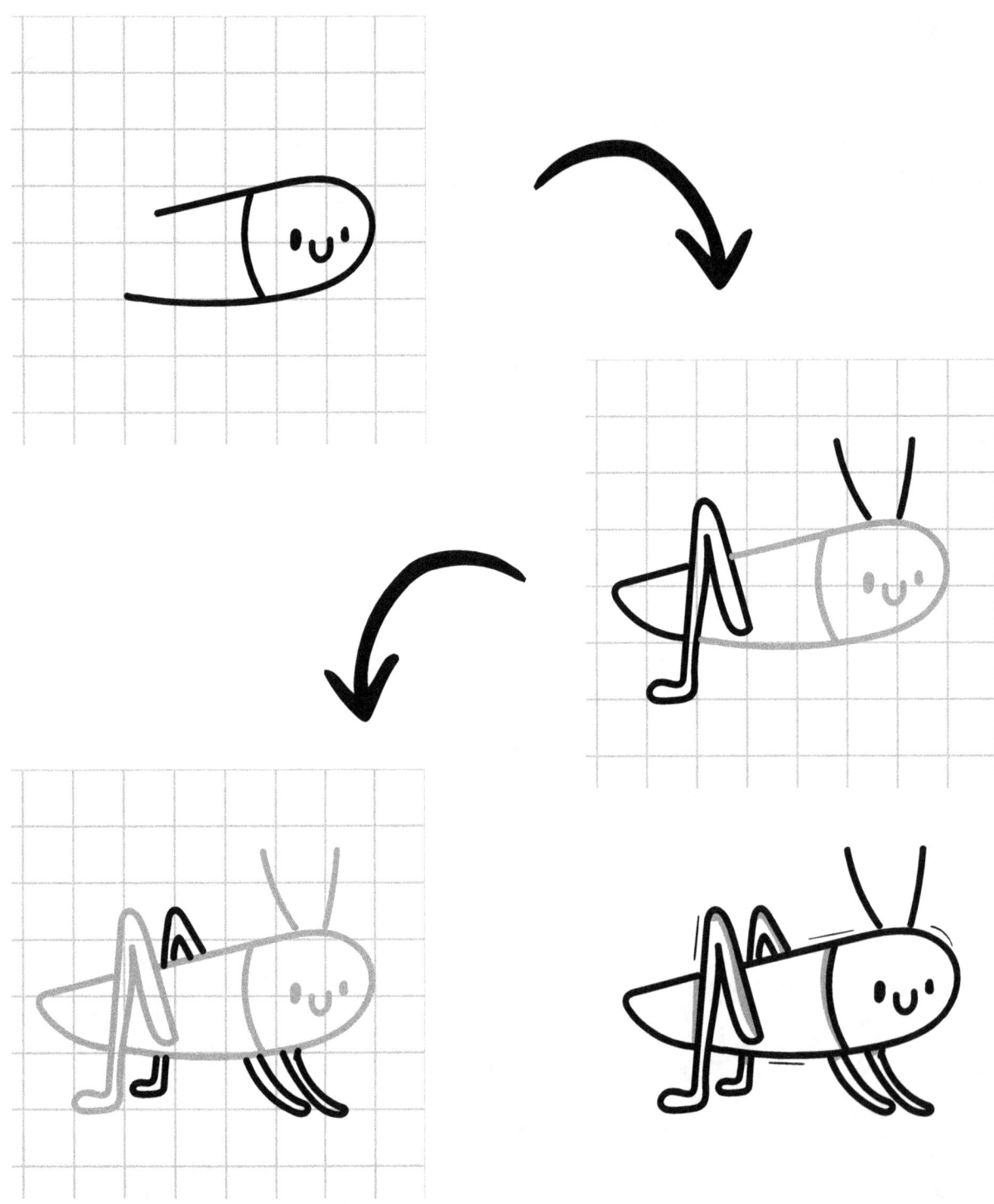

Try it

I hope you enjoy the journey !

Now, show everyone your new drawing skills